Whatever Happened to Inclusion?

Disability
Studies in
Education

Susan L. Gabel and Scot Danforth
General Editors

Vol. 7

PETER LANG
New York • Washington, D.C./Baltimore • Bern
Frankfurt am Main • Berlin • Brussels • Vienna • Oxford

Whatever Happened to Inclusion?

The Place of Students with Intellectual Disabilities in Education

EDITED BY PHIL SMITH

PETER LANG
New York • Washington, D.C./Baltimore • Bern
Frankfurt am Main • Berlin • Brussels • Vienna • Oxford

Library of Congress Cataloging-in-Publication Data

Whatever happened to inclusion?: the place of students
with intellectual disabilities in education / edited by Phil Smith.
p. cm. — (Disability studies in education; vol. 7.)
Includes bibliographical references and index.
1. Inclusive education. 2. Special education.
3. Learning disabled—Education. 4. Disability studies. I. Title.
LC1200.S65   371.9′046—dc22   2009044580
ISBN 978-1-4331-0435-0 (hardcover)
ISBN 978-1-4331-0434-3 (paperback)
ISSN 1548-7210

Bibliographic information published by **Die Deutsche Nationalbibliothek**.
Die Deutsche Nationalbibliothek lists this publication in the "Deutsche
Nationalbibliografie"; detailed bibliographic data is available
on the Internet at http://dnb.d-nb.de/.

The paper in this book meets the guidelines for permanence and durability
of the Committee on Production Guidelines for Book Longevity
of the Council of Library Resources.

© 2010 Peter Lang Publishing, Inc., New York
29 Broadway, 18th floor, New York, NY 10006
www.peterlang.com

Printed in the United States of America

For Sara and Marilla, for all the reasons that you both know.

TABLE OF CONTENTS

ACKNOWLEDGEMENTS

Projects like this sometimes look to the reader as if they were completed by a single person. They never are. Behind the scenes are always a bunch of folks who make a particular work possible. Here are mine.

Susan Gabel, Valerie Owen, and Missy Morton came to an infinitesimally small session I did at the American Association for Educational Research conference in 2007, where I began talking about the ideas that ended up here. They told me to make it a book. I have. Thanks for pointing me in the right direction.

Series editors Susan Gabel and Scot Danforth held my hand, shouted encouragement, and provided thoughtful suggestions and comments about my writing and the project as a whole. When I grow up, I want to be just like them. Really.

Thank goodness for undergraduate and graduate students. They keep me fresh, sane, and on my toes. Over the past number of years, a bunch of them have made me think new things and defend what I take for granted. I can't possibly list them all, but the best have definitely included Kelli Bracken, Pamela Colton, Dené Granger, Casey Harhold, John Harnois, John Planck, Christie Routel, and Liz Turek. They are the most bestest cool people I know.

I began working at Eastern Michigan University with a cohort of new faculty in the Department of Special Education. While we don't always (or even often) agree about things (perhaps especially the topic of this book), their comraderie and friendship have kept me sane. To Steve Camron, Ann Orr, Linda Polter, Karen Schulte, and Gil Steifel, I can only say, it really *is* stupid.

Among my other colleagues there, Jackie McGinnis, John Palladino, and Lynne Rocklage are really swell. You rock.

Every year, I make it a point to go to several conferences and professional meetings, both to present my work and to learn. One that has been important to me is the Disability Studies in Education conference, which began in Chicago and has moved to other places. Going there is like going home: the people who attend and present at it are a community of brothers and sisters, who disagree and agree about all the right (and wrong) things. Thank you all for making me feel welcome.

INTRODUCTION

Whatever Happened to Inclusion?

The Place of Students with Intellectual Disabilities in Education

PHIL SMITH

> Inclusive education is not a sub-branch of special education. (Len Barton, 2007)
>
> The question is not, Is it possible to educate all children well? but rather, Do we want to do it badly enough? (Deborah Meier, 2002, p. 4)
>
> What is unfair to everyone is to segregate students on the basis of their abilities. (Frank Smith, 1998, p. 99)

This is a book about the inclusion of students with intellectual disabilities in general education classrooms—what I and my colleagues here have come to know and think about that over the last four to five years. Let me tell you a story about how this book and the ideas here emerged.

I came to the ideas, thinking, and exploration embedded in this book after moving to Michigan from Vermont, where I had lived and worked for many years supporting people with disabilities. Vermont has had a long history of including people with intellectual and developmental disabilities—as well as others—in civil and educational communities (Aichroth et al., 2002). There, I worked as an inclusion specialist (among a variety of other roles, both in and out of schools). My responsibility was to make it possible for students with intellectual, developmental, and multiple disabilities to be fully included in general education classrooms. Inclusion of students with significant disabilities was seen as the norm in school districts in which I worked.

The training I had received as a special educator had prepared me for just this role. My mentors, advisors, and colleagues at university provided me with knowledge and experience in collaboration, systems change, community building, and teaching best practices—a host of tools for my ever-expanding educational tool belt.

Not that my work in Vermont was easy. I faced resistant teachers and toxic school cultures. I was called into the principal's office a lot. In fact, I began to realize I was probably doing the right work if, on my drive to work in the morning, I felt like I was going to get fired that day. But even when teachers and principals and paraeducators didn't have the skills and knowledge to create inclusive environments—there was some underlying belief that it was the right thing to do.

Even for students like John (not his real name), my beliefs held strong. John was in third grade and had cerebral palsy, couldn't use speech to communicate, and was fed through a stomach tube. He'd roll his eyes up to say yes. When he didn't want to do something or was upset, he'd start to cry—he could turn tears on like he had a switch. You could tell when he was happy because he had this great smile, ear-to-ear. When the world was especially awesome—as when he was running repeatedly over my shoe with his motorized wheelchair—he'd shriek and holler and wave his arms around (while I pretended my foot didn't hurt like the dickens).

John learned with every other third grader in a general education classroom. He did the same math that other students did and went to reading group with them. John had figured out that if he didn't want to take a test—like an assessment of his reading ability—he'd just shut down and not respond. A different tactic, perhaps, than those used by his peers—but pretty much standard third-grade behavior, for all that. I worked with a terrific teacher and a paraeducator to make sure he was in the classroom every possible second, and mostly we did okay. It wasn't perfect, but it was okay.

I knew that inclusion was not always seen in the same way in other places, but in Michigan, as I sought to place student teachers in nearby school districts, I was struck by how few opportunities there were for them to work and learn in environments that I thought of as truly inclusive. My students at the university would describe to me particular students, or students with particular disabilities, that they thought would be impossible to teach in general education classrooms. These were often the same kinds of students who were on my caseload in Vermont, and with whom I worked to ensure that they spent all of their time in exactly such environments—students like John.

Robert (again, not his real name) is a high school student with spina bifida I met in Michigan. He rarely uses speech to communicate—it is usually too difficult for others to understand him. He is included in a couple of his general education classrooms, but his school district wants to place him in a segregated setting for most of the day, a classroom with only students with intellectual disabilities. They argue that the work asked of him in his general education classes was much too difficult for him and pointed out that he frequently falls asleep in class. When I observed him in school, I discovered a well-behaved, casually dressed young man who was never given an opportunity to use his augmentative communication device the whole time I was there; was socially isolated in his general education classes, sitting in the back of the class, separated from other students, with a paraprofessional hovering over him; and given work that was stiflingly, excruciatingly boring. *Of course,* he was falling asleep—I would, too, given the circumstances. I know that the well-understood skills and techniques for including students with intellectual disabilities that I had been using for years would make Robert a candidate for *increasing* his level of inclusion, not decreasing it.

I asked myself, why are teachers seeing Robert as someone who should be separated rather than included in ways in which I was used to? What is different about the culture of Michigan schools? Why are experienced educators—and even some of my own students—so resistant to including students in schools and communities? What is going on?

My colleague Linda Ware once described the research and analysis in which I engage to unpack these questions as pissed-off research. Because I identify myself as a person with a disability and as the parent of a young woman with a disability—and because I have friends, colleagues, and students with intellectual and developmental disabilities—the questions that I ask here have a personal and immediate stake for me. When I think about the ways in which people are segregated, persecuted, and denied basic human rights, I get pissed off. My research and analysis reflect that; my words, thinking, and results reflect that. Passion, I think, is a good thing—it can drive us to explore ideas and thinking and understandings in ways that others take for granted.

I began talking to people. I did some research, looked at some numbers, did some analysis. I wrote an article, did a few presentations at conferences. I started to see parts of the picture, but I couldn't put it all together. I needed other stories, local stories. What was going on in different states, different environments? Why and how were some places more successful than others at making inclusion happen for students with intellectual disabilities? What was working, what was not? What needed to change in order for inclusion to be implemented more universally? This book is a beginning of an answer to those questions.

The answers are about changing education. Maybe that's too simple a phrase—the answers are about changing the meanings, the metaphors, about what we think about education. Maybe even about whether education as we understand it is even a good thing.

Some Facts about Inclusion for Students with Intellectual Disabilities

During 2006–2007, approximately 6.686 million students lived in special education land in the United States, receiving so-called special education services and supports (I say so-called because they aren't being supported, and those being served aren't students with disabilities—more about that later). That amounted to about 13% of the total population of students in our public schools. Of the total number of youth aged 3–21, 1.1% receive special education because they are labeled as having intellectual disabilities—a pretty weighty label to have hung around one's neck. Nationally, although educated through public school funding in the United States, most students with intellectual disabilities don't graduate from high school in the same way as their peers—only 36.7% of students with intellectual disabilities graduated from high school with a regular diploma in 2005–2006; 59% completed their schooling but received no diploma, and another 22.3% dropped out before graduating (Planty et al., 2008).

Given the kind of segregation they experience in schools, I'd say it's no wonder so many drop out. In the United States, only 11.66% of students labeled as having intellectual disabilities were fully included (spent 79% of the time or more) in general education classrooms in 2003–2004. Over half—51.8%—were in general education settings for 40% of the time or less. Because of the ways schools count these things, those general education settings sometimes include things such as lunchtime and recess. The data wonks who think that students with disabilities are "included" during lunch and recess obviously haven't been in the same cafeterias and playgrounds as I have—places where what other students call "tards" sit at the "sped"[1] table over in the corner, and who get picked on or beaten up or ignored during recess. Often, in general classroom landscapes, the only places where students labeled as having intellectual disabilities spend time with their peers without disability labels are in art, gym, or music classes.

A disturbing number of students with cognitive impairments receive much or all of their education in completely segregated learning terrains—separate classrooms, separate schools, sometimes even separate residential facilities or hospital environments (Office of Special Education and Rehabilitative Services, 2007). Why, I wonder? After decades of work seeking to include students with intellectual disabilities in general education classrooms, they continue to be segregated within educational communities, left off the maps of general education. What is going on?

Different Perspectives: An Alternative View of Inclusion

This book is founded in post-critical theory and disability studies perspectives. These frameworks for looking at the world offer new tools for unpacking how and why some schools and districts embrace democratic notions such as equality and community, while others don't—tools that embrace a rigorous cultural and cross-cultural analysis. But what are these tools—what do those frameworks look like, what views do they open up for those looking in?

I understand critical theory to mean an exploration of the complexity of social and cultural power structures. Critical theory is an activist critique seeking "to empower the powerless and transform existing social inequalities and injustices" (McLaren, 2007, p. 186) and to "examine social and political contradictions" (McLaren, 2007, p. 11). It follows on the work of the so-called Frankfurt school as well as more current critical theorists who applied this work more specifically to the world of education. Here, Giroux defines what he understands as a critical pedagogy:

Critical pedagogy attempts to understand how power works through the production, distribution, and consumption of knowledge within particular institutional contexts and seeks to constitute students as particular subjects and social agents. It is also invested in the practice of self-criticism about the values that inform our teaching and a critical self-consciousness regarding what it means to equip students with analytical skills to be self-reflective about the knowledge and values they confront in classrooms. (2006, p. 31)

Critical pedagogy—whether in theory, practice, or research—is about the "fundamental interruption of common sense" (Apple, 2004, p. 14). In some ways, it's like the practice of anthropologists who seek to make the typical unusual, and the unusual typical. Kincheloe

(2004) says that critical pedagogy is "the educational articulation of critical theory buoyed by the work of feminist theorists and Brazilian educator, Paulo Freire" and that through it, "advocates have confronted the positivistic, decontextualized, and depoliticized education often found in mainstream teacher education and higher education in general, and elementary and secondary schools" in particular (p. 55). In this work, critical pedagogy scholars have looked closely at social and cultural issues such as race, gender, and class, but, unfortunately, only rarely at disability (Danforth & Gabel, 2006; Danforth & Smith, 2005; Giroux, 1997; McLaren, 2007; Smith, 2005; 2008a; Ware, 2009).

In addition to subscribing to the scholarship of critical theory, I align myself with a post(modernist) perspective, working the terrain of cultural and social cartography with the tools of a bricoleur. I put the word "modernism" in post(modernism) within parentheses to indicate that my thinking has moved beyond postmodernism itself, to being post-whatever or just post, or perhaps even to dismodernism (Davis, 2002). Although individual authors, here and elsewhere, will define it differently (and often in useful conflict), I define a post perspective (others will approach this differently) as one that acknowledges and encourages plundering (Betts, 2005) and bricolage, in which words ≠ worlds (Smith, 2008a). And it asserts that "all readings are misreadings" (Lather, 2003, p. 1). The ideas I outline here have really just skimmed the surface of a pretty wide-ranging and complicated discussion—for a fuller look at them, it might be helpful to look at Smith (2001b; 2008a) and Gabel (2005).

Some find post and critical theory positions to be in opposition to each other (Giroux, 2004; Smith, 2004). I seek a way out of such dueling dualisms, to find a way forward through black-and-white binaries that benefit no one. The tools of each of these ways of thinking are too useful, and too interesting, to discard one or the other because of offalic ideological putrescence. Instead, with others, I seek a way through, in order "to avoid the modern/postmodern divide that suggests that we can do either culture or economics but that we cannot do both" (Giroux, 2004, p. 32). This requires, encourages, and allows me to place myself in a terrain of scholarship that is filled with complexity, tension, and conflict—elements that encourage, not dissuade, creativity; a place of interpenetration, synergy, and active learning.

One way through the intersection of critical theory and postmodernism is the thinking proposed by Kincheloe and Steinberg (1993) regarding postformalism and later explored in more depth by Kincheloe (2008) as a critical complex epistemology. Kincheloe argues that "we must possess and be able to deploy multiple methods of producing knowledge of the world" (2008, p. 41).

Researcher Margaret McLean, with a twinkle in her eye, calls those of us who profess to be disability studies scholars "upstarts with books" (Wills & McLean, 2007)—as apt a description as any, I suppose, especially for those of us engaged in pissed-off research. When I think about the meaning of disability studies, I see it as a way of exploring and understanding issues of disability in cultural contexts (Gabel, 2005; Smith, 2001a; 2001b; 2004; 2006; 2008b). A disability studies view understands disability as a social construction (Taylor, 2006; Smith, 2001a; 2001b; 2006). And it explores the meaning of disability across a variety of disciplines and perspectives (Gabel, 2005; Danforth & Gabel, 2006).

The implications of a social model of disability, as understood by disability studies scholars, are wide:

The social model offers a sociopolitical analysis that describes disability as an ideological construction used to justify not only the oppressive binary cultural constructions of normal/pathological, autonomous/dependent, and competent citizen/ward of the state, but also the social and racial divisions of labor... In other words, Disability Studies scholars describe disability as a socially constructed category that has historical, cultural, political, and economic implications for social life. (Watts & Erevelles, 2004, p. 276)

The understanding of disability as a social construction is not a unified, singular thing—there is no single social model of disability, but rather a number of them, reflecting a variety of analyses and discourses. The social model of disability expressed by many disability studies scholars in England, for example, is very different from that discussed by many of their counterparts in the United States. There are, for example, difficult and worrisome differences in understandings about the nature of disability as a social phenomenon and of impairment as a physical reality (Smith, 2004). In my view, this lack of common agreement around the world about the definition of a social model is not a bad thing—it allows for multiple understandings, multiple perspectives, multiple possibilities for exploration.

Disability studies understands that people with disabilities— including those with intellectual disabilities—are systematically oppressed and marginalized by a dominating, hegemonic culture, founded in an essentializing ableism. Ableism might be described as the persecution and discrimination of people with so-called disabilities by the dominant, normate culture. In the case of people with disabilities, it creates Others in order to support and advance the social, economic, and cultural goals of the normative (in the United States, the normative might be said to come in the form of White, middle and upper class, patriarchal, heterosexual, neoliberal, capitalist power elites) (Smith, 1999; 2004).

Disability studies is *not* special education. In fact, some scholars within the field of disability studies equate special education with negative values of segregation and stigmatization (Conway, 2005). Still, disability studies can be an essential and pivotal tool for informing special education in particular and education in general, looking at them in new, fresh, and invigorating ways.

Labeling People: Constructing Intellectual Disability

What are intellectual disabilities? Language has changed over time in the ways that we call people who are said to have intellectual disabilities (Smith, 1999). Currently, in professional special education literature, intellectual disabilities are assumed to represent people having an IQ of 70 or below and concurrent deficits in what is known as adaptive behavior, all arising before the age of 18 (American Psychiatric Association, 2000).[2] This definition is based in a medical model.

The medical model of disability is based in normative and ableist understandings of people (Smith, 2004). It asserts that labeled people have real and objectively quantifiable deficits, located in their bodies and minds (rather than in physical or social environments). These deficits can be measured and understood, so this story of disability goes, through rigorous Cartesian taxonomies of difference, a process that might be described as a numbering of people. According to this model, these deficits and the people they inhabit can and should be fixed, eliminated, or ameliorated through the use of instructional and other professionally controlled technologies. In essence, it posits that people with disabilities are broken, needing to be fixed. They are, if you will, diseased in ways that are thought by the dominant normative discourse to be curable (Smith, 1999). Disability studies scholars and activists have long held that the medical model uses the institutionalized power of professionals and experts to maintain control over people with disabilities (Finkelstein, 1997; Union of the Physically Impaired Against Segregation, 1976).

It's important to briefly unpack the notion of IQ. It is, most significantly, "a measurement technology" (Shelton, 1997, p. 92). Like all technologies, it is inherently ideological, value laden, and socially constructed. One's IQ, given that a society or culture uses IQ as a measure of something (or even that measuring itself is worth doing), says at least as much about the culture as it does about the individual, and probably more.

I view intellectual disabilities in ways different from the medical construct view. I see them as culturally constructed, and I often describe people as "being labeled as" or "said to have" or "described as being" to point to this cultural and social construction (Smith, 2005). With others, I see intellectual disability as a metaphor. Approached from understandings coming from cognitive-linguistic research, metaphors are portrayed as foundational to human thought and experience. Disability is seen as one such trope, one that has done substantial harm to those so labeled (Danforth, 2007). Others further explore the construct of disability as metaphor, looking specifically at intellectual disabilities:

Traditional deficit models of disability assume an objective reality to the labeled conditions. Thus, "intellectual disability" (i.e., mental retardation) is considered an objective manifestation of impaired capacity to know and think that can be measured and grouped according to severity. In contrast, we view labels as metaphors … However … its metaphoric quality, was quickly forgotten and the label reified as an actual condition. We do not believe a person has an intellectual disability; rather, the person is defined by others as having the condition. (Kliewer, Biklen, & Kasa-Hendrickson, 2006, p. 187–188)

What This Book Is About

In this book, we'll explore the place of students with intellectual disabilities in general education classrooms, and the trajectories of practice, policy, teacher education, and leadership at state and national levels.

In Chapter 1, "Trends for Including Students with Intellectual Disabilities in General Education Classrooms," I update, revise, and extend my previous work looking critically at the state of inclusion for students with intellectual disabilities in general education classrooms (Smith, 2007a; 2007b). Drawing on new federal data, I show that little, if any, progress has been made in including students with intellectual and other developmental disabilities. Using historical and the most recent available federal data, I explore trends, from a national perspective and across almost two decades, in the percentage of students with intellectual disabilities who are fully included in general education classrooms.

Research on inclusion for students with intellectual and other disabilities shows a slow and halting crawl forward, with little to show for all the policy and practice that's been put in place. Negative attitudes and stigma continue to be associated with students labeled as having intellectual disabilities. Over the course of the ten years of data that were explored, only tiny, incremental gains have been made towards including students with intellectual disabilities in general education classrooms. Most students are not fully included, and many states have lost ground. In the most recent five years for which there is data, the national percentage of students with intellectual disabilities who were fully included went down by 2.39%. If this represents a trend, then the full inclusion of students with intellectual disabilities is in retreat. If I were to grade the states in terms of their inclusion of students with intellectual disabilities, I'd have to give every state an F for their efforts. And, of course, these kinds of statistics are replicated in other disability areas.

Chapter 2, "Defining Inclusion: What Is It? Who Does It Benefit?", begins to define the meaning of inclusion and who benefits from it. The beneficiary of special education is not the student with intellectual and other disabilities, but rather the educational industrial complex and the larger normate culture in which it resides. Instead, children and adults with intellectual disabilities are forced to the marginalia (and sometimes entirely off the page) of maps of normative cultures, outside boundaries patrolled by special education and human service gatekeepers.

Defining inclusion is a difficult proposition—there is no single, agreed-upon definition. And although it is referred to (obliquely) in the most recent re-authorization of federal special education law (the Individuals with Disabilities Educational Improvement Act [IDEIA] of 2004), there is no federal definition that is stated clearly and concisely. Rather, law and regulation at the federal level (replicated at state and local levels) implies that inclusion is a place, not a process. This, in spite of the fact that there is a substantial body of research that is quite explicit about the benefits of inclusive education for students labeled as having intellectual (and other) disabilities, as well as for their peers without disabilities, both academically and socially. And there is also a substantial body of research that outlines the kind of educational practices that ensure the success of inclusion, with many examples of that success from around the United States. Among these positive practices are co-teaching and the Universal Design for Learning.

In this chapter, I also propose a common definition of inclusion that might be adopted by policymakers and outline some of the arguments used by those who are ideologically opposed to inclusive education (though they would deny that their arguments are in the arena of ideology). I end the chapter by exploring who (if anyone) benefits from special education.

Clearly, labeling and segregated practices benefit only people without disabilities, and the dominating, hegemonic, normate culture of the northern Western Hemisphere. Special education practices, founded as they are in the ongoing pseudo-science of eugenics, have substantial deleterious effects on people with disabilities, and ultimately on all who are their allies and supporters. Through processes of commodification and reification, substantial financial and social benefits accrue to the neoliberalist, capitalist disability and education industrial complex.

Chapter 3, entitled "Barriers to Inclusion: Does Special Education Work?" looks at the numerous barriers to including students with disabilities in general education classrooms. It is clear that what are sometimes portrayed as inclusive educational practices do not always meet the criteria held by many researchers and practitioners. This has led to unwarranted critique of inclusive education, poor implementation of inclusion, and a general lack of understanding of the goals and strategies of those who seek to create opportunities for inclusive structures.

Educational leaders remain ambivalent at best about including students with intellectual disabilities in general education classrooms on a full-time basis. Perhaps partly as a result of this and other factors, educators often have inadequate training, support, and experience regarding teaching students with disabilities in general education settings. Money does not appear to be a barrier to including students with intellectual and other disabilities in general education.

I outline the wide-ranging and varied research that shows that special education has done little to effect the achievement of students with disabilities; I then explore the ways in which the high-stakes testing and student performance accountability measures of No Child Left Behind (NCLB) legislation have had a negative impact on the inclusion of students with intellectual disabilities.

The following set of chapters begin to look at how inclusion for students with intellectual disabilities plays out in individual states at a more micro-level. First up, Chapter 4, entitled "Lack of Vision? Lack of Respect? Exclusion in Illinois," is written by Valerie Owen and Susan Gabel, both from National-Louis University in Chicago; they outline a history of inclusion (and exclusion) in Illinois schools. They note that the history of education in Illinois is a history of systematic segregation of students with disabilities, especially those with intellectual disabilities. This segregation is found at all levels, including ways in which the Illinois Board of Education is organized, state statutes, and policy regulations. They describe important systemic change efforts, including Illinois Board of Education Initiative (Project CHOICES) and an influential federal lawsuit (*Corey H. v. Board of Education*, 1998), that seek ways out of the trap of segregated schooling for students with intellectual disabilities. In spite of this work, they report, the state's record of providing inclusive educational opportunities is quite dismal.

In the next chapter, Barbara LeRoy (director of the Developmental Disabilities Institute, Wayne State University's University Center for Excellence in Developmental Disabilities) and Krim Lacey (a postdoctoral fellow working at the University of Michigan) take a close look at "The Inclusion of Students with Intellectual Disabilities in Michigan." Michigan has a long history of providing special education to students with disabilities, enacting model legislation in 1971, years before the federal law 94-142. Called P.A. 198, Michigan's special education law created an extremely categorical, dual education system that continues to encourage the exclusion of students with disabilities, and perhaps especially those with intellectual disabilities. Still, LeRoy and Lacey call the period from 1989 to 1999 "the decade of inclusion" and outline ways in which a statewide systems change initiative (the result of a substantial federal grant) resulted in significant change for the education of students with disabilities. As a result of collaboration across a wide variety of stakeholder groups, intensive statewide training and technical assistance to schools, notable policy analysis and development work, and leadership development among parents and other groups were done around the state. In spite of substantial success, after the initiative ended, the percentage of students with intellectual disabilities who were included in general education classrooms dropped precipitously. LeRoy and Lacey outline the "storms of change" that wiped out gains for inclusion in Michigan.

In Chapter 6, "Fighting Professional Opinions: Stories of Segregation by Three California Families," Emily Mintz takes a different tack as she explores the inclusion of students with intellectual disabilities in California schools. Mintz, who lectures and supervises student teachers at San Francisco State University, begins with a brief examination of national data related to inclusive educational placement for students with intellectual disabilities and their access to it. She also looks at data specific to the state of California, arguing that monitoring of the implementation of federal special education law is largely ineffective. She notes that placement rates for students labeled as having intellectual disabilities within and across the state of California vary too much to be accounted for by variations in students' needs, given the large numbers of students served within the state. Therefore, she says, factors other than student needs impact locally based teams as they make student placement decisions. Mintz provides a set of case studies of students and their families in several school districts representative of California's diverse student body in order to highlight the range of factors that influence IEP teams in making placement decisions. She uses critiques from the field of disability studies in education to develop a nuanced understanding of these factors and recommends potential alternatives to the current practices that seem to perpetuate them.

Kagendo Mutua and Jim Siders ask an important question in their chapter, "'What Is This Inclusion Thing?' Who Dumped These Kids on Me? How Am I Supposed to Do This? Tracing the Contours of Inclusion in Alabama." Mutua and Siders, who both teach at the University of Alabama, describe the history of inclusion in Alabama for students with intellectual disabilities, ranging from the Regular Education Initiative of the early 1980s, to IDEIA of 2004 as well as the so-called No Child Left Behind Act and the resulting policies at the state level. They adopt a disability studies perspective in order to look behind statistics on inclusion, in order to reflect on how views on inclusion as outlined in federal and state policy are played out within schools in Alabama. Mutua and Siders examine the impact that teaching, learning, and access to inclusive educational environments have on students labeled as having intellectual and other developmental disabilities. Finally, they offer some thoughts on practices within schools that lend hope for meaningful inclusion of students with intellectual and other developmental disabilities in schools across Alabama and look at the implications for policy, practice, and research.

In Chapter 8, David Connor (who teaches in the School of Education, Hunter College, City University of New York) looks at ways of "Adding Urban Complexities into the Mix: Continued Resistance to the Inclusion of Students with Cognitive Impairments (or *New York, New York: So Bad They Segregated It Twice*)." Connor points out that the inclusion of students with cognitive impairments is a troubling idea for educators. Inclusion is seen as possible only for students with so-called mild disabilities, those who are closer to cultural understandings of the normate. Those labeled as having cognitive impairments are more often placed in segregated, even institutional, environments. Connor looks at the ways in which students with cognitive impairments are included (or not) in New York City. He uses Kincheloe's (2007) mapping of twelve aspects of urban education, in which urban schools

operate in areas with high population density

are bigger (urban school districts serve more students)

function in areas marked by profound economic disparity

have a higher rate of ethnic, racial, and religious diversity

experience factionalized infighting on school boards over issues concerning resources and influence

are undermined by ineffective business operations

are more likely to work with students who experience health problems

experience higher student, teacher, and administrator mobility

serve higher immigrant populations

are characterized by linguistic diversity

experience unique transportation problems

employ teachers who are less likely to live in the poor communities surrounding the schools than teachers in suburban and rural systems

Students with cognitive impairments make up 4.6% (6, 341) of New York City's student population, with only one in twenty students placed in general education classes for 80% or more of their school day. Another 1.03% were placed out of general education classes for 21–60% of their day, but 61.91% were placed in segregated settings for more than 60% of their program. Connor notes that New York City is the only place in the United States with a separate superintendency for students with moderate and severe disabilities, called District 75, in which only 8% of students receive their schooling in general education buildings. Connor uses New York City as an example of the urban experience exploring the variety of issues that have produced such poor results and outlines ways to create and sustain systemic change for inclusive education.

In Chapter 9, I describe "The Story(s) of the States: What Does It All Mean?" Here, I explore the meanings of what has gone on in these places—Michigan, Illinois, Alabama, California, and New York City—in terms of including students with intellectual and developmental disabilities in general education classrooms. What are the common themes? Why has one state been successful where another has seen limited or declining numbers? What works and what doesn't? I analyze the histories and constructions of inclusion and disability to uncover the meaning of these stories—at research, policy, and practice levels.

In the next chapter, "Preparing Educators for Inclusion: What We're Doing Right, What We're Doing Wrong," I outline what little is known about the effectiveness of teacher preparation practices designed to prepare educators to create and function in inclusive classrooms for students with intellectual or other disabilities. Typically around the country, preservice general educators receive only a single 2 to 3-credit course in special education; this class is often a survey course with insufficient time to go into details about instructional strategies and methods. And states do little to ensure that teacher preparation programs provide appropriate training to future special educators. Current teacher preparation and certification programs reinforce the segregation of special education, so that neither general nor special education preparation programs, whether inservice or preservice, provide future teachers with sufficient experience and training to work successfully and collaboratively in inclusive classrooms. I look at the kinds of knowledge and experience that general and special educators as well as their educational leaders need in order to create truly inclusive classrooms, schools, and districts. This will require teacher education programs to transform and restructure themselves, putting disability studies and critical theory approaches at their foundation.

Chapter 11, the final chapter of the book, explores "Future Directions: Policy, Practice, and Research." As I've outlined in earlier chapters, educators know how to include students with so-called intellectual disabilities in general education classrooms. Depending on the state, we also have plenty of experience in doing it (and even in states that have been less successful, we know some of the pitfalls and traps to avoid). Money doesn't seem to be a legitimate barrier, at least in terms of whether there is enough of it. In this chapter, I explore the specific policy, practice, and research concerns that need to be addressed to ensure that increasing (not declining) numbers of students labeled as having intellectual disabilities are included in general education classrooms.

First, at minimum, the United States Office of Special Education and Rehabilitative Services will need to adopt a clear definition of inclusion (I've suggested Giangreco's) and collect appropriate data related to it. Second, funding and definitional disincentives to inclusion need to be eliminated, probably by starting with inserting specific language into IDEIA (using the actual word "inclusion"). Changing NCLB to ensure that it harbors no disincentives to inclusion will also be important. Funding incentives for inclusion, at state and federal levels (including in future reauthorizations of IDEIA and NCLB), would go a long way to encourage reform supporting inclusion across a variety of levels.

Inclusion is clearly hindered by categorical disability determination and education. Moving federal and state legislation in non-categorical directions and eliminating barriers between special and general education will be essential to alleviate this issue.

Teacher and administrator preparation, both preservice and inservice, will need to change as well, with an increased emphasis on the skills, dispositions, experiences, and attitudes needed to enable general and special educators to work collaboratively to educate students with disabilities in general education classrooms, and for educators and administrators to implement inclusive school reform measures at micro- and macro-levels. This will require substantive change in much of current university teacher and administrator education structures—instead of departments of special education, we'll need schools of inclusive education that stretch across disciplinary boundaries and focus more on disability studies. Programs in educational leadership will need to explore how to create learning communities and constructivist leadership models.

Continued policy and practice research will be essential if we really want inclusion to be a goal for all students. In creating incentives for inclusion, we'll need to look more at what works and what doesn't. We'll need to explore educational reform issues at state and federal levels, and at both systems and school-building levels. We'll need to look at the kinds of teacher education practices that increase opportunities for inclusion. We'll need to find out what kinds of supports, administrative and otherwise, schools and educators need to satisfactorily include students with disabilities in general education classrooms, and how best to implement them. And we'll need to explore what it means for people with disabilities to take on important leadership roles in educational and other communities.

The Arc of the United States (2008) position statement on inclusion makes clear what families and professionals believe is an important value in the lives of students with disabilities: "Children should … learn in their neighborhood school in a regular classroom that contains children of the same age without disabilities" (p. 1). We know what we should be doing, and why, to create real opportunities for social justice in the lives of students with intellectual (and other) disabilities in schools.

The kind of piecemeal, incremental changes that have taken place over the last few decades to create inclusive opportunities for students labeled as having intellectual disabilities have clearly not been enough. The kinds of changes discussed in this book may take years to implement—realistically, they probably will.

But here's the thing about being realistic. The first job I got in the field of supporting people with developmental disabilities was at a small agency supporting people in the community. Fresh out of the university, the ink on my master's degree barely dry, I interviewed with the executive director. I gave him my usual rant about inclusion, in both schools and communities. He looked at me and said, "That's all great, Phil. But do you know how long that will take? It took us thirty years to close down institutions for people with developmental disabilities in this state. It'll take another thirty years to do what you're suggesting." At the time, I just looked at him. I didn't have a ready answer. But driving home that afternoon, I realized what I should have said—and what I continue to say to my students and anybody else who will listen: yes, it may, in fact, take a long time. But I can't work like its going to take thirty years. I have to work—have the drive, the energy, the chutzpah—to make it happen tomorrow. Why? Because my friends Kathy, Jacob, and Frank—people with developmental disabilities—and Pam, Kathryn, and John—parents of students—don't have thirty years. They need it to happen now. Tomorrow. In the worst case, the day after. Absolutely, by the end of the week. So they can have a real life, with real friends, with a job, and a home. People who love them.

Tomorrow. Not thirty years from today.

In fall 2008, I was presenting some of these ideas to some potential funders. The wonderful, wise old man who sat across the table looked down at the notepad in front of him when I was done, and then up at me with a small grin. "Phil," he said, "What you're proposing will take a great deal of naïveté to accomplish. There will be all kinds of people who will be upset with you as you do this. You just have to go ahead and do it anyway."

That sounds about right to me. So, let's roll up our sleeves, get to work, and make it happen.

Notes

1   This is harsh language, words that I do not typically—do not ever—use. In my world, they represent reprehensible, objectionable hate language. I use this language here because I want to be clear about the climate and culture that students with disabilities face in many schools, and to describe the kind of persecution that students with disabilities—perhaps especially students with intellectual disabilities—face on a daily basis. I hope that my self-advocate colleagues—who I hold in great honor and respect—will forgive me for using such words.

2   The American Association on Intellectual and Developmental Disabilities (AAIDD) is a preeminent national professional organization in the United States. It has recently changed its definition of intellectual disability, from one that relies on IQ, to one that explores it from the perspective of the kinds and levels of supports required to meet the needs of individuals. It has not yet gained a foothold in federal and state special education policy, which continues to rely on IQ. While it might be argued that AAIDD's definition is more progressive and a move away from a deficit, medical model understanding of disability, I would suggest that it continues to create taxonomies of intelligence, through the reified construct of support. Some states are using it as a means of deciding who gets what kind of support in community services, an unproductive use of such a tool (Thompson et al., 2004; Wehmeyer et al., 2009).

References

Aichroth, S., Carpenter, J., Daniels, K., Grassette, P., Kelly, D., Murray, A., Rice, J., Rivard, B., Smith, C., Smith, P., & Topper, K. (2002). Creating a new system of supports: The Vermont self-determination project. *Rural Special Education Quarterly, 21* (2), 16–28.

American Psychiatric Association (2000). *Diagnostic and statistical manual of mental disorders* (4th Ed., Text Revision). Arlington, VA: Author.

Arc of the United States (2008). Position statement on inclusion. Retrieved on 10/22/2009 from http://www.thearc.org/NetCommunity/Page.aspx?pid=1359

Apple, M. (2004). Creating difference: Neo-liberalism, neo-conservatism and the politics of educational reform. *Educational Policy, 18*, 12–44.

Barton, L. (2007). Inclusive education and disability studies: Observations and issues for debate. 7th Annual Second City Disability Studies in Education Conference, Chicago.

Betts, G. (2005). Plunderverse: A cartographic manifesto. *Poetics.ca, 5* (n.p.). Retrieved

August 24, 2006 from http://www.poetics.ca/poetics05/05betts.html

Conway, M. (2005). Introduction: Disability studies meets special education. *Review of Disability Studies, 1,* 3–8.

Danforth, S. (2007) Disability as metaphor: Examining the conceptual framing of emotional behavioral disorder in American public education. *Educational Studies: A Journal of the American Educational Studies Association, 42,* 8–27.

Danforth, S., & Gabel, S. (2006). Introduction. In S. Danforth & S. Gabel (Eds.) *Vital questions facing disability studies in education* (pp. 1–15). New York: Peter Lang.

Danforth, S. & Smith, T. (2005). *Engaging troubling students: A constructivist approach.* Thousand Oaks, CA: Corwin Press.

Davis, L. (2002). *Bending over backwards: Disability, dismodernism, and other difficult positions.* New York: NYU Press.

Finkelstein, V. (1997). *Modeling disability.* Leeds, England: University of Leeds Centre for Disability Studies. Retrieved on February 28, 2009 from http://www.leeds.ac.uk/disability-studies/archiveuk/finkelstein/models/models.htm

Gabel, S. (2005). An aesthetic of disability. In S. Gabel (Ed.), *Disability studies in education: Readings in theory and method.* New York: Peter Lang.

Giroux, H. (1997). *Pedagogy and the politics of hope.* Boulder, CO: Westview.

—— (2004). Critical pedagogy and the postmodern/modern divide: Towards a pedagogy of democratization. *Teacher Education Quarterly, 31,* 31–47.

—— (2006). Academic freedom under fire: The case for critical pedagogy. *College Literature, 33*(4), 1–42.

Kincheloe, J. (2004). The knowledges of teacher education: Developing a critical complex epistemology. *Teacher Education Quarterly, 31,* 49–66.

—— (2007). Why a book on urban education? In S. R. Steinberg & J. L. Kincheloe (Eds.), *19 urban questions: Teaching in the city* (pp. 1–27). New York: Peter Lang.

—— (2008). *Knowledge and critical pedagogy: An introduction.* New York: Springer.

Kincheloe, J., & Steinberg, S. (1993). A tentative description of post-formal thinking: The critical confrontation with cognitive thinking. *Harvard Educational Review, 63,* 296–320.

Kliewer, C., Biklen, D., & Kasa-Hendrickson, C. (2006). Who may be literate? Disability and resistance to the cultural denial of competence. *American Educational Research Journal, 43,* 163–192.

Lather, P. (2003). Applied Derrida: (Mis)reading the work of mourning in educational research. Annual Meeting of the American Educational Research Association, Chicago.

McLaren, P. (2007). *Life in schools: An introduction to critical pedagogy in the foundations of education* (5th ed.). New York: Pearson.

Meier, D. (2002). *The power of their ideas: Lessons for America from a small school in Harlem.* Boston: Beacon Press.

Office of Special Education and Rehabilitative Services (2007). *27th annual report to Congress on the implementation of the Individuals with Disabilities Education Act.* Washington, DC: Author.

Planty, M., Hussar, W., Snyder, T., Provasnik, S., Kena, G., Dinkes, R., KewalRamani, A., and Kemp, J. (2008). *The condition of education, 2008* (NCES 2008–031). Washington, DC: National Center for Education Statistics, Institute of Education Sciences, U.S. Department of Education.

Shelton, A. (1997). The ape's IQ. In J. Kincheloe, S. Steinberg, & A. Gresson (Eds.) *Measured lies: The Bell Curve examined* (pp. 91–105). New York: St. Martin's Press.

Smith, F. (1998). *The book of learning and forgetting*. New York: Teacher's College Press.

Smith, P. (1999). Drawing new maps: A radical cartography of developmental disabilities. *Review of Educational Research, 69*(2), 117–144.

——— (2001a). Inquiry cantos: A poetics of developmental disability. *Mental Retardation, 39,* 379–390.

——— (2001b). MAN.i.f.e.s.t.o.: A Poetics of D(EVIL)op(MENTAL) Dis(ABILITY). *Taboo: The Journal of Education and Culture, 5*(1), 27–36.

——— (2004). Whiteness, normal theory, and disability studies. *Disability Studies Quarterly,* 24(2).

——— (2005). Off the map: A critical geography of intellectual disabilities. *Health and Place, 11,* 87–92.

——— (2006). Split——ting the rock of {speci [ES]al} e.ducat.ion: flowers of lang[ue]age in >DIS<ability studies. In S. Danforth and S. Gabel (Eds.), *Vital Questions in Disability Studies in Education,* (pp. 31-58). New York: Peter Lang.

——— (2007a). Have we made any progress? Including students with intellectual disabilities in regular education classrooms. *Intellectual and Developmental Disabilities, 45,* 297–309.

——— (March 2007b). What progress in Michigan? Including students with intellectual disabilities in regular education classrooms. Annual Meeting of the Michigan Academy of Science, Arts and Letters, Big Rapids, MI.

——— (2008a). an ILL/ELLip(op)tical *po—ETIC/EMIC/Lemic/litic post®* uv ed DUCAT ion *recherché repres©entation. Qualitative Inquiry, 14,* 706–722.

——— (2008b). Cartographies of eugenics and special education: A history of the (ab)normal. In S. Gabel & S. Danforth (Eds.), *Disability and the politics of education: An international reader* (pp. 33-61). New York: Peter Lang.

Taylor, S. (2006). Forward: Before it had a name: Exploring the historical roots of disability studies in education. In S. Gabel & S. Danforth (Eds.), *Disability and the politics of education: An international reader* (pp xiii-xxiii). New York: Peter Lang.

Thompson, J., Bryant, B., Campbell, E., Craig, E., Hughes, C., Rotholz, D., Schalock, R., Silverman, W., Tassé, M., & Wehmeyer, M. (2004). *Supports Intensity Scale.* Washington, DC: American Association on Mental Retardation.

Union of the Physically Impaired Against Segregation (1976). *Policy Statement.* Leeds, England: University of Leeds Centre on Disability Studies. Retrieved on February 28, 2009 from http://www.leeds.ac.uk/disabilitystudies/archiveuk/UPIAS/UPIAS.htm

Ware, L. (2009). Writing, identity, and the Other: Dare we do disability studies? In A. Darder, M. Baldodano, & R. Torres (Eds.) *The critical pedagogy reader* (2nd ed.) (pp. 397–416). New York: Routledge.

Watts, I. & Erevelles, N. (2004). These deadly times: Reconceptualizing school violence by using Critical Race Theory and Disability Studies. *American Educational Research Journal, 41,* 271–299.

Wehmeyer, M., Chapman, T., Little, T., Thompson, J., Schalock, R., & Tassé, M. (2009). Efficacy of the Supports Intensity Scale (SIS) to predict extraordinary support needs. *American Journal on Intellectual and Developmental Disabilities, 114,* 3–14.

Wills, R. & McLean, M. (2007). Drafting—Who is in, who is out, and how decisions are shaped. 7th Annual Second City Disability Studies in Education Conference, Chicago

CHAPTER 1

Trends for Including Students with Intellectual Disabilities in General Education Classrooms

PHIL SMITH

Inclusive education in the United States and elsewhere is under challenge. (Weber, 2007, p. 30)

Federal special education law—established in 1975 in the Education for All Handicapped Children Act and then continued through a series of reauthorizations up through 2004 in what is now called the Individuals with Disabilities Education Improvement Act (IDEIA)—has long held that students with disabilities, including those with intellectual disabilities, have a right to receive a free and appropriate public education (FAPE) in a Least Restrictive Environment (LRE). But to what extent are students with intellectual disabilities educated in general education classrooms and schools? Has the number of students with intellectual disabilities included in general education classrooms changed over time? What states successfully provide the supports schools need in order to make sure that students are included in general education? This chapter provides a progress report on the extent to which educational systems include students with intellectual disabilities in general education classrooms. Here, I will update, revise, and extend my previous work looking critically at the state of inclusion (Smith, 2007a; 2007b). Drawing on new federal data, I will show that little, if any, progress has been made in this area. Using historical and the most recent available federal data, I explore, from a national perspective and across almost two decades, trends in the percentage of students with intellectual disabilities who are fully included in general education classrooms.

Although I see myself principally as a qualitative researcher, as those who've read some of my work may know (Smith, 1999a; 1999b; 1999c; 2001a; 2001b; 2005), my concern here is less about the research approach I'll use than with its outcome: policy analysis and systems change. I come to this work, in the words of my colleague Diane Ferguson (1995), as a "rabid inclusionist." This is a value that has become for me an ethical imperative—a matter of moral concern in which, as a person with a disability and as the parent of a student on an IEP, I have a personal stake. Here, I will tell a story in numbers about the inclusion of students with intellectual disabilities that is disturbing at the least and of great importance to our field, as well as to the lives of people with intellectual and developmental disabilities and their families.

Data about Including Students with Intellectual Disabilities in General Education Classrooms

Progress—if you can call it that—in advancing the social justice and human rights project of including students with intellectual disabilities in general education classrooms can only be described as slow. Even that description is generous and does not begin to adequately describe the extraordinary inertia—even active opposition—for essential cultural, policy, and education change. Downing notes that "the majority of those with the more severe disability labels still receive most of their education in specialized educational settings, either special classrooms or special schools" (2008, p. 8).

One study, using data from the United States Department of Education, found that, in the period between 1988 and 1995, school districts had been relatively successful in moving students with intellectual disabilities out of separate schools into classrooms in neighborhood and local schools but had less success in moving further to include them in general education classrooms with their peers (McLeskey, Henry, & Hodges, 1999). And although many students now receive their education in local schools, nearly all of them are in highly segregated classrooms within those schools. And a remarkable 6.7% of all public schools in the United States are completely segregated settings, providing education only to students with disabilities (National Council on Teacher Quality, 2004)—islands, if you will, of disability. These schools are set aside only for students with disabilities—separate but (not) equal dumping grounds for people left off the maps of normative, industrial education, in complete defiance of court cases such as *Brown v. Board of Education of Topeka* (1954) that have otherwise, at least de jure, redone the cartography of education as we understand it in the United States.

Another study found that, in the twelve years between 1977 and

1990, the number of students with disabilities in general education or resource classrooms increased by a meager 1.2% (Karagiannis, Stainback, & Stainback, 1996). One analysis of the inclusion of students labeled as having intellectual disabilities found that, nationally, their numbers seems to have plateaued in the school year 1997–1998 (Williamson, McLesky, Hoppey, & Rentz, 2006).

A national research project exploring the attitudes of students without disabilities regarding those with intellectual disabilities, across rural, suburban, and urban settings, found that fewer than 40% of students without disabilities had any contact in school with students with intellectual disabilities, either at the time of the project or during their prior educational experiences, and only 10% reported having a friend with an intellectual disability. Most of their knowledge about students with intellectual disabilities came from secondary sources, including media representations and interactions with peers and adults. Overall, students without disabilities reported negative attitudes about those with intellectual disabilities, seeing them as incapable. Researchers found little change in perception over the course of 30 years of similar research (Siperstein, Parker, Bardon, & Widaman, 2007). Clearly, because of the continued segregation of students with intellectual disabilities in schools, negative attitudes and high levels of stigma remain attached to the notion of intellectual disability in U.S. culture.

This data is only for educational communities. The situation for people with intellectual and developmental disabilities who are included in civic communities is only somewhat less grim. In 2008, only nine states had completely closed their large state-operated institutions of more than 16 people with intellectual and developmental disabilities—Alaska, Hawaii, Maine, New Hampshire, New Mexico, Rhode Island, Vermont, West Virginia, and the District of Columbia—a number that hasn't changed for several years. A total of 41 states still had 37,711 people living in 173 state-run institutions. Disturbingly, by 2008, the number of people living in private institutional settings went up to over 72,000 for a combined state-private total of over 109,000 people. In addition, fewer people with intellectual and developmental disabilities were engaged in competitive employment than in the previous year (Bragden, 2008). And the rate at which people with intellectual and developmental disabilities were leaving state-run institutions has "fallen to historically low levels" (Lakin, Prouty, and Alba, 2007, p. 30).

Well over a decade ago, in 1992, The Arc, a national organization focused on issues related to people with intellectual disabilities and their families, published a summary entitled *Report Card to the Nation on Inclusion in Education of Children with Mental Retardation* (Davis, 1992). In 1995, they updated it with a *Report Card on Inclusion in Education of Children with Mental Retardation* (The Arc of the United States, 1995). In these report cards, the Arc, using federal education data, rank ordered the states by the percentage of students (age 6–21) with intellectual disabilities educated in general education classrooms and graded states on their inclusion of students with intellectual disabilities. The highest grade attained in 1995 was a B, obtained by one state (Vermont). No state received a grade of C; 16 states received a D, and the rest—almost two-thirds—received an F.

What, I wondered, were current levels of inclusion of students with intellectual disabilities compared with this earlier data? The most recent official data available at the time of writing, collected by the U.S. Department of Education, was from the 2003–2004 school year (OSERS, 2005). While more recent data is sometimes available, this information is not the data formally presented to Congress and is subject to change as individual states modify or correct statistics that they have submitted. Unfortunately, the data that the federal Department of Education's Office of Special Education and Rehabilitative Services (OSERS) uses does not correlate with any good definition of inclusion I found in the literature—it is primarily derivative (more about that later).

So I looked at data that came as close as I could come to an understanding of full inclusion in schools, that is, in situations in which students with disabilities spend all or most of their time in general education classrooms. OSERS collects information about the percentage of time that students with various disability labels spend outside of general education classrooms, in increments: those who are outside general education classrooms less than 21% of the time, 21–60% of the time, and greater than 60% of the time. Information is collected also about the number of students who do not receive their education in schools but instead receive services in public separate facilities, private separate facilities, public residential facilities, private residential facilities, prisons, and home or hospital environments.

I used information available from this federally collected data that showed by state[1] the percentage of students with intellectual disabilities who received their education in general education classrooms

for more than 79% of the time as the closest measure of the full inclusion of students with intellectual disabilities (OSERS, 2005).

I then rank ordered the states from those with the highest percentage to those with the lowest percentage of students with intellectual
disabilities included in general education classrooms, based on the
most recent, formally published 2003–2004 school year data. Finally, I
compared these percentages, by state, to the same kind of data from
the previous five-year increment (1998–1999 school year), data for the
increment roughly five years before that (1994–1995 school year), and
the five-year increment previous to that (1989–1990), to see how the
numbers had changed over time (OSERS, 2005; 2001; 1993) (see Table
1 for a representation of this data). Using this data allowed me to look
at almost 15 years of information about inclusion, over roughly five-
year increments, including the most recent formally published data,
to explore changes and trends in the inclusion of students with intellectual disabilities in general education classrooms.

What Do the Numbers Say about Inclusion in the United States?

Nationally, for the 50 states plus Washington DC and Puerto Rico,
between the 1986–1987 and the 2003–2004 school years (offering almost two decades of information), the percentage of students with
intellectual disabilities who received their education in general education classrooms for more than 79% of the time grew by a very small
amount from an almost nonexistent 3.22% to a mere 11.66%. What
does that change represent in terms of actual children? 45,478 young
human beings. Compared to the number of children served in special
education during 2003–2004, almost 6 million, that's an infinitesimal
number of kids—about three-quarters of 1% of that total number. Almost nothing, you might say.

One way of framing those numbers is to say that the percentage of
students with intellectual disabilities who were fully included came
close to quadrupling in that time period. Such a description, however,
does not do justice to those numbers: the change in percentage is
really almost infinitesimal; the change is almost comic in proportion
to the effort and research expended to make it happen—comic only if
one can ignore the impact it has had on the lives of students with intellectual disabilities and their families. Although it certainly represents an increase, the numbers are trivially, ridiculously, preposter-
ously small, given the policy goals outlined by the Arc. I'd call the
change tiny.

Table 1: Percentage of Students with Intellectual Disabilities (Mental Retardation) Included in General Education Classrooms More Than 79% of the Time

Rank Order 2003–2004	State	Percentage 1989–1990	1994–1995	1998–1999	2003–2004
1.	Vermont	54.06	77.99	67.39	59.11
2.	New Hampshire	25.22	21.88	56.68	39.53
3.	Colorado	2.18	40.41	34.35	37.31
4.	Iowa	0.33	60.85	31.99	35.92
5.	Rhode Island	1.36	2.42	2.28	33.76
6.	Kentucky	6.20	20.73	20.91	26.26
7.	Oregon	7.19	27.64	29.71	23.37
8.	Nebraska	15.50	19.79	23.70	20.29
9.	Ohio	2.25	2.62	28.48	16.29
10.	South Dakota	1.48	17.26	18.75	16.19
11.	Idaho	18.50	31.85	27.42	16.09
12.	Indiana	0.30	12.22	15.68	15.71
13.	North Dakota	7.94	24.92	32.29	15.69
14.	Alabama	8.10	5.44	12.34	14.82
15.	Alaska	5.76	13.85	17.63	14.71
16.	Florida	0.58	2.09	20.70	14.15
17.	Oklahoma	7.85	11.38	11.36	13.20
18.	Connecticut	2.50	6.85	8.95	13.04
19.	Kansas	5.29	7.35	20.13	13.00
20.	North Carolina	11.53	13.60	14.26	12.85
21.	Minnesota	2.95	21.42	18.25	12.71
22.	Montana	7.79	17.95	18.53	12.51
23.	Louisiana	1.39	2.05	9.85	12.03
24.	Massachusetts	29.25	23.05	24.60	11.70
25.	Mississippi	0.82	1.76	6.95	11.02
26.	Wisconsin	3.38	5.81	6.57	10.95
27.	Delaware	4.83	6.19	6.83	10.59
28.	Georgia	0.27	7.60	5.41	10.26
29.	Arkansas	11.54	10.67	9.63	9.94
30.	Tennessee	7.97	6.86	7.07	9.84
31.	West Virginia	4.97	2.25	8.73	9.35
32.	Maryland	3.58	8.19	7.66	9.32
33.	Pennsylvania	1.37	4.79	6.43	9.07
34.	Maine	8.41	7.51	7.03	7.95
35.	California	3.16	4.07	6.31	7.88
36.	New York	0.26	4.75	8.34	7.81
37.	South Carolina	5.27	5.34	6.29	7.47
38.	Missouri	5.17	10.90	6.04	7.31
39.	New Jersey	0.51	1.11	3.16	6.93

Rank Order 2003–2004	State	Percentage			
		1989–1990	1994–1995	1998–1999	2003–2004
40.	Wyoming	36.02	7.2	8.50	6.67
41.	Washington	8.14	20.12	14.69	6.59
42.	Arizona	1.26	8.66	7.03	5.90
43.	Michigan	6.13	7.92	18.28	5.41
44.	New Mexico	3.18	4.67	17.88	5.17
45.	Nevada	5.31	7.96	6.86	4.67
46.	Hawaii	1.75	9.74	9.42	4.24
47.	Illinois	0.31	1.52	6.66	4.05
48.	Texas	1.62	2.06	1.40	3.65
49.	Virginia	2.32	2.99	2.05	3.46
50.	Utah	6.25	3.44	5.12	2.55
	U.S. Total	6.74	9.68	9.60	11.66

Note: Data for "Percentage, 1989–1990" is from the *15th annual report to Congress on the implementation of the Individuals with Disabilities Education Act, Appendix A,* by the Office of Special Education and Rehabilitative Services, Table AB2, p. A-62, and reflects the percentage of students with intellectual disabilities (mental retardation) who received their education in general classes. Data for "Percentage, 1994–1995" is from the *18th annual report to Congress on the implementation of the Individuals with Disabilities Education Act, Appendix A,* by the Office of Special Education and Rehabilitative Services, Table AB2, p. A-56, and reflects the percentage of students with intellectual disabilities (mental retardation) who received their education in general classes. Data for "Percentage, 1998–1999" is from the *23rd annual report to Congress on the implementation of the Individuals with Disabilities Education Act, Appendix A,* by the Office of Special Education and Rehabilitative Services, Table AB2, p. A-87, and reflects the percentage of students with intellectual disabilities (mental retardation) who were outside of general classes less than 21% of the time. Data for "Percentage, 2003–2004" is from the *27th annual report to Congress on the implementation of the Individuals with Disabilities Education Act, Part 2,* by the Office of Special Education and Rehabilitative Services, Table 2–2c, p. 186, and reflects the percentage of students with intellectual disabilities (mental retardation) who were outside of general classes less than 21% of the time in the fall of 2003.

The percentage of students with intellectual disabilities who are outside of general education less than 21% of the time (data used from the *23rd* and *27th* reports) and the percentage of students with intellectual disabilities who received their education in general classes (data used from the *15th* and *18th* reports) appear to reflect percentages of students with intellectual disabilities who are outside of general education less than 21% of the time (that is, the numbers compared are apples to apples, not apples to oranges) or are treated as the same by the Office of Special Education and Rehabilitative Services, based on my analysis of data in the *25th report,* Table 3–8, p. 234. U.S. totals noted in the table reflect data for the 50 states, Washington DC, and Puerto Rico from the *15th, 18th,* and *23rd* reports and reflect data for the 50 states, Washington DC, and Bureau of Indian Affairs schools from the *27th* reports. Ranking of the states is by the author.

What do those numbers mean? They indicate that almost 90% of students with intellectual disabilities still spend substantive time outside of classrooms in which all students, regardless of disability label, might be included (see Figure 1 for a graphic representation of the level of exclusion they experience). In other words, almost all students with intellectual disabilities are not fully included. Also disappointing is that, over the course of the years between 1994 and 2003, a full 21 states—nearly half—lost ground in this regard, in some cases dramatically.

Figure 1: Percentage of Students with Intellectual Disabilities Fully Included in General Education Classrooms in the United States, 2003–2004

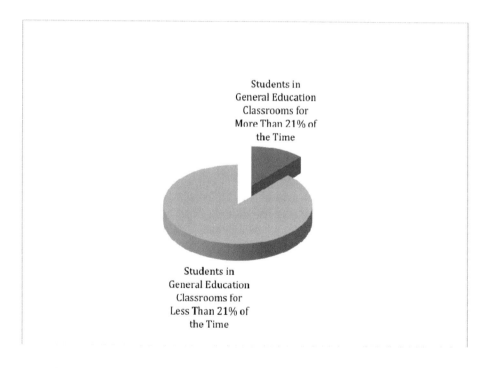

The state with the greatest percentage of students with intellectual disabilities fully included in general education classrooms has been the same over time—Vermont. Somewhat startlingly, because it has a powerful reputation around the country—indeed, the world—as a place solidly committed to inclusion, it was one of the almost one-half of states that lost ground in inclusion performance. The number of students with intellectual disabilities fully included in Vermont in the years 1994–1995 (when it reached its peak at 77.99%) dropped by an alarming 18.88%, leaving the state with the highest percentage at only 59.11% in 2003–2004.

Figure 2: Percentage of Students with Intellectual Disabilities Fully Included in General Education Classrooms in Vermont

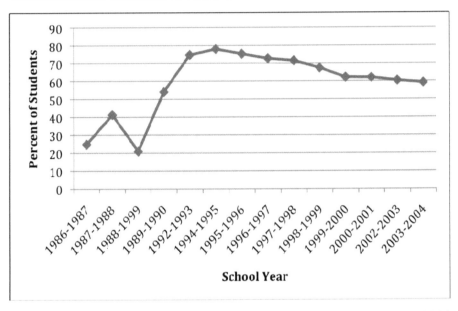

Note: Data for Figure 2 comes from the 11th, 12th, 13th, 15th, 16th, 18th, 20th, 21st, 22nd, 23rd, 24th, 25th, 26th, and 27th annual reports to Congress on the implementation of the Individuals with Disabilities Education Act. Data from the 14th, 17th, and 19th reports are not included, because they are for the same school year as that in the immediately preceding report. See note for Table 1 for additional comments regarding this data.

Looking at other data, the numbers go from bad to worse. Nationally, during the period between 1999–2000 and 2003–2004, the number of students with intellectual disabilities fully included in general education went down by 2.39% overall, from 14.05% to 11.66% (see Figure 2 for a graphic representation of the percentage of students with intellectual disabilities fully included in general education classrooms over time, nationally). If this represents a trend—and I worry that it does—then sometime during the late 1990s the United States reached a peak in the number of students with intellectual disabilities who were fully included (at a number still substantially less than the extent of inclusion advocates, families, and people with disabilities want and need) and then started a slide toward increased segregation. This appears to be not just a plateauing—as Williamson, McLesky, Hoppey, & Rentz (2006) indicated, based on their analysis of slightly less recent data than is looked at here—but a downward turn. This slide is not just at the national level but is replicated at the micro-level in half of all individual states.

What Do These Numbers Mean?

In its 1992 report, the Arc called for the full inclusion of 50% of students with intellectual disabilities by 1995, and for the full inclusion of all students with intellectual disabilities by the year 2000. By any measure, efforts to reach that goal have been not just a dismal failure but a failure of the grossest magnitude—in policy terms, in human rights terms, in moral and legal terms. Instead, just a hair's-breadth more than one-tenth of all students with intellectual disabilities in the United States were fully included by the year 2003. In fact—looked at in the best light possible, seeing the last two decades or so as a whole— the states, local school districts, and the federal government have moved at an extraordinarily pathetic slow pace toward the goal of full inclusion. Looking at the more recent five years, and in a more pessimistic view, the pace has not just slowed—it has stopped and, worse, reversed direction.

Further, Vermont, the state with the highest percentage of fully included students with intellectual disabilities, is now doing a poorer job—substantially poorer—at including those students than it did in the early 1990s; the top is no longer anywhere near where it was at its peak. The movement toward full inclusion has reversed direction (even if, more generously, one takes a broader view, the pace of change has slowed from a snail's pace to one that is foot-draggingly slow). If the state that has been the most successful at including students with intellectual disabilities can be considered a kind of canary in a coal mine and if the most recent five years of official data reported to Congress can be considered any sort of trend, then there are signs that the future of inclusion in the United States is very bleak indeed.

Figure 3 Percentages of Students with Intellectual Disabilities Fully Included in General Education Classrooms in the United States

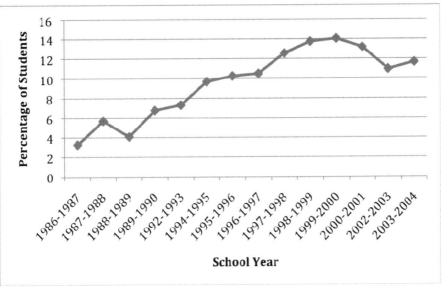

Note: Data for Figure 3 comes from the 11th, 12th, 13th, 15th, 16th, 18th, 20th, 21st, 22nd, 23rd, 24th, 25th, 26th, and 27th annual reports to Congress on the implementation of the Individuals with Disabilities Education Act. Data from the 14th, 17th, and 19th reports are not included, because they are for the same school year as that in the immediately preceding report. Data reflects the percentage of students in the 50 states as well as Washington, DC and Puerto Rico for the 11th through 25th reports and the percentage of students in the 50 states, Washington, DC, and Bureau of Indian Affairs schools for the 26th and 27th reports. See note for Table 1 for additional comments regarding this data.

I'm not going to perform the statistical analysis that the Arc did in the mid-1990s to develop an inclusion score for individual states. But in looking at the raw percentages of students with intellectual disabilities included in general classrooms in 2003–2004, by state, no state could get the highest grade the Arc gave in 1995, a B (given to only one state—again, Vermont). In fact, using the kind of scoring rubric that I use for my students, there would be no Cs in my grade book, or Bs, nor certainly any As. If I were to give grades a year ago, Vermont would have been given a D, though I would have said that it was hanging onto that grade by its fingernails (Smith, 2007a). Today, I can say not even that—in 2008, no state would get even a D, instead of the 16 states who received that grade from the Arc in 1995. Using the grading rubric that I use in my classes, I would have to give every state in the Union an F. Some would say I should give Vermont a break—that I should give the state a couple of points for the equivalent of good attendance. It is, after all, the second state in the United States to have fully closed its large state-run institution for people with intellectual and developmental disabilities (Aichroth et al., 2002). But, in fairness, I can't. All Fs.

Inclusion for Students with Other Disabilities

Is inclusion just an issue for students with intellectual disabilities? Of course, not. Less than half of students aged 6–21 receiving special education services spent most of their time (80% or more) in general education classrooms in 2000, and almost 20% spent more than 60% of their schooltime in segregated classes, outside of general education classrooms. A full 4.2% of students with all kinds of disabilities in the 6–21 age range received their education in completely segregated settings outside of general education buildings (residential facilities and other separate facilities, or in homebound or hospital environments). Students with deaf-blindness, multiple disabilities, and emotional impairments were the most likely to receive educational services in those completely segregated settings. Even when receiving their education in general education buildings, just like students with intellectual disabilities, students with autism, multiple disabilities, deaf-blindness, and emotional impairments were likely to spend most of their time in segregated classes outside of general education classrooms (OSERS, 2003).

In order to understand better the trends surrounding inclusion, I did an analysis similar to the one that I did for students with intellectual disabilities, looking at the numbers of students with, in this case, a high incidence disability who were included in general education classrooms in the United States—students with emotional disabilities (described as emotional disturbance by the federal government). The numbers were revealing (see Table 2).

What do these numbers tell us? Only a tiny bit more than 30% of one of the largest groups of students with disabilities in the country are fully included in general education classrooms; only slightly less than 70% remain in highly segregated settings. Although the change in terms of inclusion over the decade I looked at was more steady than that for students with intellectual disabilities, when you look at the total percentage of students with emotional disabilities who were fully included in general education classrooms, these numbers can be somewhat deceiving.

Table 2: Percentage of Students with Emotional Disabilities (Emotional Disturbance) Included in General Education Classrooms More Than 79% of the Time

Rank Order 2003–2004	State	Percentage			
		1989–1990	1994–1995	1998–1999	2003–2004
1.	New Hampshire	43.72	42.35	63.61	60.43
2.	North Dakota	38.81	47.82	55.22	66.67
3.	Vermont	69.90	74.16	67.06	58.50
4.	Colorado	19.86	19.80	48.60	50.92
5.	Oregon	28.75	42.26	45.31	49.17
6.	Minnesota	9.84	46.29	51.30	48.36
7.	Alabama	45.90	37.03	38.43	45.06
8.	South Dakota	7.84	14.27	40.43	44.00
9.	Texas	5.06	6.32	13.37	42.04
10.	Nebraska	38.01	38.24	37.65	41.81
11.	Idaho	41.84	36.82	39.03	40.00
12.	Wisconsin	19.70	35.45	27.75	39.90
13.	Kansas	30.06	30.00	40.07	38.84
14.	Missouri	14.67	4.68	33.22	37.15
15.	West Virginia	10.67	13.83	31.78	36.51
16.	Iowa	2.11	55.31	33.74	36.47
17.	Florida	13.81	9.50	36.10	36.37
18.	Montana	32.17	44.98	36.42	35.52
19.	Rhode Island	22.36	19.94	22.10	35.19
20.	Indiana	11.38	31.19	31.97	34.72
21.	Maine	36.28	36.11	32.18	34.66
22.	North Carolina	31.86	32.35	29.13	34.43
23.	Alaska	17.41	22.03	27.59	34.12
24.	Nevada	8.65	14.56	32.26	33.38
25.	Mississippi	7.66	9.20	15.17	32.50
26.	Georgia	31.22	34.40	23.07	32.22
27.	Connecticut	31.28	36.75	30.53	31.95
28.	Kentucky	5.03	10.41	19.72	31.62
29.	Washington	27.52	19.20	34.51	30.60
30.	Michigan	27.90	32.45	45.14	29.89
31.	Wyoming	40.51	30.29	27.55	28.81
32.	Utah	34.36	41.13	35.19	28.18
33.	Arizona	0.90	14.87	23.75	27.93
34.	New Mexico	26.95	25.40	32.19	27.71
35.	Oklahoma	8.52	13.34	20.25	27.42
36.	New Jersey	4.18	12.21	17.17	27.12
37.	Maryland	11.38	18.58	17.57	26.34
38.	Tennessee	23.77	24.50	23.63	25.36
39.	Delaware	26.46	9.40	14.40	23.70
40.	Pennsylvania	10.17	11.68	13.56	23.20
41.	Hawaii	18.03	29.74	24.87	22.85

Rank Order 2003–2004	State	Percentage			
		1989–1990	1994–1995	1998–1999	2003–2004
42.	New York	1.95	16.04	17.80	22.84
43.	Louisiana	7.92	10.07	11.36	22.07
44.	Virginia	15.91	12.20	17.77	20.26
45.	Ohio	4.93	8.50	23.63	20.19
46.	Illinois	2.54	3.23	12.88	18.91
47.	Arkansas	11.28	14.41	14.55	18.53
48.	South Carolina	10.43	11.16	10.74	17.60
49.	California	3.57	9.13	12.62	17.39
50.	Massachusetts	60.65	20.61	21.22	15.50
	U.S. Total:	16.80	24.14	25.51	30.33

Note: Data for "Percentage, 1989–1990" is from the 15th *annual report to Congress on the implementation of the Individuals with Disabilities Education Act, Appendix A,* by the Office of Special Education and Rehabilitative Services, Table AB2, p. A-61. Data for "Percentage, 1994–1995" is from the 18th *annual report to Congress on the implementation of the Individuals with Disabilities Education Act, Appendix A,* by the Office of Special Education and Rehabilitative Services, Table AB2, p. A-55. Data for "Percentage, 1998–1999" is from the 23rd *annual report to Congress on the implementation of the Individuals with Disabilities Education Act, Appendix A,* by the Office of Special Education and Rehabilitative Services, Table AB2, p. A-89. Data for "Percentage, 2003–2004" is from the 27th *annual report to Congress on the implementation of the Individuals with Disabilities Education Act, Part 2,* by the Office of Special Education and Rehabilitative Services, Table 2–2c, p. 188.

The percentage of students with emotional disabilities who are outside of general education less than 21% of the time (data used from the 23rd and 27th reports) and the percentage of students with emotional disabilities who received their education in general classes (data used from the 15th and 18th reports) appear to reflect percentages of students with emotional disabilities who are outside of general education less than 21% of the time (that is, the numbers compared are apples to apples, not apples to oranges) or are treated as the same by the Office of Special Education and Rehabilitative Services, based on my analysis of data in the 25th report. U.S. totals noted in the table reflect data for the 50 states, Washington DC, and Puerto Rico from the 15th, 18th, and 23rd reports; and reflect data for the 50 states, Washington DC, and Bureau of Indian Affairs schools from the 27th reports.

Ranking of the states is by the author.

Two out of three of the top-ranked states for fully including students with emotional disabilities showed a fair amount of slippage in the last five years that were examined. Vermont, which had been ranked as number one for the full inclusion of students with emotional disabilities for a decade and a half, slipped down to the number three position, in spite of having climbed to an incredible 74% in the mid-1990s. While many states showed steady growth over the period explored, thirteen states peaked *before* the most recent data point, dropping since then. In 2003–2004, eight states were below where they had started in 1989–1990 (Massachusetts dropped an almost incredible 45%).

If I were to give states grades based on these percentages, again using the grading rubric I use with my own students, only two states would get the passing grade of D (with those two barely at that level) based on the 2003–2004 data—all the rest would get Fs. Every single one. At the beginning of the roughly 15-year-long period that I looked at, there were two states that were passing. At the end of that time—still two states were passing, but those were not the same states.

And there were some interesting things that were *not* revealed by the data I've presented here. For example, while South Dakota ranked highly (at number 8) in 2003–2004 for full inclusion, it also had 16% of students with emotional disabilities receiving their education in residential facilities, followed closely by California. In New Hampshire, the highest-ranked state for the full inclusion of students with emotional disabilities in the United States in 2003–2004, 7% of students received their education in residential facilities. Such facilities can be described only as among the most highly segregated and separate settings imaginable. It is simply amazing to me that the state ranked as having the best capacity for including students with emotional disabilities still has so many that are so completely segregated.

These trends are clearly disappointing. What's going on here? What is the history and meaning of inclusion? How did we end up in this place? These are questions that my fellow authors and I will explore in the next few chapters of this book.

Notes

1   Translated from the way OSERS describes it, in terms of those who are outside those classrooms for less than 21% of the time.

References

Aichroth, S., Carpenter, J., Daniels, K., Grassette, P., Kelly, D., Murray, A., Rice, J., Rivard, B., Smith, C., Smith, P., & Topper, K. (2002). Creating a new system of supports: The Vermont self-determination project. *Rural Special Education Quarterly, 21*(2), 16–28.

The Arc of the United States (1995). *Report Card on inclusion in education of children with mental retardation.* Silver Springs, MD: Author. Retrieved on April 4, 2006 from http://www.thearc.org/report/95RPTCD.html

Bragden, T. (2008). The case for inclusion 2008: An analysis of Medicaid for Americans with intellectual and developmental disabilities. Washington, DC: United Cerebral Palsy.

Brown v. Board of Education, 347 U.S. 483, 47 S. Ct. 686, 98 L. Ed. 873 (1954).

Davis, S. (1992). Report card to the nation on inclusion in education of students with mental retardation. Arlington, TX: The Arc.

Downing, J. (2008). Inclusive education: Why is it not more prevalent? *TASH Connections, 34*(2), 8–10, 13.

Ferguson, D. (1995). The real challenge of inclusion: Confessions of a "rabid inclusionist." *Phi Delta Kappan, 77,* 281–287

Karagiannis, A., Stainback, S., & Stainback, W. (1996). Historical overview of inclusion. In S. Stainback & W. Stainback (Eds.), *Inclusion: A guide for educators* (pp. 17–28). Baltimore: Brookes.

Lakin, K., Prouty, R., & Alba, K. (2007). Status and trends in institutional services for persons with intellectual and developmental disabilities. *TASH Connections, 33*(11/12), 28–30.

McLeskey, J., Henry, D., & Hodges, D. (1999). Inclusion: What progress is being made across disability categories? *Teaching Exceptional Children, 31*(4), 60–64.

National Council on Teacher Quality (2004). Attracting, developing and retaining effective teachers: Background report for the United States. Washington, DC: Author.

Office of Special Education and Rehabilitative Services (1989). Implementation of the Education of the Handicapped Act Public Law 94-142: Eleventh annual report to Congress. Washington, DC: Author.

————— (1990). Implementation of the Education of the Handicapped Act: Twelfth annual report to Congress. Washington, DC: Author.

————— (1991). Implementation of the Individuals with Disabilities Education Act: Thirteenth annual report to Congress. Washington, DC: Author.

————— (1993). Implementation of the Individuals with Disabilities Education Act: Fifteenth annual report to Congress. Washington, DC: Author.

————— (1994). Implementation of the Individuals with Disabilities Education Act: Sixteenth annual report to Congress. Washington, DC: Author.

————— (1996). Implementation of the Individuals with Disabilities Education Act: Eighteenth annual report to Congress. Washington, DC: Author.

————— (1998). Implementation of the Individuals with Disabilities Education Act: Twentieth annual report to Congress. Washington, DC: Author.

————— (1999). To assure the free appropriate public education of all children with disabilities (Individuals with Disabilities Education Act, Section 618). Twenty-first annual report to Congress on the implementation of the Individuals with Disabilities Education Act. Washington, DC: Author.

————— (2000). To assure the free appropriate public education of all children with disabilities (Individuals with Disabilities Education Act, Section 618). Twenty-second annual report to Congress on the implementation of the Individuals with Disabilities Education Act. Washington, DC: Author.

————— (2001). To assure the free appropriate public education of all children with disabilities (Individuals with Disabilities Education Act, Section 618). Twenty-third annual report to Congress on the implementation of the Individuals with Disabilities Education Act. Washington, DC: Author.

————— (2002). To assure the free appropriate public education of all children with disabilities (Individuals with Disabilities Education Act, Section 618). Twenty-fourth annual report to Congress on the implementation of the Individuals with Disabilities Education Act.. Washington, DC: Author.

——— (2003). 25th annual report to Congress on the implementation of the Individuals with Disabilities Education Act. Washington, DC: Author.

——— (2004). 26th annual report to Congress on the implementation of the Individuals with Disabilities Education Act. Washington, DC: Author.

——— (2005). 27th annual report to Congress on the implementation of the Individuals with Disabilities Education Act. Washington, DC: Author.

Siperstein, G., Parker, R., Bardon, J., & Widaman, K. (2007). A national study of youth attitudes toward the inclusion of students with intellectual disabilities. *Exceptional Children, 73,* 435–455.

Smith, P. (1999a). Ideology, politics, and science in understanding developmental disabilities. *Mental Retardation, 37,* 71–72.

——— (1999b). Drawing new maps: A radical cartography of developmental disabilities. *Review of Educational Research, 69*(2), 117–144.

——— (1999c). "I know how to do": Stories of choice, control, and power in the lives of people with developmental disabilities. *Dissertation Abstracts International, 60* (11) A (University Microfilms No. 9951862).

——— (2001a). Inquiry cantos: A poetics of developmental disability. *Mental Retardation, 39,* 379–390.

——— (2001b). MAN.i.f.e.s.t.o.: A Poetics of D(EVIL)op(MENTAL) Dis(ABILITY). *Taboo: The Journal of Education and Culture, 5*(1), 27–36.

——— (2005). Off the map: A critical geography of intellectual disabilities. *Health and Place, 11,* 87–92.

——— (2007a). Have we made any progress? Including students with intellectual disabilities in general education classrooms. *Intellectual and Developmental Disabilities, 45,* 297–309.

——— (2007b). What progress? The inclusion of students with intellectual disabilities in regular education. Annual Conference of TASH, Seattle, WA.

Weber, M. (2007). Inclusive education in the United States and internationally: Challenges and response. *Review of Disability Studies, 3*(1–2), 19–32.

Williamson, P., McLeskey, J., Hoppey, D., & Rentz, T. (2006). Educating students with mental retardation in general education classrooms. *Exceptional Children, 72,* 347–361.

CHAPTER 2

Defining Inclusion

What Is It? Who Does It Benefit?

PHIL SMITH

> What are schools for anyway? ... is it the task of the teacher to supply cannon fodder for the military-industrial complex? Are we shaping packages for the corporate assembly line? (McCourt, 2005, p. 211)

In this chapter, I will begin to define the meaning of inclusion for students with intellectual disabilities in schools. More important than this definition, of course, is a beginning outline of who that definition benefits. It will be clear from this exploration that the beneficiary of special education is not students with intellectual and other disabilities, but rather the educational industrial complex and the larger normate culture in which it resides. Instead, children and adults with intellectual disabilities are forced to the marginalia (and sometimes entirely off the page) of maps of normative cultures, outside boundaries patrolled by special education and human service gatekeepers.

Defining Inclusion

Arriving at a single, unifying, clear, useful, and practical definition of inclusion for students with disabilities, intellectual or otherwise, in schools and other educational contexts, is no small task, for there is no clear consensus about what, in fact, inclusion is (Snyder, Garriott, & Aylor, 2001). Frankly, definitions are all over the place, representing diverse perspectives and ideologies (e.g., see Ainscow, 2007; Begeny & Martens, 2007; Brown, 1997; Clair, Church, & Batshaw, 2002; Damer, 2001; Falvey & Givner, 2005; Fuchs & Fuchs, 1998; Gee, 2004; Hagan-Burke & Jefferson, 2002; Hall, 2002; Keefe & Davis, 1998; King, 2003; Lewis & Doorlag, 2006; Marchbanks, Richardson, & Flanagan, 2001; Ruef, 2003; Ryndak, Jackson, & Billingsley, 2000; Shapiro-Barnard, 1998; B. Smith, 2007; Stockall & Garten, 2002; Turnbull, Turnbull, Erwin, & Soodak, 2006).

Unfortunately, inclusion is not defined—or even referenced—in the Individuals with Disabilities Educational Improvement Act (IDEIA). One result of this is that the formal data available to us concerning the inclusion of students with intellectual disabilities in schools—about the inclusion of students with *any* disability—that the Office of Special Education and Rehabilitation Services (OSERS) collects is derivative. The numbers I presented in chapter 1 are not based on a definition of inclusion per se—they're based on the data that OSERS collects (not to belabor the obvious, this is unquestionably a circular, almost incestuous description at best). The information provided by the federal government describes the amount of time students with disabilities spend in particular educational environments. In a way, the data has created the definition, rather than working the other way around. Because OSERS collects data about environments, that's the way we can understand inclusion.

This is in part a reflection of the way that education for students with disabilities has been described and understood for the past more than thirty years, formalized in the language of the IDEIA. There, education is framed as a place—an environment, one that is portrayed as more or less restrictive. IDEIA does not describe inclusion, so OSERS does not collect information about it. One of the traps that the original designers of P.L. 94-142 (the precursor of IDEIA) fell into—a trap that has been maintained for several decades—is the portrayal of special education (and, for that matter, education more broadly) as a place, rather than seeing it as a process or set of practices (Kluth, Villa, & Thousand, 2002). For OSERS, special education is where things occur, not what is done there.

In short, then, to truly collect information about the inclusion of students with intellectual (or any other) disabilities, OSERS needs to adopt a (hopefully progressive) definition of inclusion. Without this, the information we get doesn't really help much.

Why Do Inclusion?

In spite of the fact that there is no clear consensus on the meaning of inclusion, there is a diverse body of research about inclusion—about what it means and what it does—that has been explored over a long period of time. As early as 1951, researchers explored ways to include students with disabilities in regular education classrooms (Haring, 2002). The history of inclusive education has a long and powerful story, with substantial success, not just for students with so-called mild disabilities, but for students with intellectual and significant disabilities as well (Stainback & Smith, 2005; Tomlinson, 2004; Villa & Thousand, 2002).

Researchers have found many reasons, including those that are legal, moral, procedural, and philosophical, for asserting that inclusion is a best practice in education (Baglieri & Knopf, 2004; Baker, Wang, & Walberg, 1995; Dixon, 2005; Villa & Thousand, 2002; Villa & Thousand, 2005). Downing notes that there is "strong legislative backing and empirical evidence of the benefits of inclusive education" (2008, p. 8). A number of exemplary schools and districts have built inclusive models, across pre-, elementary, middle, and high school levels including the Twin Valley Middle School in Elverson, Pennsylvania; the Arnold Schwarzenegger Charter Elementary School in Woodland Hills, California; and the Ravenswood City School District in East Palo Alto, California, to name some very recent examples (Downing, 2008; Haney & Cox, 2008; Fabrocini & Hanreddy, 2008; Taschner & Donahue, 2008).

Doyle (2003) outlines a useful framework for understanding the capacity for inclusion to serve as an overarching theme that unifies what might otherwise be fragmented metaphors within education. She notes that

> inclusion for students with disabilities provides the power to weave together educational leaders as moral stewards, builders of democratic leadership, and educators ... Inclusion (a) facilitates leadership for social justice, (b) models democracy, (c) shifts power, (d) involves school-wide reform, (e) restructures and recultures, (f) enhances strategies for teaching and learning, and (g) provides support and resources. In these ways, inclusion of students with disabilities has the potential to facilitate inclusion for students of all diversities. (p. 4)

A wide variety of evidence-based educational strategies are available to enable students with disabilities to be included in regular education classrooms (e.g., see Conway & Gow, 1988; Carter, Sisco, Brown, Brickham, & Al-Khabbaz, 2008; Downing & Eichinger, 2003; Eiserman, 1988; Giangreco, 1997; Hardin & Hardin, 2002; Hasbrouck & Christen, 1997; Hunt, Doering, Hirose-Hatae, Maier, & Goetz, 2001; Hunt, Soto, Maier, & Doering, 2003; Jameson, McDonnell, Polychronis, & Riesen, 2008; Jenkins, Antil, Wayne, & Vadasy, 2003; Idol, 2006; King-Sears & Bradley, 1995; Lawrence-Brown, 2004; Lohrman & Bambara, 2006; Maheady, Harper, & Sacca, 1988; Mastropieri, & Scruggs, 2001; McCormick, Noonan, Ogata, & Heck, 2001; McDonnell, 1998; Morocco, 2001; Putnam, 1993; McLeskey & Waldron, 2007; Schmidt, Rozendal, & Greenman, 2002; Slavin, 1991; Udvari-Solner,

Thousand, Villa, Quiocho, & Kelly, 2005; Villa, Thousand, & Chapple, 1996; Villa & Thousand, 2003; Villa, Thousand, Nevin, & Liston, 2005; Willis, 2007).

Inclusive practices bring clear, unequivocal academic and social benefits for students with and without disabilities, across a variety of age ranges and educational disciplines (see, for example, Agran, Blanchard, Wehmeyer, & Hughes, 2002; Austin, 2001; Burstein, Sears, Wilcoxen, Cabello, & Spagna, 2004; Cole, 2006; Cole, Waldron, & Majd, 2004; Cushing & Kennedy, 1997; Dore, Dion, Wagner, & Brunet, 2002; Downing, 2008; Downing & Eichinger, 2003; Downing and Peckham-Hardin, 2007; Downing, Spencer, & Cavallaro, 2004; Dymond & Orelove, 2001; Fisher & Meyer, 2002; Freeman & Alkin, 2000; George & Duquette, 2006; Giangreco & Putnam, 1991; Halvorsen & Sailor, 1990; Hunt, Hirose-Hatae, Doering, Karasoff, & Goetz, 2000; Hunt & Goetz, 1997; Hunt, Staub, Alwell, & Goetz, 1994; Idol, 2006; Jenkins, Antil, Wayne, & Vadasy, 2003; Karagiannis, Stainback, & Stainback, 1996; Kennedy & Itkonen, 1994; Peck, Staub, Gallucci, & Schwartz, 2004; Rea, Mclaughlin, & Walther-Thomas, 2002; Sax, Fisher, & Pumpian, 1996; Scott, Jellison, Chappell, & Standridge, 2007; B. Smith, 2007; Staub & Peck, 1995; Waldron & McLeskey, 1998).

Strikingly, general educators, school psychologists, school administrators, and teacher educators all report that they see important, positive academic and/or social gains for students with disabilities (Cowan, McGoey, & Quallich, 2007; Crockett, Myers, Griffin, & Hollandsworth, 2007; Griffin, Jones, & Kilgore, 2007; Ornelles, Cook, & Jenkins, 2007; Tankersley & Cook, 2007). As Downing notes, "such findings counter fears that students without disabilities will endure any negative impact as a result of inclusive practices" (2008, p. 8).

Co-teaching is an important strategy for enabling the inclusion of students with disabilities in general education classrooms (Bouk, 2007; Cramer & Nevin, 2006; Fontana, 2005; Friend, 2007; Mastropieri, Scruggs, Graetz, Norland, Gardizi, & McDuffie 2005; Murawski & Dieker, 2008; Rice, Drame, Owens, & Frattura, 2007; Scruggs, Mastropieri, & McDuffie, 2007; Villa, Thousand, & Nevin, 2004). Developed as a practice in the 1960s, co-teaching benefits a wide variety of students with diverse learning styles and needs and leads to positive outcomes for schools across numerous axes (Villa, Thousand, & Nevin, 2004). Quantitative research indicates that it is an effective method of instruction (Murawski & Swanson, 2001). Qualitative research reveals that it has both academic and social benefits for students with and without disabilities, along with professional benefits for educators, although it is often poorly implemented (Scruggs, Mastropieri, & McDuffie, 2007).

A Universal Design for Learning approach is another important tool for building inclusive models of education from the ground up (Hehir, 2007; Sabia, 2008; Smith, Kozleski, & King, 2008). One parent of a student with Down syndrome described Universal Design for Learning

> as a framework for education that makes the curriculum accessible for all students, including students with intellectual disabilities, by providing cognitive as well as physical access to the information being taught and the assessments that measure what has been learned. It mirrors the universal design movement for architecture and products ... The term "Universal" in UDL does not imply that any one educational method is universal for all students. Instead, it emphasizes the need for multiple educational approaches that provide diverse learners with accessible learning opportunities. (Sabia, 2008, p. 14)

Universal Design for Learning builds on the growing body of work that explores differentiated instruction and the theory of multiple intelligences (Smith, Kozleski, & King, 2008).

The effectiveness of inclusion for students with disabilities, including those labeled as having intellectual disabilities, hinges not just on instruction, but also on elements of classroom climate/culture. Berry (2006) asserts,

> Attributes of classroom culture underlying successful inclusive classrooms are believed to include valuing of student voices, authority sharing, accountability of students to each other, presence of relevant resources, attention to individual differences, positive interpersonal relationships, preparation for integration, participation in shared routines, school-wide community spirit, and high levels of acceptance and expectations for all students. (p. 491)

These are the qualities that Noddings (2003) identified as being part of caring classroom communities (Smith, 2007).

The framework for those who believe inclusion to be a useful goal in education is one that "privileges subjective, multiple truths and complex rather than simple analyses" (Ware, 2004, p. 4). Brantlinger (1997) comments that

> inclusionists ideology can be considered organic, in that it dwells on emancipatory or transformative ideas for eliminating oppression from social structures ... they are explicit about values, educational philosophies, theories of learning, and goals for society ... inclusionist's accept nontraditional learning theories, instructional practices, and research methods ... and perhaps most importantly, they are optimistic about school reform and individual transmutability. (pp. 448–449)

A number of practices appear to have a positive impact on the achievement gap (as measured by statewide assessments) between students with disabilities and students without disabilities. Among these are the inclusion of students with disabilities in general education contexts (Donahue Institute, 2004). In fact, among state responses, inclusion was the second most commonly reported practice having a positive impact on moving the performance of students with disabilities closer to that of students without disabilities (Altman, Lazarus, Thurlow, Quenemoen, Cuthbert, & Cormier, 2008).

A Modest Proposal for a Definition of Inclusion

If the OSERS were to ask me what definition of inclusion they should use in order to develop the kind of data they need to collect, I'd recommend the one Giangreco (2006) proposed based on his in-depth research over decades, one that he's revised and added to over time. Usefully, it holds to the working definition developed by Ryndak, Jackson, and Billingsley (2000), who looked at common themes across a variety of expert definitions—at least in scope, if not always in precise detail. Here, I quote the definition in its entirety:

All students are welcomed in general education. The general education class in the school the student would attend if not disabled is the first placement option considered. Appropriate supports, regardless of disability type or severity, are available.

Students are educated in classes where the number of those with and without disabilities is proportional to the local population (e.g., 10%–12% have identified disabilities).

Students are educated with peers in the same age groupings available to those without disability labels.

Students with varying characteristics and abilities (e.g., those with and without disability labels) participate in shared educational experiences while pursuing individually appropriate learning outcomes with necessary supports and accommodations.

Shared educational experiences take place in settings predominantly frequented by people without disabilities (e.g., general education classes, community work sites, community recreational facilities).

Educational experiences are designed to enhance individually determined valued life outcomes for students and therefore seek an individualized balance between the academic-functional and social-personal aspects of schooling.

Inclusive education exists when each of the previously listed characteristics occurs on an ongoing, daily basis. (Giangreco, 2006, p. 4)

Giangreco's definition is a powerful one because: it speaks about all students, not just those with disabilities; it describes special education as a process, not as a place; it speaks to the rights of students; it describes students, both with and without disabilities, as being a shared responsibility for all schools and educators; and finally, it describes schools as a place of community, and as a place within which to create community.

Opposing Inclusion

There are some for whom full inclusion is not seen as a useful goal, principle, or value. Their perspective represents a particular ideology (Brantlinger, 1997; 2004; Smith, 1999a; 2008a; 2008b; Ware, 2004). However, many of these authors would deny that their position is ideological (Bouck, 2006; Foxx & Roland, 2005; Heward & Silvestri, 2005; Jacobson, Mulick, & Foxx, 2005; Kavale & Forness, 2000; Kozloff, 2005; Zigmond, 2003). Instead, they remain trapped in a modernist, Cartesian understanding of science, refusing to recognize that all science is ideological. This kind of positivist science purports to be neutral, obfuscating its inherent value-based ideology (Brantlinger, 1997; Smith, 1999a; 1999b). Brantlinger (1997) describes these writers as traditionalists. Ware (2004) notes that

> traditionalists challenge the research knowledge base that informs the inclusion movement because they claim it lacks rigor and scientific objectivity and fails to conform to the linear model of positivist research privileged in their own scholarship. Their conceptual approach to understanding assumes objectivity through measured observation, calibrated interventions, and pursuit of singular truth that rests on an appeal to facts. (p. 4)

Some of these authors critique the kind of postmodernist, critical, and disability studies approaches in (special) education reflected in (parts of) this book (Favell, 2005; Heward & Silvestri, 2005; Hockenbury, Kauffman, & Hallahan, 2000; Kauffman, 1999; 2003; Kauffman, Bantz, & McCullough, 2002; Kavale & Forness, 2000; Kavale & Mostert, 2003; Newsom & Hovanitz, 2005; Zane, 2005). Researchers in this group have critiqued my own scholarship in this area, again failing to recognize the way they position themselves from an ideological perspective, asserting that they are neutral and scientific instead of neo-conservative, functionalist, essentialist, positivist, and Cartesian (Heward & Silvestri, 2005; Hockenbury, Kauffman, & Hallahan, 2000; Kavale & Mostert, 2003). Rather than being scientific, their work reflects an inherent scientism.

Leading the charge for the ideological opposition to inclusion has long been James Kauffman. Now emeritus at the University of Virginia, he has written much in an attempt to denigrate inclusive approaches, again denying his own value-based position (Crockett & Kauffman, 1998; Kauffman, 1999; 2003; 2004; Kauffman, Bantz, & McCullough, 2002; Kauffman, Landrom, Mock, Sayeski, & Sayeski, 2005; Kauffman, Lloyd, & Riedel, 1995; Kauffman, McGee, & Brigham, 2004; Kauffman & Hallahan, 2005; Mock & Kauffman, 2002; Mock & Kauffman, 2005; Mostert, Kavale, & Kauffman, 2007). He and colleagues assert that full inclusion "is contrary to common sense, inconsistent with what we know about disabilities, and devoid of credible supporting evidence" (Mock & Kauffman, 2005, p. 113).

Somewhat astoundingly (from a disability studies perspective), Kauffman (2007a) recently argued for the benefits of a medical model in special education. He contrasts this with what he calls a "legal" model, which seeks to protect the rights of people. He asserts that a medical model based on scientific and empirical knowledge can resolve problems for people with disabilities—locating those problems within people with disabilities, rather than seeing issues related to disabilities as located within cultural projects. My own and others work over more than a decade has long pointed to fundamental problems with a medical model of special (and other) education and disability, arguing instead for a complexifying social model (Smith, 1999b; Danforth, 1997). Kauffman and his colleagues have created an ideology of radical exclusion that denies people with disabilities the benefits of social, cultural, and educational institutions.

Brantlinger (2004) asserts that there are two sets of ideologies:

> (1) those related to establishing social hierarchies through interpersonal competition and stratifying practices, and (2) those based on the communal ideals that recognize human dignity, commonality, equality, equity, and reciprocity. (p. 20)

She refers to these as hierarchical and communal ideologies respectively. Although recognizing that such an ordering is simplistic and binaric, she notes that hierarchical ideologies result in the kinds of practices espoused by Kauffman and his colleagues: "ability-based reading groups, secondary school tracking or streaming, special education pull-out, class/race segregated schools, property-tax-based school funding... [and] within-district disparities in school funding and human resource distribution" (Brantlinger, 2004, p. 21). Opposed to these practices, she notes that "communal ideology articulates ways for people to relate across race, language usage, ethnicity, sexual orientation, gender, and other personal attributes and be equal" (p. 21) and that, in alignment with models of distributive justice, students with disabilities "are entitled to fair portions of resources and respect and have the right to have access to the general curriculum and be part of the comprehensive school community" (p. 22).

Kincheloe (2006a) critiques the particular brand of positivism espoused by those critical of inclusion (among others), noting that it "is a monocultural way of seeing the world that emphasizes the knowledges produced by patriarchy, white Europeans, and individuals from the upper middle/upper classes" (p. 11). He notes that "White, male, class-elitist, heterosexist, imperial, and colonial privilege often operates by asserting the power to claim objectivity and neutrality. Indeed the owners of such privilege often own the 'franchise' on reason, rationality, and truth" (Kincheloe, 2007, p. 19).

Who Benefits?

Education as a modernist enterprise within the twentieth and twenty-first centuries is nestled snugly within the ideology and scientism of the eugenics movement; it "carries a legacy informed and created by eugenic ideology, which has defined, sorted, and categorized students on the basis of a heretofore unexamined yardstick of 'scientific' racialism" (Winfield, 2007, p. 3). More specifically, special education is founded in the eugenics movement of the early modernist period during the late nineteenth and early twentieth centuries (Smith, 2008a). Early eugenicists developed a set of statistical tools with which to sort those who are Normal from those who are Different, locating difference in their bodies and their minds. Describing these differences in moral terms, they found ways to describe and separate the Good (white, upper-class, rich, male, heterosexual, able-bodied, reasonable) inhabitants of the land of the Normal from the Evil (non-white, lower-class, impoverished, female, queer, disabled, mad) inhabitants of the land of the Different (Smith, 2001; 2004; 2008a). Although an extremely important ideology of the early modernist period, this kind of Social Darwinism still holds remarkable currency in an increasingly rightist American culture and dominates present educational thinking and policy (Apple, 2003; Giroux, 2001; 2005; Winfield, 2007).

The eugenicist science of modernist, positivist psychology creates and enforces both the Normal and the Different through numbering testing procedures in order to differentiate students; they provide and extend the "normalizing gaze" of their makers ... Students are compared and ordered in ever finer degrees of "normal" and "abnormal," which the technologies of the modern sciences have made available ... On the basis of their behavior and their scores, students are sorted and selected in and out of programs, receiving unequal and unjust opportunities to learn high-status knowledge that is unsurprisingly akin to the perspective of the test-makers. Teachers are assigned the position of "gatekeepers" ... as they become skilled in using the technologies of the discipline. (Gallagher, 1999, p. 80).

Labeling has negative impacts on students with intellectual disabilities (Bailey, 1998; Forts, 1998; Smith, 1999b; Smull, 1998; Snow, 1998). Unfortunately, though we have known that for some time, some continue to insist that labeling is an important and useful process in special education (Kauffman, 2007b). This is, undoubtedly, a function of an ableist ideology inherent in education, the notion that "disability is negative and tragic and that 'overcoming' disability is the only valued result" (Hehir, 2007, p.10). Students labeled as having disabilities, including those with so-called intellectual disabilities, when placed in special education, rather than receiving any benefit from that education, are instead routinely humiliated publicly, contained and segregated, denied access to knowledge afforded to those without disability labels, made dependent, and devalued (Connor, 2004). In one qualitative research project, 8 of 10 college students with learning disabilities who were asked to reflect on their experiences in K–12 special education cried when describing the sometimes horrible consequences of being in special education. They reported that special education had a negative impact on self-esteem and made them feel stupid. Special education is a set of practices that "scars people," creating "a wound that never heals" (Orr, 2008).

Labeling, and the process of measuring people in order to engage in labeling, is an inherently colonialist project, one that is essentialist, Eurocentric, and positivist. It "proves" the presumed superiority of white intellectual abilities, and the inferiority of those who do not fall into such neatly pre- (and pro-) scribed boundaries. It is an effort "to 'recover' white supremacy, patriarchy, class privilege, heterosexual 'normality,' Christian dominance, and the European intellectual canon" (Kincheloe, 2006b, p. 33).

Other researchers describe special education as socially isolating and stigmatizing (Conway, 2005), disempowering, reducing expectations, stressful, shameful, and focused on deficits (Kellner & Freden, 2006) and typically delivering poor quality services (Weber, 2007). For those for whom a medical model of disability is the right approach (especially for educators such as Kauffman), the problems experienced by some students—especially those who are African American or poor—resides in their so-called disability, rather than being, as more progressive educational theorists would suggest, the result of

> regressive government policies, the growing militarization of urban space, the attack on basic social provisions for the poor and young, the disinvestment in such public goods as public schools, or the growing criminalization of social policy. (Giroux, 2001, p. 70)

Knowledge and education are created by and serve the needs of those in powerful, hegemonic, and dominating cultural positions, subjugated by the needs of neoliberal capitalism and the so-called free market (Apple, 2003; Brantlinger, 2004; Cruz, 2008; Giroux, 2001; 2004; 2005; 2006b). Kincheloe (2008) describes some of the ways in which globalizing and hegemonic capitalism exploit education for its own ends:

> Utilizing a crypto-positivistic, evidence-based science that excludes complexity; context; power; multiple modes of research design; the ever-changing, in-process nature of the phenomena of the social world; subjugated and indigenous knowledges from diverse social and geographical locales; and the multiple realities perceived and constructed by different peoples at divergent historical times and cultural places, dominant power brokers attempt with a great deal of success to regulate what people view as legitimate knowledge. (p. 2)

This is a particular kind of knowledge, serving a particular kind of culture: one in which the needs of a dominating white, male, heterosexual, rich, and ableist class are held in the highest regard. Schools support, create, and teach this knowledge, and knowledge that is outside culturally inscribed boundaries literally does not exist (Smith, 2008b). As a result of national testing requirements (just one example of how globalizing market economies are subverting educational structures), concerns regarding class, gender, ability, and race literally begin to disappear (Apple, 2003; Giroux, 2005). Such testing practices are one more way for education to control students and make even more clear the powerful and increasing similarities between schools and prisons—schools

> which are marked by the foreboding presence of hired armed guards in the corridors, patrolled cafeterias, locked doors, video surveillance cameras, electronic badges, police dogs, and routine drug searches. (Giroux, 2001, p. 88)

Students who fall outside of increasingly tighter definitions of normal are labeled as having disabilities (Watts & Erevelles, 2004).

This knowledge-making and sustaining creates social and cultural hierarchies, reinforcing the status quo of dominating hegemonies (Smith, 1999b; Kincheloe, 2008). Increasingly, social, cultural, and economic resources go to the ultra-rich and corporations, while residents of middle- and lower-class or racialized landscapes face higher taxes, fewer social services, no health care, political disenfranchisement, fewer jobs, poor education, and a lower quality of life (Giroux, 2005; 2006a; 2006b; 2007). These residents have become disposable in an economy in which those who are otherized are mere waste (Giroux, 2007).

Brantlinger (2004) asserts that

> in education and other social service contexts, dominant classes gain salary and status from "delivering services," while recipients receive stigmatizing labels and segregated low status programs—that subordinates continue to be oppressed. (p. 19)

The commodification of supports for adults and students with intellectual disabilities insures that they will continue to require those supports, thus guaranteeing that institutions that provide those supports are maintained. Bureaucrats, educators, related service providers, administrators, and parents with sufficient cultural capital all benefit from the provision of special education supports for students with intellectual disabilities (Smith, 1999b).

It is apparent that educational institutions distribute benefits in a way that can only be described as unequal (Apple, 1996; Stone, 1997). In schools, for students labeled as having intellectual and developmental disabilities,

> intelligence is a code word used by educators, psychologists, and other human-service workers to explain the current distribution of benefits from publicly supported programs ... Special education programs relying on the construct of intelligence (e.g., programs for those labeled retarded [sic] or learning disabled) distribute benefits to students, teachers, parents, teacher trainers, and other participants. In general, those who are said to have intellectual deficits receive fewer profits, advantages, or opportunities than do others associated with these programs. (Heiny, 1981, pp. 309–310)

One important outcome of this mal-distribution of benefits is that groups that are otherwise in minority and oppressed groups receive labels of intellectual disabilities at much higher rates. African American students, for example, are 2.9 times more likely to be given a label of intellectual disability and substantially less likely to be included in general education classrooms. These issues result in inappropriate services and supports, low expectations, emotional difficulties, social problems, and negative postsecondary life outcomes (National Alliance of Black School Education & ILIAD Project, 2002). So how do these factors impact education in general and special education in particular as well as ultimately the inclusion of students with disabilities, especially those with intellectual disabilities? Kauffman and his colleagues reflect the ways neoliberalism operates in special education, creating a rationale for excluding students with intellectual and other disabilities. The work of Kauffman and his colleagues reflects the rise of neoliberalist thinking in both educational and special educational spheres. Giroux (2005) notes,

> At the center of neoliberalism is a new form of politics in the United States, a politics in which radical exclusion is the order of the day, and in which the primary questions no longer concern equality, justice, or freedom, but are now about the survival of the slickest in a culture marked by fear, surveillance, and economic deprivation. This is a politics that hides its own ideology by eliminating the traces of its power in a rhetoric of normalization, populism, and the staging of public spectacles. (p. 12)

Countering these moves by globalizing, dominating, demonizing capitalism is "the power of difference, alterity, and diversality" (Kincheloe, 2008, p. 7) inherent in critical, post, and bricolagic approaches to education. It is the work of these approaches and how they might be understood, experienced, and portrayed by (and with) people with intellectual and other disabilities, both inside and outside of special education, that can and must be the work of a critical disability studies.

References

Agran, M., Blanchard, C., Wehmeyer, M., & Hughes, C. (2002). Increasing the problem-solving skills of students with developmental disabilities participating in general education. *Remedial and Special Education, 23,* 279–288.

Ainscow, M. (2007). Taking an inclusive turn. *Journal of Research in Special Educational Needs, 7,* 3–7.

Altman, J., Lazarus, S., Thurlow, M., Quenemoen, R., Cuthbert, M., & Cormier, D. (2008). *2007 survey of states: Activities, changes, and challenges for special education.* Minneapolis, MN: University of Minnesota, National Center on Educational Outcomes.

Apple, M. (1996). *Cultural politics and education.* New York: Teacher's College Press.

———(2003). Competition, knowledge, and the loss of educational vision. *Philosophy of Music Education Review, 11,* 3–22.

Austin, V. (2001). Teacher's beliefs about co-teaching. *Remedial and Special Education, 22,* 245–255.

Baglieri, S., & Knopf, J. (2004). Normalizing difference in inclusive teaching. *Journal of*

Learning Disabilities, 37, 525–529.

Bailey, J. (1998) Medical and psychological models in special needs education. In C. Clark, A. Dyson, and A. Millward (Eds.), *Theorising special education* (pp. 44–60). New York: Routledge.

Baker, E., Wang, M., & Walberg, H. (1995). The effects of inclusion on learning. *Educational Leadership, 52,* 33–35.

Begeny, J., & Martens, B. (2007). Inclusionary education in Italy: A literature review and call for more empirical research. *Remedial and Special Education, 28,* 80–94.

Berry, R. (2006). Inclusion, power, and community: Teachers and students interpret the language of community in an inclusion classroom. *American Educational Research Journal 43,* 489–529.

Bouck, E. (2006). How educational placements impact classroom interactions: Experiences of six secondary students with mild mental impairment. *Journal of Classroom Interaction, 41,* 4–14.

——— (2007). Co-teaching … Not just a textbook term: Implications for practice. *Preventing School Failure, 51,* 46–51.

Brantlinger, E. (1997). Using ideology: Cases of nonrecognition of the politics of research and practice in special education. *Review of Educational Research, 67,* 425–459.

——— (2004). Ideologies discerned, values determined: Getting past the hierarchies of special education. In L. Ware (Ed.) *Ideology and the politics of (in)exclusion* (pp. 11–31). New York: Peter Lang.

Brown, D. (1997). Full inclusion: Issues and challenges. *Journal of Instructional Psychology, 24,* 24–28.

Burstein, N., Sears, S., Wilcoxen, A., Cabello, B., & Spagna, M. (2004). Moving toward inclusive practices. *Remedial and Special Education, 25,* 104–116.

Carter, E., Sisco, L., Brown, L., Brickham, D., & Al-Khabbaz, Z. (2008). Peer interactions and academic engagement of youth with developmental disabilities in inclusive middle and high school classrooms. *American Journal on Mental Retardation, 113,* 479–494.

Clair, E., Church, R., & Batshaw, M. (2002). Special education services. In M. Batshaw (Ed.) *Children with disabilities* (5th ed.) (pp. 589–606). Baltimore, MD: Paul H. Brookes Publishing Co.

Cole, C. (2006). Closing the achievement gap series, part III: What is the impact of NCLB on the inclusion of students with disabilities? *Center for Evaluation and Education Policy Brief, 4*(11), 1–12.

Cole, C., Waldron, N., & Majd, M. (2004). Academic progress of students across inclusive and traditional settings. *Mental Retardation, 42,* 136–144.

Connor, D. (2004). Infusing disability studies into "mainstream" educational thought: One person's story. *Review of Disability Studies, 1*(1), 100–120.

Conway, M. (2005). Introduction: Disability studies meets special education. *Review of Disability Studies, 1*(3), 3–8.

Conway, R., & Gow, L. (1988). Mainstreaming special class students with mild handicaps through group instruction. *Remedial and Special Education 9,* 34–40, 49.

Cowan, R., McGoey, K., & Quallich, K. (2007). The side effects of inclusion for students with learning disabilities: The perceptions of practicing school psychologists. *Learning Disabilities, 14,* 167–176.

Cramer, E.,1 & Nevin, A. (2006). A mixed methodology analysis of co-teacher assessments. *Teacher Education and Special Education, 29,* 261–274.

Crockett, J., & Kauffman, J. (1998). Taking inclusion back to its roots. *Educational Leadership, 56,* 74–77.

Crockett, J., Myers, S., Griffin, A., & Hollandsworth, B. (2007). The unintended side effects of inclusion for students with learning disabilities: The perspectives of school administrators. *Learning Disabilities, 14,* 155–166.

Cruz, M. (2008). What if I just cite Graciela? Working toward decolonizing knowledge through a critical ethnography. *Qualitative Inquiry, 14,* 651–658.

Cushing, L., & Kennedy, C. (1997). Academic effects of providing peer support in general education classrooms on students without disabilities. *Journal of Applied Behavior Analysis, 30,* 139–151.

Damer, L. (2001). Inclusion and the law. *Music Educators Journal, 87,* 19–22.

Danforth, S. (1997). On what basis hope? Modern progress and postmodern possibilities. *Mental Retardation, 35,* 93–106.

Dixon, S. (2005). Inclusion—Not segregation or integration is where a student with special needs belongs. *Journal of Educational Thought, 39,* 33–53.

Donahue Institute (2004). A study of MCAS achievement and promising practices in urban special education: Report of field research findings. Hadley, MA: University of Massachusetts Donahue Institute.

Dore, R., Dion, E., Wagner, S., & Brunet, J.-P. (2002). High school inclusion of adolescents with mental retardation: A multiple case study. *Education and Training in Mental Retardation and Developmental Disabilities, 37*(3), 253–261

Downing, J. (2008). Inclusive education: Why is it not more prevalent? *TASH Connections, 34*(2), 8–10, 13.

Downing, J., & Eichinger, J. (2003). Creating learning opportunities for students with severe disabilities in inclusive classrooms. *Teaching Exceptional Children, 36*(1), 26–31.

Downing, J., & Peckham-Hardin, K. (2007). Inclusive education: What makes it a good education for students with moderate to severe disabilities? *Research and Practice for Persons with Severe Disabilities, 32,* 16–30.

Downing, J., Spencer, S., & Cavallaro, C. (2004).The development of an inclusive charter elementary school: Lessons learned. *Research & Practice for Persons with Severe Disabilities, 29,* 11–24.

Doyle, L. (2003). Inclusion: The unifying thread for fragmented metaphors. Annual Meeting of the American Association of Educational Research, Chicago, IL.

Dymond, S., & Orelove, F. (2001). What constitutes effective curricula for students with severe disabilities? *Exceptionality, 9,* 109–122.

Eiserman, W. (1988). Three types of peer tutoring: Effects on the attitudes of students with learning disabilities and their regular class peers. *Journal of Learning Disabilities 21,* 249–52.

Fabrocini, J., & Hanreddy, A. (2008). When all children learn: CHIME Charter School's collaborative model for special education. *TASH Connections, 34*(2), 14–19.

Falvey, M., & Givner, C. (2005). What is an inclusive school? In R. Villa & J. Thousand (Eds.) *Creating an inclusive school* (2nd ed.) (pp.12–26). Alexandria, VA: Association for Supervision and Curriculum Development.

Favell, J. (2005). Sifting sound practice from snake oil. In J. Jacobson, R. Foxx, & J. Mulick (Eds.) *Controversial therapies for developmental disabilities: Fad, fashion, and science in professional practice* (pp. 19–30). Mahwah, NJ: Lawrence Erlbaum Associates, Publishers.

Fisher, M., & Meyer, L. (2002). Development and social competence after two years for students enrolled in inclusive and self-contained educational programs. *Research and Practice for Persons with Severe Disabilities, 27*, 165–174.

Fontana, K. (2005). The effects of co-teaching on the achievement of eighth grade students with learning disabilities. *The Journal of At-Risk Issues, 11*, 17–23.

Forts, A. (1998). Status and effects of labeling. *TASH Newsletter, 24*(10), 13.

Foxx, R., & Roland, C. (2005). The self-esteem fallacy. In J. Jacobson, R. Foxx, & J. Mulick (Eds.) *Controversial therapies for developmental disabilities: Fad, fashion, and science in professional practice* (pp. 101–112). Mahwah, NJ: Lawrence Erlbaum Associates, Publishers.

Freeman, S., & Alkin, M. (2000). Academic and social attainments of children with mental retardation in general education and special education settings. *Remedial and Special Education, 21*, 3–18.

Friend, M. (2007). The co-teaching partnership. *Educational Leadership, 64*(5), 48–52.

Fuchs, D., & Fuchs, L. (1998). Competing visions for educating students with disabilities: Inclusion versus full inclusion. *Childhood Education, 74*, 309–316.

Gallagher, S. (1999). An exchange of gazes. In J. Kincheloe, S. Steinberg, & L. Villaverde (Eds.), *Rethinking intelligence: Confronting psychological assumptions about teaching and learning* (pp. 69–83). New York: Routledge.

Gee, K. (2004). Developing curriculum and instruction. In F. Orelove, D. Sobsey, & R. Silberman (Eds.) *Educating children with multiple disabilities: A collaborative approach* (4th ed.) (pp. 67–114). Baltimore, MD: Paul H. Brookes Publishing Co.

George, A., & Duquette, C. (2006). The psychosocial experiences of a student with low vision. *Journal of Visual Impairment and Blindness, 100*, 152–163.

Giangreco, M. (1997). Key lessons learned about inclusive education: Summary of the 1996 Schonell Memorial Lecture. *International Journal of Disability and Development, 44*, 193–206.

— — — (2006). Foundational concepts and practices for educating students with severe disabilities. In M. Snell & F. Brown (Eds.) *Instruction of students with severe disabilities* (6th ed.) (pp. 1–27). Upper Saddle River, NJ: Pearson Prentice Hall.

Giangreco, M., & Putnam, J. (1991). Supporting the education of students with severe disabilities in regular education environments. In L. Meyer, C. Peck, & L. Brown (Eds.), *Critical issues in the lives of people with severe disabilities* (pp. 245–270). Baltimore: Paul H. Brookes Publishing Co.

Giroux, H. (2001). Mis/education and zero tolerance: Disposable youth and the politics of domestic militarization. *boundary 2, 28*, 61–94.

— — — (2004). What might education mean after Abu Ghraib: Revisiting Adorno's politics of education. *Comparative Studies of South Asia, Africa and Middle East, 24*, 3–22.

— — — (2005). The Terror of neoliberalism: Rethinking the significance of cultural politics. *College Literature, 32*, 1–19.

— — — (2006a). Dirty democracy and state terrorism: The politics of the new authoritarianism in the United States. *Comparative Studies of South Asia, Africa and Middle East, 26*, 163–177.

— — — (2006b). The emerging authoritarianism in the United States: Political culture under the Bush/Cheny administration. *symploke, 14*, 98–151.

―――― (2007). Violence, Katrina, and the biopolitics of disposability. *Theory Culture Society, 24,* 305–309.

Griffin, C., Jones, H., & Kilgore, K. (2007). The unintended side effects of including students with learning disabilities for teacher educators. *Learning Disabilities, 14,* 195–204.

Hagan-Burke, S., & Jefferson, G. (2002). Using data to promote academic benefit for included students with mild disabilities. *Preventing School Failure, 46,* 112–118.

Hall, J. (2002). Narrowing the breach: Can disability culture and full educational inclusion be reconciled? *Journal of Disability Policy Studies, 13,* 144–152.

Halvorsen, A., & Sailor, W. (1990). Integration of students with severe and profound disabilities. In R. Gaylord-Ross (Ed.), *Issues and research in special education* (pp. 110–172). New York: Teachers College Press.

Haney, M., & Cox, A. (2008). Preschool inclusion: Strategies for implementing effective programs. *TASH Connections, 34*(2), 11–13.

Hardin, B., & Hardin, M. (2002). Into the mainstream: Practical strategies for teaching in inclusive environments. *The Clearing House, 75,* 175–178.

Haring, N. (2002). Prologue. In R. Villa & J. Thousand (Eds.) *Restructuring for caring and effective education: Piecing the puzzle together* (2nd ed.) (pp. xvii–xxix). Baltimore, MD: Paul H. Brookes Publishing Co.

Hasbrouck, J., & Christen, M. (1997). Providing peer coaching in inclusive classrooms: A tool for consulting teachers. *Intervention in School and Clinic, 32,* 172–177.

Hehir, T. (2007). Confronting ableism. *Educational Leadership, 64*(5), 8–14.

Heiny, R. (1981). Focusing on benefits: A policy beyond intelligence and interventions. *The Journal of Special Education, 15,* 307–316.

Heward,, W. & Silvestri, S. (2005). The neutralization of special education. In J. Jacobson, R. Foxx, & J. Mulick (Eds.) *Controversial therapies for developmental disabilities: Fad, fashion, and science in professional practice* (pp. 193–214). Mahwah, NJ: Lawrence Erlbaum Associates, Publishers.

Hockenbury, J., Kauffman, J., & Hallahan, D. (2000). What is right about special education. *Exceptionality, 8,* 3–11.

Hunt, P., Doering, K., Hirose-Hatae, A., Maier, J., & Goetz, L. (2001). Across-program collaboration to support students with and without disabilities in a general education classroom. *Journal of the Association for Persons with Severe Handicaps, 26,* 240–256.

Hunt, P., & Goetz, L. (1997). Research on inclusive educational programs, practices and outcomes for students with severe disabilities. *The Journal of Special Education, 31,* 3–29.

Hunt, P., Hirose-Hatae, A., Doering, K., Karasoff, P. & Goetz, L. (2000). "Community" is what I think everyone is talking about. *Remedial and Special Education, 21,* 305–317.

Hunt, P., Soto G., Maier, J., & Doering, K. (2003). Collaborative teaming to support students at risk and students with severe disabilities in general education classrooms. *Exceptional Children, 69,* 315–332.

Hunt, P., Staub, D., Alwell, M., & Goetz, L. (1994). Achievement by all students within the context of cooperative learning groups. *Journal of the Association for Persons with Severe Handicaps, 19,* 290–301.

Idol, L. (2006). Toward inclusion of special education students in general education:

A program evaluation of eight schools. *Remedial and Special Education, 27, 77–94.*

Jacobson, J., Mulick, J., & Foxx, R. (2005). Historical approaches to developmental disabilities. In J. Jacobson, R. Foxx, & J. Mulick (Eds.) *Controversial therapies for developmental disabilities: Fad, fashion, and science in professional practice* (pp. 61–84). Mahwah, NJ: Lawrence Erlbaum Associates, Publishers.

Jameson, J., McDonnell, J., Polychronis, S., & Riesen, T. (2008). Embedded, constant time delay instruction by peers without disabilities in general education classrooms. *Intellectual and Developmental Disabilities, 46,* 346–363.

Jenkins, J., Antil, L., Wayne, S., & Vadasy, P. (2003). How cooperative learning works for special education and remedial students. *Exceptional Children, 69,* 279–292.

Karagiannis, A., Stainback, W., & Stainback, S. (1996). Rationale for inclusive schooling. In S. Stainback & W. Stainback (Eds.), *Inclusion: A guide for* educators (pp. 3–16). Baltimore, MD: Paul H. Brookes Publishing Co.

Kauffman, J. (1999). Today's special education and its messages for tomorrow. *The Journal of Special Education, 32,* 244–254.

Kauffman, J. (2003). Reflections on the field. *Education and Treatment of Children, 26,* 323–329.

— — — (2004). The President's Commission and the devaluation of special education. *Education and Treatment of Children, 27*(4), 307–324.

— — — (2007a). Conceptional models and the future of special education. *Education and Treatment of Children, 30,* 241–258.

— — — (2007b). Labels and the nature of special education: We need to face realities. *Learning Disabilities, 14,* 245–248.

Kauffman, J., Bantz, J., & McCullough, J. (2002). Separate and better: A special public school class for students with emotional and behavioral disorders. *Exceptionality, 10,* 149–170.

Kauffman, J., & Hallahan, D. (2005). The illusion of full inclusion: A comprehensive critique of a current special education bandwagon (2nd ed.). Austin, TX: Pro-Ed.

Kauffman, J., Landrum, T., Mock, D., Sayeski, B., & Sayeski, K. (2005). Diverse knowledge and skills require a diversity of instructional groups: A position statement. *Remedial and Special Education, 26*(1), 2–6.

Kauffman, J., Lloyd, J., & Riedel, T. (1995). Inclusion of all students with emotional or behavioral disorders? Lets think again. *Phi Delta Kappan, 76,* 542–546.

Kauffman, J., McGee, K., & Brigham, M. (2004). Enabling or disabling? Observations on changes in special education. *Phi Delta Kappan, 85,* 613–620

Kavale, K., & Forness, S. (2000). History, rhetoric, and reality: Analysis of the inclusion debate. *Remedial and Special Education, 21,* 279–296.

Kavale, K., & Mostert, M. (2003). River of ideology, islands of evidence. *Exceptionality, 11,* 191–208.

Keefe, C., & Davis, R. (1998). Inclusion Means... *NASSP Bulletin, 82,* 54–64.

Kellner, L., & Freden, L. (2006). "If they could see me now!": College students reflect on their experiences as special education students in the K–12 system. *Review of Disability Studies, 2*(1), 58–75.

Kennedy, C., & Itkonen, T. (1994). Some effects of regular class participation on the social contacts and social networks of high school students with severe disabilities. *Journal of the Association for Persons with Severe Handicaps, 19,* 1–10.

Kincheloe, J. (2006a). What you don't know *is* hurting you and the country. In S. Steinberg & J. Kincheloe (Eds.) *What you don't know about schools* (pp. 1–29). New

York: Palgrave Macmillan.

————— (2006b). How did this happen? The right-wing politics of knowledge and education. In S. Steinberg & J. Kincheloe (Eds.) *What you don't know about schools* (pp. 31–68). New York: Palgrave Macmillan.

————— (2007). Critical pedagogy in the twenty-first century: Evolution for survival. In P. McLaren & J. Kincheloe (Eds.) *Critical pedagogy: Where are we now?* (pp. 9–42). New York: Peter Lang.

————— (2008). Critical pedagogy and the knowledge wars of the twenty-first century. *International Journal of Critical Pedagogy, 1,* 1–22.

King, I. (2003). Examining middle school inclusion classrooms through the lens of learner-centered principles. *Theory Into Practice, 42,* 151–158.

King-Sears, M., & Bradley, D. (1995). Classwide peer tutoring: Heterogeneous instruction in general education classrooms. *Preventing School Failure 40,* 29–35.

Kluth, P., Villa, R., & Thousand, J. (2002). "Our school doesn't offer inclusion" and other legal blunders. *Educational Leadership, 59*(4), 24–27.

Kozloff, M. (2005). Fads in general education: Fad, fraud, and folly. In J. Jacobson, R. Foxx, & J. Mulick (Eds.) *Controversial therapies for developmental disabilities: Fad, fashion, and science in professional practice* (pp. 159–173). Mahwah, NJ: Lawrence Erlbaum Associates, Publishers.

Lawrence-Brown, D. (2004). Differentiated instruction: Inclusive strategies for standards-based learning that benefit the whole class. *American Secondary Education, 32*(3), 34–62.

Lewis, R., & Doorlag, D. (2006). *Teaching special students in general education classrooms* (7th ed.). Upper Saddle River, NJ: Pearson Prentice Hall.

Lohrman, S., & Bambara, L. (2006). Elementary education teachers' beliefs about essential supports needed to successfully include students with developmental disabilities who engage in challenging behaviors. *Research & Practice for Persons with Severe Disabilities, 31,* 157–173.

Maheady, L., Harper, G. & Sacca, K. (1988). A classwide peer tutoring system in secondary resource room program for the mildly handicapped. *Journal of Research and Development in Education, 21,* 76–83.

Marchbanks, S., Richardson, M., & Flanagan, J. (2001). Inclusion: A process of curriculum improvement. *Catalyst for Change, 30*(3), 9–11.

Mastropieri, M., & Scruggs, T. (2001). Promoting inclusion in secondary classrooms. *Learning Disability Quarterly, 24,* 265–274.

Mastropieri, M., Scruggs, T., Graetz, J., Norland, J., Gardizi, W., & McDuffie, K. (2005). Case studies in co-teaching in the content areas: Successes, failures, and challenges. *Intervention in School and Clinic, 40,* 260–270.

McCormick, L., Noonan, M., Ogata, V., & Heck, R. (2001). Co-teacher relationship and program quality: Implications for preparing teachers for inclusive preschool settings. *Training in Mental Retardation and Developmental Disabilities, 36,* 119–132.

McCourt, F. (2005). *Teacher man.* New York: Scribner.

McDonnell, J. (1998). Instruction for students with severe disabilities in general education settings. *Education and Training in Mental Retardation and Developmental Disabilities, 33,* 199–215.

McLeskey, J., & Waldron, N. (2007). Making differences ordinary in inclusive classrooms. *Intervention in School and Clinic, 42,* 162–168.

Mock, D., & Kauffman, J. (2002). Preparing teachers for full inclusion: Is it possible?

The Teacher Educator, 3, 202–215.
— — — (2005). The delusion of full inclusion. In J. Jacobson, R. Foxx, & J. Mulick (Eds.) *Controversial therapies for developmental disabilities: Fad, fashion, and science in professional practice* (pp. 113–128). Mahwah, NJ: Lawrence Erlbaum Associates, Publishers.
Morocco, C. (2001). Teaching for understanding with students with disabilities: New directions for research on access to the general education curriculum. *Learning Disability Quarterly, 24,* 5–13.
Mostert, M., Kavale, K., and Kauffman, J. (2007). *Challenging the refusal of reasoning in special education.* Denver, CO: Love Publishing.
Murawski, W., & Dieker, L. (2008). 50 ways to keep your co-teacher: Strategies for before, during, and after co-teaching. *Teaching Exceptional Children, 40*(4), 40–48.
Murawski, W., & Swanson, H. (2001). A meta-analysis of co-teaching research. *Remedial and Special Education, 22,* 258–267.
National Alliance of Black School Educators & ILIAD Project (2002). Addressing over-representation of African American students in special education: The pre-referral intervention process—An administrator's guide. Arlington, VA: Council for Exceptional Children, and Washington, DC: National Alliance of Black School Educators.
Newsom, C., & Hovanitz, C. (2005). The nature and value of empirically validated interventions. In J. Jacobson, R. Foxx, & J. Mulick (Eds.) *Controversial therapies for developmental disabilities: Fad, fashion, and science in professional practice* (pp. 31–44). Mahwah, NJ: Lawrence Erlbaum Associates, Publishers.
Noddings, N. (2003). *Caring: A feminine approach to ethics and moral education* (2nd ed.). Berkeley, CA: University of California Press.
Ornelles, C., Cook, L., & Jenkins, A. (2007). Middle school general education teachers' perspectives on including students with learning disabilities. *Learning Disabilities, 14,* 145–154.
Orr, A. (2008). Postsecondary students with learning disabilities: Profiles, problems, and possibilities. Cedarville, OH: 20th Annual Ethnographic and Qualitative Research Conference.
Peck, C., Staub, D., Gallucci, C., & Schwartz, I. (2004). Parent perception of the impacts of inclusion on their nondisabled child. *Research & Practice for Persons with Severe Disabilities, 29,* 135–143
Putnam, J. (1993). The process of cooperative learning. In J. Putnam (ed.) *Cooperative learning and strategies for inclusion: Celebrating diversity in the classroom,* (pp. 15–40). Baltimore: Brookes Pub. Co.
Rea, P., Mclaughlin, V., & Walther-Thomas, C. (2002). Outcomes for students with learning disabilities in inclusive and pullout programs. *Exceptional Children 68,* 203–222.
Rice, N., Drame, E., Owens, L., & Frattura, E. (2007). Co-instructing at the secondary level: Strategies for success. *Teaching Exceptional Children, 39*(6), 12–18.
Ruef, M. (2003). Including students with disabilities: Let's move forward together. *Action in Teacher Education 25*(1), n.p..
Ryndak, D., Jackson, L., & Billingsley, F. (2000). Defining school inclusion for students with moderate to severe disabilities: What do experts say? *Exceptionality, 8,* 101–116.
Sabia, R. (2008). Universal design for learning and meaningful access to the curricu-

lum. *TASH Connections*, 34(3), 14–16, 21.

Sax, C., Fisher, C., & Pumpian, I. (1996). Outcomes for students with severe disabilities: Case studies on the use of assistive technology in inclusive classrooms. *Technology and Disability, 5*, 327–334.

Schmidt, R., Rozendal, M., & Greenman, G. (2002). Reading instruction in the inclusion classroom: Research-based practices. *Remedial and Special Education, 23*, 130–140.

Scott, L., Jellison, J., Chappell, E., & Standridge, A. (2007). Talking with music teachers about inclusion: Perceptions, opinions and experiences. *Journal of Music Therapy, 44*, 38–56.

Scruggs, T., Mastropieri, M., & McDuffie, K. (2007). Co-teaching in inclusive classrooms: A metasynthesis of qualitative research. *Exceptional Children, 73*, 392–416.

Shapiro-Barnard, S. (1998). A rationale for inclusive high schools. In C. M. Jorgensen (Ed.), *Restructuring high schools for all students: Taking inclusion to the next level.* (pp. 1–14). Baltimore, MD: Paul H. Brookes Publishing Co.

Slavin, R. (1991). Synthesis of research of cooperative learning. *Educational Leadership 48*, 71–82.

Smith, A., Kozleski, E., & King, K. (2008). Framework for organizing inclusive K–12 environments: Universal designs for learning, differentiated instruction, and multiple intelligences. *TASH Connections, 34*(3), 11–13, 21.

Smith, B. (2007). Increasing the comfort level of teachers toward inclusion through use of school focus groups. Unpublished Dissertation, Nova Southeastern University.

Smith, P. (1999a). Ideology, politics, and science in understanding developmental disabilities. *Mental Retardation, 37*, 71–72.

——— (1999b). Drawing new maps: A radical cartography of developmental disabilities. *Review of Educational Research, 69*(2), 117–144.

——— (2001). MAN.i.f.e.s.t.o.: A Poetics of D(EVIL)op(MENTAL) Dis(ABILITY). *Taboo: The Journal of Education and Culture, 5*(1), 27–36.

——— (2004). Whiteness, normal theory, and disability studies. *Disability Studies Quarterly, 24* (2), n.p.

——— (2007). "Circles" of support offer lifeline. *Eastern Educator*, Fall, 13.

——— (2008a). Cartographies of eugenics and special education: A history of the (ab)normal. In S. Gabel & S. Danforth (Eds.), *Disability and the politics of education: An international reader.* New York: Peter Lang.

——— (2008b). (2008). an ɪʟʟ/ᴇʟʟip(op)tical *po*—ETIC/ᴇᴍɪᴄ/Lemic/litic *post*® uv ed DUCAT ion *recherché repres©entation*. *Qualitative Inquiry, 14*(5).

Smull, M. (1998). Escaping from the label trap. *TASH Newsletter, 24*(10), 22–23.

Snow, K. (1998). To achieve inclusion, community, and freedom for people with disabilities, we must use people first language. *TASH Newsletter, 24*(10). 14–16.

Snyder, L., Garriott, P., & Aylor, M. (2001). Inclusion confusion: Putting the pieces together. *Teacher Education and Special Education, 24*, 198–207.

Stainback, S., & Smith, J. (2005). Inclusive education: Historical perspective. In R. Villa & J. Thousand (Eds.) *Creating an inclusive school* (2ⁿᵈ ed.) (pp. 12–26). Alexandria, VA: Association for Supervision and Curriculum Development.

Staub, D., & Peck, C. A. (1995). What are the outcomes for nondisabled students? *Educational Leadership, 52*(4), 36–40.

Stockall, N., & Garten, B. (2002). The nature of inclusion in a blue ribbon school: A revelatory case. *Exceptionality, 10,* 171–188

Stone, D. (1997). *Policy paradox: The art of political decision making.* New York: W. W. Norton and Company.

Tankersley, M., & Cook, B. (2007). An overview of the side effects of including students with learning disabilities. *Learning Disabilities, 14,* 217–223.

Taschner, C., & Donahue, K. (2008). Whose mountain is it? Twin Valley Middle School: "The Mountain Movers." *TASH Connections, 34*(2), 26–28.

Tomlinson, C. (2004). The Mobius effect: Addressing learner variance in schools. *Journal of Learning Disabilities, 37,* 516–524.

Turnbull, A., Turnbull, R., Erwin, E., & Soodak, L. (2006). *Families, professionals, and exceptionality: Positive outcomes through partnerships and trust.* Upper Saddle River, NJ: Pearson Prentice Hall.

Udvari-Solner, A., Thousand, J., Villa, R., Quiocho, A., & Kelly, M. (2005). Promising practices that foster inclusive education. In R. Villa & J. Thousand (Eds.) *Creating an inclusive school* (2nd ed.) (pp. 97–123). Alexandria, VA: Association for Supervision and Curriculum Development.

Villa, R., & Thousand, J. (2002). Setting the context: History of and rationales for inclusive schooling. In R. Villa & J. Thousand (Eds.) *Restructuring for caring and effective education: Piecing the puzzle together* (2nd ed.) (pp. 7–37). Baltimore, MD: Paul H. Brookes Publishing Co.

——— (2003). Making inclusive education work. *Educational Leadership, 61*(2), 19–23.

——— (2005). The rationales for creating and maintaining inclusive schools. In R. Villa & J. Thousand (Eds.) *Creating an inclusive school* (2nd ed.) (pp. 41–56). Alexandria, VA: Association for Supervision and Curriculum Development.

Villa, R., Thousand, J., & Chapple, J. (1996). Preparing teachers to support inclusion: Preservice and inservice programs. *Theory into Practice, 35,* 42–50.

Villa, R., Thousand, J., & Nevin, A. (2004). *A guide to co-teaching: Practical tips for facilitating student learning.* Thousand Oaks, CA: Corwin Press.

Villa, R., Thousand, J., Nevin, A., & Liston, A. (2005). Successful inclusive practices in middle and secondary schools. *American Secondary Education, 33,* 33–50.

Waldron, N. L., & McLeskey, J. (1998). The effects of an inclusive school program on students with mild and severe learning disabilities. *Exceptional Children, 64,* 395–406.

Ware, L. (2004). Introduction. In L. Ware (Ed.) *Ideology and the politics of (in)exclusion* (pp. 1–8). New York: Peter Lang.

Watts, I. & Erevelles, N. (2004). These deadly times: Reconceptualizing school violence by using critical race theory and disability studies. *American Educational Research Journal, 41,* 271–299

Weber, M. (2007). Inclusive education in the United States and internationally: Challenges and response. *Review of Disability Studies, 3*(1–2), 19–32.

Willis, J. (2007). Brain-friendly strategies for the inclusion classroom: Insights from a neurologist and classroom teacher. Alexandria, VA: Association for Supervision and Curriculum Development.

Winfield, A. (2007). *Eugenics and education in America: Institutionalized racism and the implications of history, ideology, and memory.* New York: Peter Lang.

Zane, T. (2005). Fads in special education: An overview. In J. Jacobson, R. Foxx, & J. Mulick (Eds.) *Controversial therapies for developmental disabilities: Fad, fashion, and science in professional practice* (pp. 175–191). Mahwah, NJ: Lawrence Erlbaum Associates, Publishers.

Zigmond, N. (2003). Where should students with disabilities receive special education services? Is one place better than another? *The Journal of Special Education, 37,* 193–199.

CHAPTER 3

Barriers to Inclusion

Does Special Education Work?

PHIL SMITH

> Even our most simple actions in our classrooms are political and morally charged. (Huerta-Charles, 2007, p. 256)

Inclusion is at its root a social process. Although we talk about it in individual terms—this or that person being included (or excluded) in this or that classroom—it's not the person that is at the center, but the social process. Inclusion, in addition to being socially constructed, is socially and culturally mediated. The person isn't included; WE include individuals. It's about communities of inclusion or exclusion (Jahnukainen, 2005). The onus of responsibility for including (or excluding) students with intellectual disabilities is on how communities of people decide to act with others.

As a result, the inclusion of students with intellectual disabilities is a moral issue rather than, simply, an educational or scientific one. Discussing literacy for people with significant disabilities, Kliewer, Biklen, and Kasa-Hendrickson (2006) outline ways in which they perceive and create a connection with their sons and daughters:

> On the basis of this presumption of connection, families push for its manifestation through moral terrains such as school inclusion and community access. It is on these particular terrains of connectedness, then, that the skills of citizenship ... are constructed. Hence, the seismic moral shift that will precede the science of universal access ... is, ultimately, an end to human devaluation and consequential segregation in schools and the wider community. (p. 187)

Schools are social enterprises—institutions for accomplishing the goals (explicit and hidden) of societies in terms of educating its citizens (at least, that is one definition of what schools do). It is one place—one community—in which the inclusion of students with disabilities is played out, for better or worse. This chapter will explore the numerous barriers to including students with intellectual (and other) disabilities in general education classrooms (Buell, Hallam, Gamel-McCormick, & Scheer, 1999; Carter & Hughes, 2006; Laflamme, McComas, & Pivik, 2002; Villa & Thousand, 2003; Villa & Thousand, 2005). What can fail students within social processes of inclusion?

Power, Relevance, and Objectivity

Brantlinger (2004) outlines a number of specific barriers to including students with intellectual and other disabilities. The first barrier, she says, is one of power: the work of scholars is privileged over the knowledge of educators in the field, parents, and students with disabilities, creating a hierarchy of position. As I have discussed elsewhere and will show clearly throughout the rest of this book, researchers holding the epistemological power of Cartesian, behaviorist, and modernist science within the field of special education have failed to support inclusion, whether in or out of schools (Aichroth et al., 2002; Smith, 1999a; 2001a; 2001b; 2004; 2005a; 2006; 2008a; 2008b). The needs and demands of parents and students with disabilities, most especially, are ignored in this hierarchy (Smith, 1999a). And parents are certain that the quality of education for their children with disabilities is far superior in general education settings than in segregated settings (National Council on Disability, 1995).

The second barrier, according to Brantlinger, is one of relevance: scholars are often unaware of current school culture and practice. They understand the knowledge of university, not that of schooling. Brantlinger also points out that current educational models in the United States are based on traditional subject matter content, assessed through sequenced testing protocols. Finally, says Brantlinger, some scholars believe that educational practice is based on a belief in neutral, objective science. Such a belief obfuscates the reality that all research, all educational practice, is inherently value-laden, ideological, and political (Smith, 1999b).

Fear is one important barrier to including students with intellectual and developmental disabilities in general education classrooms:

> Fears concern disrupted learning of other students, content not being meaningful and too abstract to teach, and the difficulty of collaborating with other teachers. As a result, where families live in the United States as well as other countries determines to a great extent the accessibility of inclusive educational options and the quality of those options. (Downing, 2008, p. 8)

Fear is experienced by a variety of stakeholders, sometimes resulting from inadequate information or experience. For example, administrators claim that at least some parents of students without disabilities are afraid that their children will do less well in inclusive settings (Crockett, Myers, Griffin, & Hollandsworth, 2007). This finding, incidentally, is not supported by other research, which noted that parents were generally supportive of inclusive classrooms (Tichenor, Heins, & Piechura-Couture, 1998; Yssel, Engelbrecht, Oswald, Eloff, & Swart, 2007).

Danforth and Smith (2005) describe the fear held by other stakeholders. In addition to fear of students that they perceive as being very different from them—fear that is shared by the wider population—teachers are also afraid of the loss of autonomy that results with the need to collaborate. Students who have been previously educated in segregated settings also experience fear of the unknown, as they think about the possibility of moving into different, more inclusive settings. These different kinds of fear serve as a set of barriers to the creation of inclusive opportunities (Danforth & Smith, 2005).

Tradition is also a likely barrier. Because schools are used to providing education for students with intellectual disabilities in separate settings, they continue to do so in spite of the fact that evidence points to the greater efficacy of inclusive education. Lack of teacher training and experience is another important hurdle, as is the fact that students with significant disabilities receive little academic instruction, meaning that they are sometimes unprepared for general education classrooms (Downing, 2008).

Teacher attitude clearly has an important and potentially negative impact on the inclusion of students with disabilities in general education classrooms (Short & Martin, 2005; Silverman, 2007). General educators frequently pay less attention to students with disabilities in their classrooms and so provide less instruction to those who need it the most (Cook, 2004; Cook, Cameron, & Tankersley, 2007). They often have negative attitudes regarding the inclusion of students with disabilities (especially those said to be more severe, such as intellectual disabilities) in general education classrooms (Elhoweris & Al-sheikh, 2004; Mastropieri, 2001; Smith & Routel, 2008). When teachers have negative attitudes about including students with disabilities in their classrooms, they are less likely to work with those students (Pierson & Howell, 2006). Perhaps not surprisingly, negative attitudes about inclusion seems to be related to lack of experience working with and teaching students with disabilities (Reusen, Shoho, &

Barker, 2001). Weber (2007) argues that general education has failed

> to adapt to the needs of children with disabilities and to change the prejudiced
> attitudes of mainstream teachers with respect to children with learning disabili-
> ties and other conditions ... correcting the negative attitudes of teachers and the
> inflexible nature of conventional educational programming is necessary for inte-
> gration to be successful. (p. 28)

Low expectations are also an important barrier to inclusion. Because educators believe that students with intellectual disabilities will
not benefit from instruction, they don't provide it (Downing, 2008).
And, in fact, the amount of noninstructional time is greater in segregated classrooms than it is in inclusive settings (Helmstetter, Curry,
Brennan, & Sampson-Saul, 1998). Low expectations—which translates
to low accountability for performance—are more likely for students
with severe disabilities than for those with labels of mild disabilities
(Cook, 2004).

It is clear that what are sometimes portrayed as inclusive educational practices do not always meet the criteria held by many researchers and practitioners (Giangreco, 1997; Villa & Thousand, 2005).
Parents experienced increased stress, frustration, and dissatisfaction
when inclusion was handled poorly—or didn't occur at all—in local
schools (Dyson, 2007; Hehir, 2007). This has led to unwarranted critique of inclusive education, poor implementation of inclusion, and a
general lack of understanding of the goals and strategies of those who
seek to create opportunities for inclusive structures. Placement decisions regarding students with disabilities are too often made on the
basis of misunderstandings about inclusion and special education law
(Kluth, Villa, & Thousand, 2002).

Let me give a specific example from a real school district. As I
write this, Montgomery County Public School District, in Maryland,
is in the process of closing what are called Learning Centers at the
secondary level in their school district. These Learning Centers are
highly segregated settings for students with a variety of disabilities. A
recent report called into question the value of closing these centers,
however, noting that students transitioning out of them were doing
poorly on state standardized testing. What the report notes only in
passing is that only slightly more than half of a key group of educators attended an important, mandatory training program on co-
teaching during the summer of 2007, meaning that the rest did not
have necessary knowledge about an important method for including
students with disabilities in general education classrooms. Of ob-

served classrooms, most were not implementing co-teaching in ways known to be best-practice based. Even more striking, in observed classrooms, only approximately 25% of instruction was differentiated for all learners—meaning that roughly 75% of students did not receive instruction that targeted their individual learning needs (Fabel, 2009; Merchlinsky, Cooper-Martin, & McNary, 2009).

What does this all mean? It means that one school district was attempting to include more students in general education classrooms; that's a good thing. The problem is that their implementation was flawed in key ways, most particularly in providing educators with the skills and knowledge that they needed in order in adequately and appropriately include students with learning differences. The outcome? Students with disabilities did not receive the quality of instruction that they deserve, and standardized test scores went down for them. The good news is that, for this school district, good data about the change initiative was collected and analyzed; the school district has the information it needs to change, at least potentially, what it's doing in order to fix the problem.

Special educators state that they sometimes don't have enough time or resources to successfully implement inclusive models (Minke, Bear, Deemmer, & Griffin, 1996; Tankersley, Niesz, Cook, & Woods, 2007). As a result, students sometimes receive instruction that is not appropriate to their needs, are not provided with appropriate accommodations, or are provided inadequate supports and services (Hehir, 2007).

Special educators report that general educators often resist including students with disabilities in their classrooms, because they are unwilling to collaborate or won't change their ways of teaching. They say that general educators neither differentiate their instruction nor provide accommodations to students with disabilities (Tankersley, Niesz, Cook, & Woods, 2007; Smith & Routel, 2008). High school students with learning disabilities said the same thing and also felt that class size was an important issue effecting their learning (Leafstedt, Richards, LaMonte, & Cassidy, 2007).

Leadership and Inclusion

We know that support from those in leadership roles within education is absolutely essential for the successful implementation of any substantive change, such as the inclusion of students with disabilities in general education classrooms (Bartholomay, Wallace, & Mason,

2001; Cook, Semmel, & Gerber, 1999; Fullan & Steigelbauer, 2007).
Administrators need to take on the role of instructional leadership to
implement differentiated instruction for all students (National Council on Disability, 2008). Yet educational leaders remain ambivalent at
best about including students with intellectual disabilities in general
education classrooms on a full-time basis (Cook, Semmel, & Gerber,
1999; Praisner, 2003). Generally, they appear to know little about what
it takes to implement inclusive models, the kinds of leadership practices necessary to make it happen, and aren't convinced that all students can be included in general education classrooms. In fact, they
single out students with intellectual disabilities as being unlikely to
succeed in inclusive environments (Barnett & Monda-Amaya, 1998).

Special educators say that administrators sometimes don't provide enough support to insure the success of inclusion (Tankersley,
Niesz, Cook, & Woods, 2007). Administrators with less than positive
attitudes regarding inclusion provide less support for teachers in inclusive classrooms, and schools in which they are leaders have fewer
students with disabilities included in general education classrooms
than in schools with leaders with more positive attitudes (Salisbury,
2006). These issues may be, in part, a result of inadequate preservice
training and experience regarding inclusion (Brownell & Pajares,
1999). Broadly speaking, in the United States, educational leadership
development programs give future administrators neither sufficient
knowledge about the meaning of inclusion and who it can benefit nor
information about necessary supports and practices (Barnett &
Monda-Amaya, 1998; Brownell & Pajares, 1999; Praisner, 2003; Salisbury, 2006).

Administrators report that, while implementing inclusive models,
they feel intense pressure for meeting the requirements of the No
Child Left Behind Act, see increased demand for administrative support from teachers, and have increased responsibilities in terms of
administering special education (Crockett, Myers, Griffin, & Hollandsworth, 2007).

Perhaps partly as a result of the pressure experienced by administrators and other factors, educators often have inadequate training,
support, and experience regarding teaching students with disabilities
in general education settings (Ammah & Hodge, 2006; Burke & Sutherland, 2004; Garriott, Miller, & Snyder, 2003; Lohrman & Bambara,
2006; Shippen, Crites, Houchins, Ramsey, & Simon, 2005; Smith &
Routel, 2008; Tankersley, Niesz, Cook, & Woods, 2007; Titone, 2005).

Without sufficient training or experience, even when educators feel positive about the potential impact of inclusion, they lack confidence in their ability (Ammah & Hodge, 2006; Brownell & Pajares, 1999).

Is Money a Barrier to Inclusion?

Downing says that "the fear of financial obligation to provide the necessary support so students with more significant needs are fully included in general education classrooms may serve as a deterrent to do so" (2008, p. 9). Educators and administrators frequently assert that including students with disabilities—particularly those with significant disabilities, such as intellectual and developmental disabilities—is more expensive than segregated services (Smith & Routel, 2008).

Does the argument hold water? I don't think so. I'll compare two states. I ranked Vermont as the state that was still number one in the percentage of students with intellectual disabilities who were fully included for the school year 2003–2004. I ranked Michigan, on the other hand, as 43rd for the same school year—Michigan is not exactly at the very bottom of rankings, but not an awfully long way from it, in the bottom 20% of states.

When I looked at data about the two states in terms of per capita income, Michigan was ranked 23rd among the 50 states in 2004 (below the U.S. average), and Vermont, 24th (also below the U.S. average). The numbers are certainly not identical, but not so terribly far from each other, either—$32,052 and $31,737, respectively (National Education Association, 2007, Table D-3, p. 26). Generally speaking, people in neither state were making as much money as people around the country, and per capita income in the two states was quite similar.

Then I looked at how the two states were ranked in terms of the per capita expenditures made by state and local governments for all education in 2003–2004. Here, Vermont ranked 4th, at $2,836 per student, and Michigan ranked 6th, at $2,670 per student—again, not identical, but very close indeed (National Education Association, 2007, Table H-3, p. 52). Applying a broad paintbrush, you could say that people in Vermont on average made a little less money but spent a little bit more on education than people in Michigan—but the difference between the two in these two areas was really not very much. Not identical, but by no means terrifically different.

The single clear and decisive difference between the two states on these three measures—inclusion, per capita income, and per capita spending on education—is in the area of inclusion of students with intellectual disabilities. There is a huge difference between the two states in terms of their inclusion of students with intellectual disability, yet really very little difference in how they are ranked in per capita personal income and per capita expenditure for education. One could say pretty safely that, whatever the difference between the two states in terms of including students with intellectual disabilities in general education classrooms, the difference is not about money, not in terms of how much individual citizens have to spend or how much they spend on education.

There's enough money for inclusion to happen, probably in either state, at least given what Vermont was able to do. In fact, the National Council on Disability (1994) found over a decade ago that inclusion was no more expensive, perhaps often less expensive, than providing education to students with disabilities in segregated settings. More recent worldwide research shows that inclusion is substantially less expensive than segregated education, by perhaps as much as 7 to 9 times (Peters, 2004). It's not about enough—it's about whether, how, and on what. As one of my students said to me one day, "It's not about the money. We're already spending it." More precisely, the issue is not whether there is enough money, but on what the money is spent.

As a parallel, compare the cost of providing services to people with intellectual and developmental disabilities living in inclusive, community settings (receiving Home and Community-Based Services funding), and that for those living in segregated, institutional settings (receiving Intermediate Care Facility/MR funding). The cost of services in communities is less than half of the cost of services in institutions, in some cases as little as one-fifth (Lakin, Doljanac, Byun, Stancliffe, Taub, & Chiri, 2008). And life outcomes for people with disabilities in the United States and elsewhere in the world are demonstrably better when supports are provided in community settings rather than in large congregate living situations (Kozma, Mansell, & Beadle-Brown, 2009). Community inclusion, then, in addition to resulting in a better quality of life, is much less expensive.

What is given priority in both Vermont and Michigan is *not* teacher preparation. When states were ranked on their individual ability to prepare teachers in the area of special education, Vermont received a grade of F, and Michigan a grade of D (National Council on Teacher Quality, 2007).

Let me give another example of the ways we spend money and our perceptions about how we spend money. It is often suggested that making schools physically accessible for students with disabilities (e.g., providing, wheelchair ramps, bathroom stalls with grab bars and room to maneuver, elevators, signs in Braille, and the like) is too expensive. In reality, the cost of making schools accessible for new construction worldwide is less than 1% of total project costs. Not a lot, given the big picture. What is indeed more expensive is making schools accessible *after* they've been built (Steinfield, 2005). If we start at the beginning—before we've built buildings, made blueprints, hired contractors—from a mindset that everyone should be able to go to school, then solutions are neither difficult nor expensive. I'd suggest that the same is true of the idea of inclusion.

Research done some time ago by the National Council on Disability (1994; 1995) and the Center on Special Education Finance (Parrish, 1993; 1994; 1996) found that there were significant financial disincentives at state and local levels for including students in settings other than restrictive ones. Disincentives at the federal level include paperwork requirements necessary for funding applications, along with accounting requirements—both make it easier for schools and districts to pay for segregated settings rather than inclusive ones (National Council on Disability, 1994).

There are also legal and procedural disincentives to inclusion. Parents are often put in the place of having to advocate, legally and otherwise, for more inclusive settings for their children. However, due process procedures are complicated as well as expensive and place the burden of proof on families, essentially a blaming-the-victim process. The federal government has done little to enforce the law requiring students to receive their education in a least restrictive environment, either through monitoring processes, a rigorous examination of state plans of services, or other processes. Typically, parents are forced to resort to due process and other outside legal avenues in order for them to obtain what IDEIA ensures them as a right, because local school districts engage in what are segregative practices (National Council on Disability, 1994). Too often, families who want their children to be included in general education classrooms need to fight to make that happen (or for many other opportunities, for that matter) (Kluth, Villa, & Thousand, 2002).

Policymakers have chosen to fund special education and develop regulatory processes and procedures in such a way as to ensure that students with disabilities, including those with intellectual disabilities, receive supports in non-inclusive settings. Given the analysis above, there's enough money to make inclusion happen, but policymakers have simply chosen not to. The fact that this kind of research is well over a decade old speaks to the way in which traditionalist, neoliberal, modernist thinking is entrenched in education (in particular special education), funding, and policy. It also speaks to the ways in which ableism is so firmly entrenched in our culture that policymakers don't consider inclusive opportunities as valued and valuable.

Does Special Education (As We Know It) Work?

Researchers have pointed out that the body of literature outlining effective educational practices, although growing, is still small (Birman & Porter, 2002). This is, unfortunately, the foundation on which the present literature review is based: sadly, in the field of education, including special education, we know more about what we don't know than we know about what works. Still, an important question needs asking: does special education work?

Researchers and policymakers have been asking whether special education policy has been effective for over fifty years (Kidd, 1958). In the late 1960s, a former president of the Council for Exceptional Children questioned whether segregated settings in special education service provision were effective, especially for students with intellectual disabilities (Dunn, 1968). Some argue that current special education practice—including segregated settings, or the so-called differential placement—does little to positively effect the achievement and long-term outcomes of students with disabilities (M. Cook, 2002; Gottlieb & Weinberg, 1999; President's Commission on Excellence in Special Education, 2002; Reynolds & Wolfe, 1999).

One measure of the success of education—of special education—is the rate at which all students (both with and without disabilities) graduate from high school. Independent estimates (using various measures and methods, over periods ranging from one to five years, during the 1990s) show the graduation rate falling, with the dropout rate at nearly one-third of all high school students (Barton, 2004; Greene & Winters, 2002; Swanson, 2004a; 2004b). At the same time, alternatives for dropouts to resume their education are evaporating, and earnings for both male and female dropouts have gone down steadily over the last thirty years. Dropout rates are highest among minorities, among whom employment rates are also the lowest (Barton, 2005).

Against this already dismal educational and employment backdrop are data about school dropout rates for students with disabilities. Less than half of students with disabilities graduate from high school every year. In the school year 2000–2001, the dropout rate for students with disabilities over the age of 14 was 41%, substantially higher than that for students without disabilities (OSERS, 2003). One estimate of the dropout rate for students with intellectual disabilities puts the number at 26% (President's Committee for People with Intellectual Disabilities, 2004). Students with minority status, who are male, and who have disabilities, are most at risk for experiencing alienation in schools, a probable causal factor for leaving school early (Brown, Higgins, Pierce, Hong, & Thoma, 2003).

A statistical analysis using data from the Chicago Longitudinal Study looked at the effect of special education intervention on students with learning disabilities. They were generally low-income, and almost all were African American. Students with learning disabilities who received special education services in elementary grades did not, generally speaking, increase their scores in reading and math on standardized tests (Reynolds & Wolfe, 1999). For them, special education was not an effective intervention.

Special Education Elementary Longitudinal Study data indicates that 26% of students with disabilities are retained one grade. While most 4th graders are nine years old, only 4% of 9-year-old students with disabilities are with their age peers in 4th grade (OSERS, 2003). A study looking at the impact of special education on students with disabilities in an inner city, high-poverty district found that elementary students with disabilities who were retained in grade actually did worse academically following retention (Reynolds & Wolfe, 1999). Other research has found that retention has a negative impact longitudinally on academic and social achievement (Jimerson & Ferguson, 2007).

A statistical study looking at differences between low-achieving students who were referred to special education and low-achieving students who were not referred to special education found no difference in achievement between the two groups. Rather, students were more likely to be referred for special education services if their families changed schools, if they had higher rates of tardiness, and if their teachers were more likely to make special education referrals (Gottleib & Weinberg, 1999). Special education does not have a positive effect on achievement. And the education of students with disabilities and those who are at-risk is as much a general education issue as it is a special education issue.

Do traditional, segregated special education settings work for students with so-called severe disabilities? The answer is no. When outcomes between students with severe disabilities in inclusive settings were compared with students in separate settings, those in inclusive settings had better educational outcomes (Fisher & Meyer, 2002). In another study, students with profound and multiple disabilities in inclusive settings had more communication experiences and more communication opportunities with peers than those in segregated settings (Foreman, Arthur-Kelly, Pascoe, & King, 2004).

In one meta-analytical project, researchers found that the use of separate classrooms for students with disabilities has a negative effect size—that is, it is an ineffective strategy for students with disabilities—especially, researchers point out, for students labeled as having intellectual disabilities (Carlburg & Kavale, 1980). A meta-analysis of the academic achievement of students with so-called mild disabilities found that students who attended segregated settings did much worse than those who did not (Weiner, 1985). In another meta-analysis, integrated, inclusive supports and environments were found to have a positive impact on students with intellectual disabilities across grade levels and content areas (Wang & Baker, 1986). Baker, Wang, and Walberg (1995), in a review of meta-analytical research, found small to moderate positive impacts on social and academic outcomes for students with disabilities when placed in inclusive environments.

Post-School Outcomes for Students with Disabilities

One way of determining the impact of special education on students with disabilities is to explore their post-school experiences. What happens to students with disabilities after they leave school? What are their lives like? One study used data from the National Longitudinal Transition Study of Special Education Students done in 1987–1991, and the National Educational Longitudinal Study done in 1988 (Wells, Sandefur, & Hogan, 2003). Using a statistical analysis, researchers found that 40% of former special education students in the 18–26 age range lived at home, were single, were unemployed, and were not attending postsecondary education. Although many of the remaining former special education students were employed, had started families, and had attended postsecondary education, they were "doing so to different degrees relative to individuals without disabilities" (p. 826). Concluding on the basis on their research, the authors go on to comment that present special education and social service practices do "little to fully incorporate individuals with the most severe disabilities into a robust adult life ... Our results show that there is still a long way to go before individuals with disabilities are fully integrated into American society" (p. 828).

Substantial numbers of students with disabilities end up in prison after leaving school. Depending on the disability label, as many as 58% of youth will have been arrested after having been out of school for 3–5 years (Burrell & Warboys, 2000). Broadly speaking, youth with disabilities make up a large part of those in juvenile and adult correctional facilities. One estimate of the percentage of youth with disabilities in juvenile justice systems in the United States puts it at as much as 70–100% (Smith, 2005b). People with intellectual disabilities in prison are represented at much higher rates than in the general population (Cockram, Jackson, & Underwood, 1998). In some states, as many as 38% of prisoners have labels of intellectual disability (Anno, 2001).

Only 10% of people with intellectual disabilities were employed in 2002 and only 15% attended any kind of postsecondary education in 2002 (President's Committee on People with Intellectual Disabilities, 2004).

Looking at the data represented here, it is clear that special education policy is not effective in making inclusion a possibility for all students with disabilities, especially for those with intellectual disabilities. A different way of thinking about special education—what it does, what it's for, who it benefits—is essential.

Overrepresentation and the Failure of Special Education

Kauffman wrote recently that "too much of what is said about education does not acknowledge important realities" (2007, p. 245). One reality about education that we've known for a very long time is that people from racial and ethnic minorities or those living in poverty have been overrepresented in special education in the United States since the 1960s (American Youth Policy Forum and Center on Education Policy, 2002; Artiles, Klingner, & Tate, 2006; Bennett, 2001; Blanchett, 2006; Harry & Klingner, 2006; Losen & Orfield, 2002; Pollock, 2002). We've known about it, but in reality, we haven't done anything about it.

Put bluntly, racism is a barrier to inclusion for at least some students labeled as having intellectual disabilities. African American students are at substantially greater risk—2.9 times more likely—of getting a label of intellectual disabilities than white students (OSERS, 2003). Coupled with this is the fact that such students are also less likely to be placed in general education settings than white students (American Youth Policy Forum and Center on Education Policy, 2002; Losen & Orfield, 2002; National Alliance of Black School Educators & ILIAD Project, 2002). Racist ideologies are at the root of such concerns.

Federal data indicates that African American students are much more likely to be educated outside of regular education classrooms than students from other racial and ethnic backgrounds (Livingston & Wirt, 2005). More than twice the numbers of African American students with disabilities than white students spend at least 60% of their time in segregated-by-disability classrooms. Federal data also reveals that students with disabilities from impoverished backgrounds and African American students with disabilities were much more likely to be retained in grade compared to students not impoverished or who were white (OSERS, 2003).

One of the realities of the overrepresentation of people of color and poor people in special education is the underfunding of schools attended primarily by those with minority or impoverished status (Blanchett, 2006). Students from such backgrounds, not surprisingly, perform more poorly than do white students (National Council on Teacher Quality, 2004). Because they're underfunded, students there don't get the same kind of education that more privileged (white, middle- or upper-class) students receive and so may be more likely to need extra supports and accommodations through special education. The result has been what some have described as the resegregation of schools through special education (Blanchett, 2006; Losen & Orfield, 2002). Others, such as Jonathan Kozol (2007), would say that the reality is that it's not just special education that has been resegregated but all of education in general. Larger social issues, including the relationships of poverty, health, and housing to minority and racial categories, must also be addressed (Apple, 2004).

Where do these issues of overrepresentation come from? Special education, from its inception, has been based in racist ideologies

(Smith, 2008a). Founded as it is in eugenicist pseudoscience, it was designed to sort those deemed fit from those deemed unfit along racial boundaries (Gould, 1996; Selden, 1999; Smith, 2008a; Winfield, 2007). Eliminating such racist ideologies will require substantive restructuring not just of special education but of the very foundations of U.S. education as a whole.

Race is not, of course, the only bias operating within special education. Social class too has had a substantial undergirding negative influence in the area of educational research, one that some suggest may actually be more central than that of racial prejudice (Danforth, 2009).

NCLB and Inclusion

In 2001, the Elementary and Secondary Education Act (more commonly known as No Child Left Behind) was signed into law. What is the so-called No Child Left Behind Act (NCLB) really about? Some argue that it is one of the largest corporate takeovers of government and community activities in U.S. history, with huge benefits for global corporations and lobbyists. Notice how, as one small example, educational publishing representatives were at the table when NCLB policy was being crafted, ensuring their textbooks and materials would be in use. (Leistyna, 2007). Some critical educators assert that NCLB's focus is on

> guaranteeing simplistic and reductionistic forms of accountability. Such an assertion should not be taken as a rejection of school accountability; instead, it is an assertion that the *types* of accountability mandated often reconstruct school purpose in a way that promotes low-level thinking skills and reduces education to the indoctrination of unchallenged "truths." The law's claim of increased flexibility and local control is misleading doublespeak, and its focus on teaching strategies that have been scientifically proven to improve instruction raises profound issues about the nature of knowledge production in a democratic society. (Kincheloe, 2006, p. 4)

NCLB assumes a place in the long history of standards-based educational reform, a movement that has been active in educational and curricular policy throughout much of the twentieth century. Critical theorists assert that this movement, with NCLB as its most recent manifestation, is based on the neoliberal policies of the Western dominating social classes. Results of these kinds of standards-based reform efforts have not only had little positive impact on the so-called achievement gap they have been designed to address, while standards-based reform policies have been in place, the achievement gap has actually increased (McLaren & Farahmandpur, 2006; McLaren, Martin, Farahmandpur, & Jaramillo, 2004). Accountability policies embedded in NCLB, with its use of high-stakes testing approaches, are based on faulty research: "critical premises on which the movement of test-driven external accountability is based are weak" (Lee, 2008, p. 608). Although NCLB calls for practices based on evidence, the research on which it is based does not meet its own standards. And, notwithstanding protestations to the contrary, it does nothing to close the achievement gap between whites and racial minorities (Lee, 2008). Rather, its requirements ensure increased control over curriculum and information within schools and do so in ways that meet the needs of global corporations (Lipman, 2009).

So, do provisions of NCLB serve as disincentives to the inclusion of students with disabilities? Even the federal government believes it does. The Congressional Research Service has expressed concern that some provisions of NCLB are in conflict with the provisions of the IDEA. NCLB testing and accountability measures may force students with disabilities to be excluded from regular education curricula (Apling & Jones, 2005).

Allbritten, Mainzer, and Ziegler (2004) argue that NCLB legislation places students with disabilities at grave risk of failure, marking them as scapegoats in the world of educational accountability. They assert that high-stakes testing will result in increased dropout rates for students with disabilities. They outline ways in which current systems for assessing student performance are unreliable and invalid. The presence of students with what NCLB calls the most significant cognitive disabilities in schools puts those schools at risk of not meeting Annual Yearly Progress (AYP), thus raising stigma and reinforcing anti-disability perceptions, negative attitudes, and resentment.

The impact of AYP on students with disabilities was amply demonstrated in Indiana during 2005 when more than half the schools did not meet AYP and a full three-fourths of those schools did not meet AYP for students receiving special education services. Many around the country are concerned that the impact of NCLB on students with disabilities is wholly negative, given scapegoating, moving limited resources away from students with disabilities, a narrowing of curriculum, conflicts between NCLP and IDEIA, and increased dropout rates. These concerns were supported by formal survey research of Indiana schools and district administrators (Cole, 2006).

The kinds of high-stakes testing and student performance accountability required by NCLB have had a profound impact on inclusion for students with intellectual as well as other disabilities. This legislation that is designed to require schools to be increasingly accountable for the learning of their students—a goal that is inarguably appropriate—does so in ways that increase the surveillance and policing of education by neoliberal bureaucracies; create further opportunities for the commodification, marketization, privatization, militarization, and industrialization of schooling; and engage in a series of horrific "shaming practices" that cause more harm than good (Apple, 2007, p. 110)—shaming practices that we know from a long history of intellectual and developmental disabilities do substantial harm to labeled people (Smith, 1999a).

Apple points out that the kinds of policies inherent in NCLB reflect the notion

> that what counts as good teaching ... is to be evaluated only on improvements in students' scores ... is less than satisfactory and shows a profound misunderstanding of the complexity of the teaching act. The ways in which it tacitly defines what counts as legitimate knowledge as only that which can be included on such reductive tests flies in the face of decades of struggle over the politics of official knowledge. (Apple, 2007, p. 110–111)

Clearly, what NCLB has done is to legislate into practice the kind of new Social Darwinism that has had and continues to have such a negative impact on education in general and on students with intellectual (and other) disabilities in particular (Apple, 2004; Smith, 2008). For in enacting this kind of policy, there has been

> a shift of resources away from students who are labeled as having special needs or learning difficulties, with some of these needed resources now being shifted to marketing and public relations. "Special needs" students are not only expensive but also deflate test scores. (Apple, 2004, p. 20)

In essence, students with disabilities become throwaways (again, or still), and any incentive, desire, need, or value placed on their inclusion in general education classrooms becomes lost. In effect, "we are witnessing a process in which the state shifts the blame for the very evident inequalities in access and outcome it has promised to reduce, from itself onto individual schools, parents, and children" (Apple, 2004, p. 24). Using this blaming-the-victim strategy, students with intellectual disabilities are "rightly" denied their citizenship in education communities and access to the kinds of supports and services that will allow them to be real community members. And education, how schools are structured and situated, is taken off the hot seat as the culprit behind the success or failure of individual students. What are the outcomes of the kinds of national curriculum and standardized testing required by NCLB? Apple points out that, as a result of NCLB policies, "schools themselves become more similar, and more committed, to standard, traditional, whole-class methods of teaching and a standard and traditional (and often monocultural) curriculum" (2004, p. 23)—exactly the kinds of practices that we know do not work for students with intellectual and most other disabilities or, for that matter, for their peers without disabilities. Take for example schools that avoid precisely the kinds of differentiated instruction necessary to ensure that students with disabilities need to access the general curriculum (Broderick, Heeral, & Reid, 2005).

In the face of state and federal mandates in these areas, research indicates that reform and other efforts in support of inclusive education may be unsustainable (Cole, 2006; Sindelar, Shearer, Yendol-Hoppey, & Liebert, 2006). As I've outlined above, national and state data indicate important unintended consequences of NCLB legislation on students with disabilities, including in the area of inclusion (Cole, 2006). Teacher educators assert that high-stakes testing has set back the inclusion of students with disabilities (Griffin, Jones, & Kilgore, 2007).

NCLB is founded on a process-product model of education, assuming that the (only and singular) goal of schooling is to impart academic knowledge, which can be measured on standardized tests. This model, however, leaves out other (many and complex) goals of education, including goals related to creating a just society in which all members play a role as creative, emotionally healthy, culturally rich citizens—goals that are not amenable to measurement on standardized testing (Treder, Morse, & Ferron, 2000). The assumption inherent in such a model is that school test scores reveal or indicate students' success in areas in which they have gained academic knowledge, and that schools, rather naturally then, should produce steadily increasing test scores if they are doing their job right. These scores become, through a process of reification, the essence of what is important and valued in any educational experience. Put another way, what doesn't influence test scores is of no interest to educators.

Leaving out all those other (at least potential) roles of education, as it does, is a tremendous loss to our culture and our country. First, it ensures that education is all about meeting the needs of a globalized, neoliberal, capitalist economy. More importantly, it prevents— systematically and intentionally, I would argue—the development of a citizenry that is steeped in traditions of democracy, equality, equity, and support. Including students with intellectual (and other) disabilities in general education classrooms is one way, one place, one process for modeling and actively teaching those core values. Failing to do so is a loss not just for people with intellectual disabilities and their families but also for all others—a terrible, terrible loss.

References

Aichroth, S., Carpenter, J., Daniels, K., Grassette, P., Kelly, D., Murray, A., Rice, J., Rivard, B., Smith, C., Smith, P., & Topper, K. (2002). Creating a new system of supports: The Vermont self-determination project. *Rural Special Education Quarterly, 21*(2), 16–28.

Allbritten, D., Mainzer, R., & Ziegler, D. (2004). Will students with disabilities be scapegoats for school failures? *Educational HORIZONS, 82*(2), 153–160.

American Youth Policy Forum and Center on Education Policy (2002). *Twenty-five years of educating children with disabilities: The good news and the work ahead.* Washington, DC: Author.

Ammah, J., & Hodge, S. (2006). Secondary physical education teachers' beliefs and practices in teaching students with severe disabilities: A descriptive analysis. *The High School Journal, 89*, 40–59.

Anno, J. (2001). *Correctional health care: Guidelines for the management of an adequate delivery system.* Chicago, IL: National Commission on Correctional Health Care.

Apling, R., & Jones, N. (2005). *The Individuals with Disabilities Education Act (IDEA): Interactions with selected provisions of the No Child Left Behind Act (NCLBA).* Washington, DC: Congressional Research Service, The Library of Congress.

Apple, M. (2004). Creating difference: Neo-liberalism, neo-conservatism and the politics of educational reform. *Educational Policy, 18*, 12–44.

——— (2007). Ideological success, educational failure? On the politics of No Child Left Behind. *Journal of Teacher Education, 58*, 108–116.

Artiles, A., Klingner, J., & Tate, W. (2006). Representation of minority students in special education: Complicating traditional explanations. *Educational Researcher, 35*(6), 3–5.

Baker, E., Wang, M., & Walberg, H. (1995). The effects of inclusion on learning. *Educational Leadership, 52*(4), 33–36.

Barnett, C., & Monda-Amaya, L. (1998). Principals' knowledge of and attitudes toward inclusion. *Remedial and Special Education, 19*, 181–192.

Bartholomay, T., Wallace, T., & Mason, C. (2001). *The leadership factor: A key to effective inclusive high schools.* Minneapolis, MN: University of Minnesota Institute on Community Integration.

Barton, P. (2004). *Unfinished business: More measured approaches in standards based reform.* Princeton, NJ: Educational Testing Service.

Barton, P. (2005). *One-third of a nation: Rising dropout rates and declining opportunities.* Princeton, NJ: Educational Testing Service.

Bennett, C. (2001). Genres of research in multicultural education. *Review of Educational*

Research, 71, 171–217.

Birman, B., & Porter, A. (2002). Evaluating the effectiveness of educational funding streams. *Peabody Journal of Education, 77*(4), 59–85.

Blanchett, W. (2006). Disproportionate representation of African American students in special education: Acknowledging the role of white privilege and racism. *Educational Researcher, 35*(6), 24–38.

Brantlinger, E. (2004). Ideologies discerned, values determined: Getting past the hierarchies of special education. In L. Ware (Ed.) *Ideology and the politics of (in)exclusion* (pp. 11–31). New York: Peter Lang.

Broderick, A., Heeral, M-P., Reid, D. K. (2005) Differentiating instruction for disabled students in inclusive classrooms. *Theory into Practice, 44, 3*, 194–202.

Brown, M., Higgins, K., Pierce, T., Hong, E., & Thoma, C. (2003). Secondary students' perceptions of school life with regard to alienation: The effects of disability, gender and race. *Learning Disability Quarterly, 26*, 227–238.

Brownell, M., & Pajares, F. (1999). Teacher efficacy and perceived success in mainstreaming students with learning and behavior problems. *Teacher Education and Special Education, 22*, 154–64.

Buell, M., Hallam, R., Gamel-McCormick, M., & Scheer, S. (1999). A survey of general and special education teachers' perceptions and inservice needs concerning inclusion. *International Journal of Disability, Development, and Education, 46*, 143–156.

Burke, K., & Sutherland, C. (2004). Attitudes toward inclusion: Knowledge vs. experience. *Education, 125*, 163–172.

Burrell, S., & Warboys, L. (2000). *Special education and the juvenile justice system.* Washington, DC: Office of Juvenile Justice and Delinquency Prevention.

Carlberg, C., & Kavale, K. (1980). The efficacy of special versus regular class placement for exceptional children: A meta-analysis. *The Journal of Special Education, 14*, 296–309.

Carter, E., & Hughes, C. (2006). Including high school students with severe disabilities in general education classes: Perspectives of general and special educators, paraprofessionals, and administrators. *Research & Practice for Persons with Severe Disabilities 31*, 174–185.

Cockram, J., Jackson, R., & Underwood, R. (1998). People with an intellectual disability and the criminal justice system: The family perspective. *Journal of Intellectual & Developmental Disability, 23*(1).

Cole, C. (2006). Closing the achievement gap series, part III: What is the impact of NCLB on the inclusion of students with disabilities? *Center for Evaluation and Education Policy Brief, 4*(11), 1–12.

Cook, B. (2004). Inclusive teachers' attitudes toward their students with disabilities: A replication and extension. *The Elementary School Journal, 104*, 307–320.

Cook, B., Cameron, D., & Tankersley, M. (2007). Inclusive teachers' attitudinal ratings of their students with disabilities. *The Journal of Special Education, 40*, 230–238.

Cook, B., Semmel, M., & Gerber, M. (1999). Attitudes of principals and special education teachers toward the inclusion of students with mild disabilities: Critical differences of opinion. *Remedial and Special Education 20*, 199–207.

Cook, M. (2002). Outcomes: Where are we now? The efficacy of differential placement and the effectiveness of current practices. *Preventing School Failure, 46*, 54–56.

Crockett, J., Myers, S., Griffin, A., & Hollandsworth, B. (2007). The unintended side effects of inclusion for students with learning disabilities: The perspectives of school administrators. *Learning Disabilities, 14,* 155–166.

Danforth, S. (2009). *The incomplete child: An intellectual history of learning disabilities.* New York: Peter Lang.

Danforth, S., & Smith, T. (2005). *Engaging troubling students: A constructivist approach.* Thousand Oaks, CA: Corwin Press.

Downing, J. (2008). Inclusive education: Why is it not more prevalent? *TASH Connections, 34*(2), 8–10, 13.

Dunn, L. (1968). Special education for the mildly retarded—Is much of it justifiable? *Exceptional Children, 35,* 5–22.

Dyson, L. (2007). The unexpected effects on inclusion on the families of students with learning disabilities: A focus-group study. *Learning Disabilities, 14,* 185–194.

Elhoweris, H., & Alsheikh, M. (2004). Teachers attitudes toward inclusion. Annual Meeting of the New York State Federation of the Council for Exceptional Children, Albany, NY.

Fabel, L. (2009). Report: Special ed integration fails expectations. *Washington DC Examiner.* Retrieved on March 15, 2009 from http://www.dcexaminer.com/local/ Report-Special-ed-integration-fails-expectation_02_27-40396677.html

Fisher, M., & Meyer, L. (2002). Development and social competence after two years for students enrolled in inclusive and self-contained educational programs. *Research and Practice for Persons with Severe Disabilities, 27,* 165–174.

Foreman, P., Arthur-Kelly, M., Pascoe, S., & King, B. (2004). Evaluating the educational experiences of students with profound and multiple disabilities in inclusive and segregated classroom settings: An Australian perspective. *Research and Practice for Persons with Severe Disabilities, 29,* 183–193.

Fullan, M., & Steigelbauer, S. (2007). *The new meaning of educational change* (4th ed.). New York: Teachers College Press.

Garriott, P., Miller, M. & Snyder, L. (2003). Preservice teachers' beliefs about inclusive education: What should teacher educators know? *Action in Teacher Education, 25*(1), 48–54.

Giangreco, M. (1997). Key lessons learned about inclusive education: Summary of the 1996 Schonell Memorial Lecture. *International Journal of Disability and Development, 44,* 193–206.

Gottlieb, J., & Weinberg, S. (1999). Comparison of students referred and not referred for special education. *The Elementary School Journal, 99,* 187–199.

Gould, S. (1996). *The mismeasure of man.* New York: W. W. Norton & Co.

Greene, J., & Winters, M. (2002). *Public school graduation rates in the United States.* New York: Manhattan Institute for Public Research.

Griffin, C., Jones, H., & Kilgore, K. (2007). The unintended side effects of including students with learning disabilities for teacher educators. *Learning Disabilities, 14,* 195–204.

Harry, B., & Klingner, J. (2006). *Why are so many minority students in special education? Understanding race and disability in schools.* New York: Teachers College Press.

Hehir, T. (2007). Confronting ableism. *Educational Leadership, 64*(5), 8–14.

Helmstetter, E., Curry, C., Brennan, M., & Sampson-Saul, M. (1998). Comparison of general and special education classrooms of students with severe disabilities. *Education and Training in Mental Retardation and Developmental Disabilities, 33,* 216–227.

Huerta-Charles, L. (2007). Pedagogy of testimony: Reflections on the pedagogy of critical pedagogy. In P. McLaren J. Kincheloe (Eds.) *Critical pedagogy: Where are we now?* (pp. 249–261). New York: Peter Lang.

Jahnukainen, M. (2005). Education in the prevention of social exclusion. *Review of Disability Studies, 1*(3), 36–44.

Jimerson, S., & Ferguson, P. (2007). A longitudinal study of grade retention: Academic and behavioral outcomes of retained students through adolescence. *School Psychology Quarterly, 22*, 314–339.

Kauffman, J. (2007). Labels and the nature of special education: We need to face realities. *Learning Disabilities, 14*, 245–248.

Kidd, J. (1958). Special education: Fulfillment of a promise. *The Elementary School Journal, 58*, 454–456.

Kincheloe, J. (2006). What you don't know *is* hurting you and the country. In S. Steinberg & J. Kincheloe (Eds.) *What you don't know about schools* (pp. 1–29). New York: Palgrave Macmillan.

Kliewer, C., Biklen, D., & Kasa-Hendrickson, C. (2006). Who may be literate? Disability and resistance to the cultural denial of competence. *American Educational Research Journal, 43*, 163–192.

Kluth, P., Villa, R., & Thousand, J. (2002). "Our school doesn't offer inclusion" and other legal blunders. *Educational Leadership, 59*(4), 24–27.

Kozma, A., Mansell, J., & Beadle-Brown, J. (2009). Outcomes in different residential settings for people with intellectual disability: A systematic review. *American Journal on Intellectual and Developmental Disabilities, 114*, 193–222.

Kozol, J. (2007). *Letters to a young teacher.* New York: Crown.

Laflamme, M., McComas, J., & Pivik, J. (2002). Barriers and facilitators to Inclusive Education. *Exceptional Children, 69*, 97–107.

Lakin, C., Doljanac, R., Byun, S.-Y., Stancliffe, R., Taub, S., and Chiri, G. (2008). Factors associated with expenditures for Medicaid Home and Community Based Services (HCBS) and Intermediate Care Facilities for Persons With Mental Retardation (ICF/MR) services for persons with intellectual and developmental disabilities. *Intellectual and Developmental Disabilities, 46*, 200–214.

Leafstedt, J., Richards, C., LaMonte, M., & Cassidy, D. (2007). Perspectives on co-teaching: Views from high school students with learning disabilities. *Learning Disabilities, 14*, 177–184.

Lee, J. (2008). Is test-driven external accountability effective? Synthesizing the evidence from cross-state causal-comparative and correlational studies. *Review of Educational Research, 78*, 608–644.

Leistyna, P. (2007). Neoliberal non-sense. In P. McLaren & J. Kincheloe (Eds.) *Critical pedagogy: Where are we now?* (pp. 97–123). New York: Peter Lang.

Lipman, P. (2009). Beyond accountability: Toward schools that create new people for a new way of life. In A. Darder, M. Baltodano, & R. Torres (Eds.) *The critical pedagogy reader* (2nd ed.) (pp. 364–383). New York: Routledge.

Livingston, A., & Wirt, J. (2005). *The condition of education 2005 in brief.* Washington, DC: National Center for Education Statistics.

Lohrman, S. & Bambara, L. (2006). Elementary education teachers' beliefs about essential supports needed to successfully include students with developmental disabilities who engage in challenging behaviors. *Research & Practice for Persons with Severe Disabilities, 31*, 157–173.

Losen, D. & Orfield, G. (2002). *Racial inequity in special education.* Cambridge, MA:

Harvard Education Press.

Mastropieri, M. (2001). Is the glass half full or half empty? Challenges encountered by first-year special education teachers. *The Journal of Special Education, 35*, 66–74.

McLaren, P. & Farahmandpur, R. (2006). The pedagogy of oppression: A brief look at "No Child Left Behind." *Monthly Review, 58*(3), 92–99.

McLaren, P., Martin, G., Farahmandpur, R., & Jaramillo, N. (2004). Teaching in and against the empire: Critical pedagogy as revolutionary praxis. *Teacher Education Quarterly, 31*, 131–153.

Merchlinsky, S., Cooper-Martin, E., & McNary, S. (2009). *Evaluation of the phase out of the secondary Learning Centers: Final report.* Rockville, Maryland: Montgomery County Public Schools, Office of Shared Accountability.

Minke, K., Bear, G., Deemer, S., & Griffin, S. (1996). Teachers' experiences with inclusive classrooms: Implications for special education reform. *The Journal of Special Education, 30*, 152–186.

National Alliance of Black School Educators & ILIAD Project (2002). *Addressing over-representation of African American students in special education: The prereferral intervention process—An administrator's guide.* Arlington, VA: Council for Exceptional Children, and Washington, DC: National Alliance of Black School Educators.

National Council on Disability (1994). *Inclusionary education for students with disabilities: Keeping the promise.* Washington, DC: Author.

——— (1995). *Improving the implementation of the Individuals with Disabilities Education Act: Making schools work for all of America's children.* Washington, DC: Author.

——— (2008). *The No Child Left Behind Act and the Individuals with Disabilities Education Act: A progress report.* Washington, DC: Author.

National Council on Teacher Quality (2004). *Attracting, developing and retaining effective teachers: Background report for the United States.* Washington, DC: Author.

——— (2007). *2007 State Teacher Policy Yearbook.* Washington, DC: Author.

National Education Association (2007). *Rankings and estimates: Rankings of the states 2006 and estimates of school statistics 2007.* Atlanta, GA: Author.

Office of Special Education and Rehabilitative Services (2003). *25th annual report to Congress on the implementation of the Individuals with Disabilities Education Act.* Washington, DC: Author.

Parrish, T. (1993). *State funding provisions and least restrictive environment: Implications for federal policy.* (CSEF Brief #2). Palo Alto, CA: Center for Special Education Finance.

——— (1994). *Fiscal issues in special education: Removing incentives for restrictive placements* (CSEF Policy Paper #4). Palo Alto, CA: Center for Special Education Finance.

——— (1996). *Special education finance: Past, present, and future* (CSEF Brief #8). Palo Alto, CA: Center for Special Education Finance.

Peters, Susan (2004). *Inclusive education: An EFA strategy for all children.* Washington, DC: The World Bank.

Pierson, M., & Howell, E. (2006). Pre-service teachers' perceptions of inclusion. *Academic Exchange, 10*, 169–173.

Pollock, M. (2002). How the question we ask most about race in education is the very question we must suppress. *Educational Researcher, 30*(9), 2–12.

Praisner, C. (2003). Attitudes of elementary school principals toward the inclusion of students with disabilities. *Exceptional Children, 69*, 135–145.

President's Commission on Excellence in Special Education (2002). *A new era: Revitalizing special education for children and their families*. Washington, DC: U.S. Department of Education Office of Special Education and Rehabilitation Services.

President's Committee for Persons with Intellectual Disabilities (2004). *A charge we have to keep: A road map to personal and economic freedom for people with intellectual disabilities in the 21st century*. Washington, DC: Author.

Reusen, A., Shoho, A., & Barker, K. (2001). High school teacher attitudes toward inclusion. *The High School Journal, 84*, 7–20.

Reynolds, A., & Wolfe, B. (1999). Special education and school achievement: An exploratory analysis with a central-city sample. *Educational Evaluation and Policy Analysis, 21*, 249–269.

Salisbury, C. (2006). Principals' perspectives on inclusive elementary schools. *Research & Practice for Persons with Severe Disabilities, 31*, 70–82.

Selden, S. (1999). *Inheriting shame: The story of eugenics and racism in America*. New York: Teacher's College Press.

Shippen, M., Crites, S., Houchins, D., Ramsey, M., & Simon, M. (2005). Preservice teachers' perceptions of including students with disabilities. *Teacher Education and Special Education, 28*(2), 92–99.

Short, C., & Martin, B. (2005). Case study: Attitudes of rural high school students and teachers regarding inclusion. *The Rural Educator, 27*, 1–10.

Silverman, J. (2007). Epistemological beliefs and attitudes toward inclusion in preservice teachers. *Teacher Education and Special Education, 30*, 42–51.

Sindelar, P., Shearer, D., Yendol-Hoppey, D., & Liebert, T. (2006). The sustainability of inclusive school reform. *Exceptional Children, 72*, 317-332.

Smith, P. (1999a). Drawing new maps: A radical cartography of developmental disabilities. *Review of Educational Research, 69*(2), 117–144.

——— (1999b). Ideology, politics, and science in understanding developmental disabilities. *Mental Retardation, 37*, 71–72.

——— (2001a). Inquiry cantos: A poetics of developmental disability. *Mental Retardation, 39*, 379–390.

——— (2001b). MAN.i.f.e.s.t.o.: A Poetics of D(EVIL)op(MENTAL) Dis(ABILITY). *Taboo: The Journal of Education and Culture, 5*(1), 27–36.

——— (2004). Whiteness, normal theory, and disability studies. *Disability Studies Quarterly, 24*(2).

——— (2005a). Off the map: A critical geography of intellectual disabilities. *Health and Place, 11*, 87–92.

——— (2005b). "There is no treatment here:" Disability and health in a state prison system. *Disability Studies Quarterly, 25*(3).

——— (2006). Split------ting the ROCK of {speci [ES]al} e.ducat.ion: FLOWers of lang[ue]age in >DIS<ability studies. In S. Danforth and S. Gabel (Eds.), *Vital Questions in Disability Studies in Education*, (pp. 31–58). New York: Peter Lang.

——— (2008a). Cartographies of eugenics and special education: A history of the (ab)normal. In S. Gabel & S. Danforth (Eds.), *Disability and the politics of education: An international reader*. New York: Peter Lang.

——— (2008b). Reality, disability, and education. *Disability Studies Quarterly, 28*(3), n.p.

Smith, P., & Routel, C. (2008). Constructing meaning: Including students with disabilities in general education classrooms. 20th Annual Ethnographic and Qualitative Research Conference. Cedarville, IL.

Steinfield, E. (2005). Education for all: The cost of accessibility. *Education Notes* (The World Bank).

Swanson, C. (2004a). *The real truth about low graduation rates, an evidence-based commentary.* Washington, DC: Urban Institute Education Policy Institute.

— — — (2004b). *Who graduates? Who doesn't? A statistical portrait of public high school graduation, class of 2001.* Washington, DC: Urban Institute Education Policy Institute.

Tankersley, M., Niesz, T., Cook, B., & Woods, W. (2007). The unintended side effects of inclusion of students with learning disabilities: The perspectives of special education teachers. *Learning Disabilities, 14,* 135–144.

Tichenor, M., Heins, B., & Piechura-Couture, K. (1998). Putting principles into practice: Parent perceptions of a co-taught inclusive classroom. *Education, 118,* 471–477.

Titone, C. (2005). The philosophy of inclusion: Roadblocks and remedies for the teacher and the teacher educator. *Journal of Educational Thought, 39,* 7–32.

Treder, D., Morse, W. & Ferron, J. (2000). The relationship between teacher effectiveness and teacher attitudes toward issues related to inclusion. *Teacher Education and Special Education, 23,* 202–210.

Villa, R., & Thousand, J. (2003). Making inclusive education work. *Educational Leadership, 61* (2), 19–23.

— — — (2005). Preface. In R. Villa & J. Thousand (Eds.) *Creating an inclusive school* (2nd ed.) (pp. v–vii). Alexandria, VA: Association for Supervision and Curriculum Development.

Wang, M., & Baker, E. (1986). Mainstreaming programs: Design features and effects. *Journal of Special Education, 19,* 503–521.

Weber, M. (2007). Inclusive education in the United States and internationally: Challenges and response. *Review of Disability Studies, 3*(1–2), 19–32.

Weiner, R. (1985). *P.L. 94–142: Impact on the schools.* Arlington, VA: Capitol Publications.

Wells, T., Sandefur, G., & Hogan, D. (2003). What happens after the high school years among young persons with disabilities? *Social Forces, 82,* 803–832.

Winfield, A. (2007). *Eugenics and education in America: Institutionalized racism and the implications of history, ideology, and memory.* New York: Peter Lang.

Yssel, N., Engelbrecht, P., Oswald, M., Eloff, I., & Swart, E. (2007. Views of inclusion: A comparative study of parents' perceptions in South Africa and the United States. *Remedial and Special Education, 28,* 356–365.

CHAPTER 4

Lack of Vision? Lack of Respect?

Exclusion in Illinois

VALERIE OWEN AND SUSAN GABEL

Regrettably, Illinois has never been considered an inclusion state. On the contrary, the history of education in Illinois is a history of exclusion and systematic segregation of students with disabilities, particularly students with cognitive disabilities. Segregation is instantiated at all levels of the state, including the organization of the State Board of Education, state educational statutes, and teacher preparation and certification regulations. At the local level, teachers and administrators have tremendous responsibility and influence concerning educational placement decisions for students with cognitive disability. That influence was affirmed in recent litigation, through teachers' unions and through their professional preparation. Today, in spite of some efforts toward systemic change through an Illinois State Board of Education Initiative (Project CHOICES) and a federal lawsuit (*Corey H. v. Board of Education*, 1998), Illinois' record of providing inclusive education or even education in the least restrictive environment (LRE) as required by law is quite dismal.

A challenge in writing any historical account of the exclusion of a segment of the school-aged population is that the label of the group has changed over time. The Illinois State Board of Education currently uses the term "cognitive disability" to refer to students who were once labeled with mental retardation. The American Association on Intellectual and Developmental Disabilities (AAIDD) uses the term "intellectual disability" and defines it as "characterized by significant limitations both in intellectual functioning and in adaptive behavior as expressed in conceptual, social, and practical adaptive skills [originating] before the age of 18" (AAIDD, 2008, p. 1; Schalock, Luckasson, Shogren et al., 2007, p. 118). To assure that the term "intellectual disability" replaces other terms, Schalock and colleagues (2007) note that

the term … covers the same population of individuals who were diagnosed previously with mental retardation in number, kind, level, type, and duration of the
disability and the need of people with this disability for individualized services
and supports. Furthermore, every individual who is or was eligible for a diagnosis of mental retardation is eligible for a diagnosis of intellectual disability. (117)

In the history of Illinois as well as the nation, the terms "feeble-
minded" and "mental deficiency" have also been used. In all, the underlying concept is of a perceived impairment of cognitive function
and adaptive behavior. Throughout this chapter, we use the term appropriate for the historical context under discussion.

What the Numbers Show Us

Illinois is a state of 102 counties. Much of the state is rural with the
larger population centers, including Chicago and its suburbs, in the
northern part of the state. It has a long history of locally governed
schools as evidenced by its 873 separate school districts, many of
which have less than 1,000 students (Illinois State Board of Education,
2008). In addition, many districts consolidate their special education
services into special education cooperatives that constitute groups of
smaller, additional administrative units. In these administrative arrangements, the cooperatives deliver the instruction while the local
districts continue, ostensibly, to be responsible for the educational
progress of those students.

In numerous recent rankings of inclusionary practices and school
funding in U.S. states and territories, Illinois consistently ranks near
the bottom (e.g., Braddock, Hemp, & Rizzolo, 2008; CSEF, 2004; Illinois State Board of Education, 2007). Historically, in a number of
studies, Illinois ranked at the bottom for inclusive placements of students with mental retardation. For example, Danielson and Bellamy
(1989) reported that for the 1985–1986 school year Illinois not only
was one of the states with the highest percentage of disabled students
in separate classes but also was among the states with the highest
percentage of students in segregated facilities.

For the 1988–1989 school year, Hemp, Freagon, and Christensen-
Leininger (1991) reported that Illinois had a regular class or resource
room placement rate of 3% for students labeled with mental retardation and it ranked 49th when compared nationally. In 1992, the ARC
placed Illinois in its "Hall of Shame" for being among the most restrictive states in the country in how it educated students labeled with
mental retardation (Davis, 1992). Similarly, in 1992, Designs for

Change, a Chicago advocacy organization, reported that the Chicago Public Schools and the Illinois State Board of Education (ISBE) failed to educate students with disabilities in the least restrictive environment in Chicago and across the state (Designs for Change, 1992).

In comparison, the latest data for Illinois show that not much has changed. Recent ISBE data indicate a decrease in the number of students labeled with cognitive disability, an increase in the number of students so labeled in segregated settings, and below average funding for students with disabilities (ISBE, 2007). For example, in the ISBE's 2006 Annual Report (ISBE, 2007), the number of children labeled with cognitive disability in grades 6–12 steadily decreased over the previous three years (i.e., 2004, 2005, and 2006). The total number of students labeled with cognitive disability in 2006 was 26,372 or 9.19% of the students in special education, down from 9.74% in 2004. According to the report, the following targets are defined in the Illinois State Performance Plan for the 2005–2006 school year:

> At least 48% of students with disabilities receive special education services outside of the general education classroom less than 21% of the time.
>
> No more than 20.5% of students with disabilities receive special education services outside of the general education classroom more than 60% of the time. (p. 25)

However, the 2006 data show that "almost three-fourths (73.7%) of students with cognitive disabilities receive services outside of the general education classroom more than 60% of the time or in a separate facility, the highest of any disability category" (p. 25). Furthermore, in 2006, the percentage of students labeled with cognitive disability who were educated outside the general education classroom less that 21% of the time was 5.3%. In the words of the 2006 report, "Illinois serves students in less inclusive settings than the national averages for all of the six highest incidence disabilities except Speech/Language Impairment" (ISBE, 2007, p. 25).

The 2006 Annual Report also cites the year 2000 national comparison data from the Center for Special Education Finance (2004) Special Education Expenditure Project (SEEP) on total special education spending. The year 2000 national average per pupil expenditure on special education was $7,556; in the SEEP report, the average was $8,080. Using both the cited state report number and the SEEP number, however, we would conclude that Illinois lagged behind the national average in the most recent national comparison year possible, the year 2000, when per pupil spending was only $6,625 per special education student (ISBE, 2007). Although Illinois funding has increased each year, spending remains significantly lower than the national average and leaves Illinois students with disabilities, particularly cognitive disability, among the least well funded in the nation.

A History of Exclusionary Policy and Practice: The Early Years

While the Illinois Free School Act of 1825 and the Common School Act of 1845 did not mention students with disabilities, the Illinois Constitution of 1870 guaranteed good common school education for *all* children. In fact, Illinois was one of the first states to require compulsory education for students with what was then called mental deficiency (Scheerberger, 1983). By 1913, school districts were eligible to receive reimbursements from the state for children with mental deficiency and by 1923 districts were also required to set aside their own funds for educating students with disabilities (Kane, John, Bell, & Charlesworth, 1993).

In those early years, students labeled with mental deficiency attending public school were taught together with other students and using the same curriculum (Scheerberger, 1983). Five state residential institutions for students with more severe disabilities had been flourishing in Illinois since the late nineteenth century, however, and many individuals with significant disabilities were housed there (Kane, John, Bell, & Charlesworth, 1993); however, until the mid-twentieth century, if students attended public school, they attended with everyone else and were taught the same curriculum.

Segregation as Part of the Curriculum in the Mid-Twentieth Century

Segregated public school buildings began to emerge in the late 1940s and early 1950s. In 1952, the University of Illinois collaborated with the Illinois Departments of Public Welfare and Public Instruction to found the Institute for Research on Exceptional Children (IREC) at the University of Illinois (Scheerberger, 1983). Samuel Kirk, credited with coining the term "learning disability," was appointed as the first director of the IREC. Kirk and the institute focused their research on expanding their understanding of the needs and problems of exceptional children and the effectiveness of their education. In the new field of educating students with disabilities, Kirk was an advocate for segregated education for students with mental retardation. In 1953, Kirk claimed that there were a number of positive results of segregated special education including the way in which segregation allows children to avoid the frustration of competition. Other advantages cited by Kirk included modified or special academic materials, prescriptive instruction based on diagnosis, clinical teaching procedures, intensive use of learning principles (e.g., concrete examples, repetitions in various situations), systematic approaches to teach living skills and adjustment, individualized instruction, and parent education (Kirk, 1953).

In another Illinois milestone, the Illinois Department of Public Instruction (now the Illinois State Board of Education, 1955) published one of the first curriculum guides for students labeled "trainable mentally retarded." At the time, it was considered a model curriculum, as reported by Burton (1976) who wrote that *A Curriculum Guide for Teachers of Trainable Mentally Handicapped Children* (Baumgartner, 1955), "epitomizes the thrust of public school programs during this period" (p. 114). Although Kirk encouraged the teaching of academic skills, the objectives of the Illinois curriculum were defined in the non-academic areas of self-care, social adjustment, and economic usefulness as well as physical training, language development, music, and art (Burton, 1976). This curriculum was founded on the theory and belief that these students were not educable and that they could not benefit from academics.

This idea that students would not benefit from academic instruction continued to be deeply held. For example, in the 1970s, Marc Gold, a nationally recognized researcher and practitioner, advocated for vocational training for persons with mental retardation. He believed, however, that their lack of learning was due to insufficient teaching and that they had the potential for being more competent if they were just taught. His "Try Another Way System" used content task analysis (breaking down the steps), systematic cuing, and immediate feedback to teach meaningful work skills (Gold, 1980). Unfortunately, the system furthered the idea of a separate non-academic curriculum and suggested that the curriculum and instructional practices for students labeled with mental retardation would look quite different from those who did not have the label.

A Commitment to Segregation as Public Policy and Practice

Although widespread, the belief that children labeled with mental retardation were uneducable did not go unchallenged through the state's legal system. The first litigation was in 1958. In *Department of*

Public Welfare v. Haas (1958), the state of Illinois sued the father of a boy who lived at a state institution because the father had failed to make the required financial contributions toward the child's institutional maintenance. The father claimed that his child was entitled to a free public education under the 1870 constitution. The Illinois Supreme Court ruled in favor of the state, declaring that the state was not responsible for educating those who were "feeble-minded" or "mentally deficient."

Another challenge was waged in the 1970s. In 1970, an Illinois Constitutional Convention resulted in a change in the Illinois Constitutional mandate from "good common school" education to educating "all persons to the limits of their capacities" (Constitution of Illinois, X.1.A., 1970). In 1977, however, in *Pierce v. Board of Education of the City of Chicago* (1977), the Illinois Supreme Court ruled that the new language was merely a goal and not a mandate to provide education to all children. Furthermore, it ruled that it was the state that was responsible for the education of the student, not the school district. A year later, however, in somewhat of a reversal in *Eliot v. Board of Education* (1978), the court ruled that local school districts were obligated to pay the tuition of disabled children placed in private schools (Kane, John, Bell, & Charlesworth, 1993).

Following that ruling and to further emphasize this commitment to private, segregated educational placements, the state enacted Public Act 80-1405 (105 ILCS 5/14-7.02, 1978), which mandated free education for students with disabilities. Perhaps more importantly, the act stated that special private schools were an extension of the public system. In response to P.A. 80-1450, most districts joined in cooperative agreements with other districts, clustering students with disabilities together in small consolidated districts and causing students to attend school outside their neighborhoods. Districts effectively relinquished the responsibility of educating students with mental retardation to the cooperative organization, a policy that continues even today in many communities. For classroom space, these special education administrative structures rented space in wings of existing schools or built entire new buildings. Furthermore, state funding provided incentives for the building of new structures, thereby further instituting segregated education (Kane, John, Bell, & Charlesworth, 1993). As a result of the influence of those early researchers, the belief spread that those labeled with mental retardation needed to be protected from the general population and would not benefit from being exposed to what non-disabled students were learning. Furthermore, the assumption embedded in this clustering and segregation was and continues to be that the label clearly defined the deficit and that an individual educational plan (IEP) could be developed based on the label (e.g., Bogdan and Kuglemass, 1984).

In the late 1970s, after the passage of the *Education of all Handicapped Children Act* (EHA) (P.L 94-142, 1975), Illinois established a number of additional procedures and policies that were very effective in the systemic segregation of children with disabilities. These included separate funding streams and a formalized system for paying the tuition for students who left the general education classroom for private segregated schools. In fact, under the revisions, districts received more state funding the more restrictive a student's placement was.

In addition, the categorical special education teacher certification required by EHA meant that special education teachers were trained and certified to teach separately from general education teachers. Segregated teacher education reinforced segregated K–12 education and continues in Illinois even today. It is one cause of an eventual court case, *Corey H. v. Board of Education,* which has had far-reaching impact on special education teacher certification in Illinois (Kane, John, Bell, & Charlesworth, 1993).

Efforts to Support and Require Inclusionary Practices: A Small Blip of Inclusion

In the 1980s three special education cooperatives were instrumental in closing their segregated schools (Kane, John, Bell, & Charlesworth, 1993): DeKalb County Special Education Association, the LaGrange Area Department of Special Education, and the School Association for Special Education in Dupage County. As a result, in 1988 the ISBE created Project CHOICES (Children Have Opportunities in Inclusive Community Environments and Schools), a least restrictive environment (LRE) initiative. The purpose of CHOICES was to increase the capacity of school districts and educational personnel to educate and provide supports and services to children and youth with disabilities in the preschool, school, and community environments in which they would participate if not identified as having a disability. A fee for service paid by schools or districts was established for Project CHOICES services in 2005. It was not until 2005 that Project CHOICES had a new goal of gathering specific data to evaluate its effectiveness (Project CHOICES, 2008); however, data on the longitudinal effectiveness are not available. The most recent *Project CHOICES Annual Report of Outcomes* (2007) reports that the project is working with a total of 41 school sites across the state committed to creating an LRE team with a range of stakeholders who are implementing an action plan with a timeline. Although the number of active school sites that Project CHOICES has is small, it has a resource library, publishes newsletters, and conducts a well-attended statewide conference in the Chicago area and in addition, more recently, in the greater East St. Louis area (Project CHOICES, 2007).

Barriers, Disincentives, and Educational Policy Reform

Even after the creation of Project CHOICES, Illinois state statutes continued to include many disincentives and barriers to inclusion. For example, in 1993, Gail Lieberman, who was then the Illinois State Board of Education assistant superintendent for Special Education, recognized and detailed the difficulties school personnel were having implementing inclusive practices (Lieberman, 1993). In a study funded by the Illinois Council on Developmental Disabilities, Cohen (1994) identified barriers to inclusion in ten areas: information, attitudes, instruction/technology, leadership, accessibility, organization, operational and implementation problems, financial issues, regulatory barriers, and legal barriers. Cohen's "Blueprint for Change" included a broad spectrum of recommendations including increased parental involvement, accountability for school leaders, and improvements in preparation and continued training and support of teachers.

In 1992, about the time Cohen was conducting his investigation, a landmark class action lawsuit was filed by eight students (*Corey H. v. Board of Education*, 1998) on behalf of all students with disabilities in Chicago Public Schools (CPS). In that action, Chicago Public School District #299 and ISBE were charged with failing to properly educate Chicago Public School students with disabilities as required by *Individuals with Disabilities Educational Act* (IDEA, 1995).The plaintiffs alleged that the Board of Education of the City of Chicago and ISBE were not educating CPS students with disabilities in the least restrictive environment (LRE) as required by IDEA.

Chicago-based U.S. federal judge Robert Gettleman (*Corey H. v. Board of Education*, 1998) initially acted on the suit in 1998 by ruling that the Chicago Board of Education and ISBE failed to provide the proper environment to educate children with disabilities. CPS was cited for not educating students in the least restrictive environment (LRE) and ISBE was cited for not monitoring LRE in Chicago and across the state. As a result, ISBE has somewhat reluctantly implemented more consistent monitoring and documentation of LRE compliance (Mayrowitz & Lapham, 2008). CPS has implemented a remedy focusing primarily on professional development of current CPS teachers and documentation of implementation of LRE.

Gettleman also concluded that one of the reasons that students with disabilities in Illinois were being placed in restrictive, segregated settings was the categorical teacher preparation and certification. Therefore, students were being taught in settings with a teacher certified to teach students associated with a particular disability category, rather than being placed in the LRE regardless of labels. He ordered ISBE to revise its statewide system of certifying special education teachers and general education teachers. The new system retains four categorical special education certificates: Early childhood, Blind/Visually impaired, Deaf/Hard of hearing, and Speech-language pathologist. In conjunction with these categories, the system establishes a new non-categorical K–12 certificate (Learning Behavior Special 1 or LBS1) allowing its holder to teach students in all remaining disability categories (Cognitive Disability, Learning Disability, Social-Emotional Disorder, Other Health Impaired, Orthopedic Impairment, Traumatic Brain Injury, and Autism).

This certification structure sets Illinois apart from other states. According to the most recent data from the Council for Exceptional Children, over twenty states have some form of non-categorical or multi-categorical certification (R. Mainzer, personal communication, April 27, 2009). Many states, however, have certification based on level of severity such as mild/moderate and severe/profound, which de facto means that students with intellectual disabilities continue to have their teachers prepared separately from the other special education teachers. This structure has the potential for those teachers being prepared to teach in more segregated programs. In contrast, Illinois has only one certification for the standard, initial credential and all special education teachers enrolled in teacher education program receive training using unified special education standards. There is an advanced certificate in multiple disability (LBS II), however, only three of the sixty state-approved college and university teacher education programs offer this advanced certificate (ISBE, 2009) and, currently, teachers are not required to have this credential to teach students who have multiple disabilities.

In addition to making changes in Special Education teacher certification, Judge Gettleman also ruled that certification for general education teachers (Early childhood, Elementary, and Secondary) needed significant changes because general education teacher preparation insufficiently prepared teachers for meeting the needs of special education students in the least restrictive environment. As a result, the Illinois Professional Teaching Standards (ISBE, 2003), the standards for all teachers in the state, now include a significant number of indicators directly related to the needs of students receiving special education supports.

Unfortunately, while the judge's ruling mandated better monitoring of LRE by the ISBE, the primary responsibility of ensuring LRE fell to teacher preparation with little effect on school administrative structures and funding streams. Consequently, there remains an unresolved, unrecognized paradox for Illinois. On one hand, federal law, the *Individuals with Disabilities Education Improvement Act* (IDEIA, 2004; formerly IDEA), directs all special education delivery in the country and still continues to define 14 categories for identifying children who are eligible for special education funding and resources. On the other hand, Illinois is mandated through federal court order to maintain a certification system that assures that teachers are prepared to meet the needs of *all* students regardless of categorical labels.

In their analysis of the judicial proceedings and mandated policy reform resulting from *Corey H. v. Board of Education*, Mayrowitz and Lapham (2008), state,

> In traditional litigation, judgments are easily enforced and usually end the court's involvement in the dispute. By contrast, judgments in public law litigation are quite difficult to enforce and generally expand and extend the court's involvement in the dispute. Difficulties enforcing judgments in public law litigation arise because those judgments ultimately seek to reform not only the structure but also the culture of large institutions. Courts are accustomed to achieving their judgments by fiat, but achieving cultural change by fiat is impossible, essentially. (p. 401)

Mayrowitz and Lapham (2008) identify three key tensions in such litigation: (1) the connection between problem and solution, (2) the quality and breadth of representation, and (3) participation and the balance between finality and flexibility. In their analysis of *Corey H. v. Board of Education*, they criticize the CPS building level remedies (i.e., the cadre of school consultant and individual school plans). They conclude that the remedy did not reach the full class of plaintiffs. They also recognize the inherent resistance that resulted when the voices of those "interested persons," such as teachers, parents, disability advocates, and students not directly involved in the case but affected by the remedies, were dismissed by Judge Gettlemen. There also has been tremendous and lasting statewide resistance to the judge's mandated certification change decision, resulting in political tensions as the ISBE tried to appease all the "interested" parties that were attempting to delay the final action on the judgment. Mayrowitz and Lapham note that in *Corey H. v. Board of Education*, the court "opted to protect finality over flexibility" (p. 408), which means Gettlemen's decision was crafted to bring definitive closure that left little or no room for alternative solutions.

Current state data, however, show very little impact of *Corey H. v. Board of Education*. Illinois still ranks well below the national average of educating students with disabilities in the general education classroom (ISBE, 2007). The mixed results of the *Corey H. v. Board of Education* remedies, Mayrowitz and Lapham (2008) conclude, can be directly related not only to the enormity of the task but also to the "lack of participation of groups representing special educators, child study team members, and those who prepare them" (p. 413). They also recognize that this type of participation runs against traditional judicial practice that tends, as did Gettlemen, to seek efficient resolution of disputes by strictly controlling participation. The court imposed its will, rather than working with the various constituents across the state, thereby delaying the implementation of the remedies as well as resulting in tremendous resistance.

Classroom-Level Court Decisions

In a landmark inclusion decision in New Jersey, *Oberti v. Board of Education* (1993), the Third Circuit Court of Appeals determined that inclusion is a right, that the school district must consider LRE first, that it has an obligation to provide the necessary supports for inclusion, and that it is required to provide the necessary supplemental aids and services to enable the child to be educated for a majority of the time in a regular classroom while still addressing unique educational needs. In stark contrast to *Oberti* stands Illinois, where the Seventh Circuit Court of Appeals ruled in the *Beth B. v. Mark VanClay and School District #65* that even though Beth was receiving benefit in the general education classroom, a student could be segregated if the school district personnel thought it more appropriate. Deference to school district personnel is evident in the words of the court as it describes the "constraints" of inclusion:

> Instead of granting flexibility to educators and school officials, it places an extreme restriction on their policymaking authority and the deference they are owed; it essentially vitiates school districts' authority to place any disabled children in separate special education environments. (*Beth B. v. Van Clay*, 2002)

In other words, classroom-level personnel make the decision about the degree to which a student can be placed in LRE, exacerbating the political imbalance between parents or families and school officials in matters of LRE.

The "constraints" and the impact of inclusion have also been addressed by teacher unions, nationally and in Illinois. Generally, teacher unions have positioned themselves in opposition to inclusive education; for example, the former American Federation of Teachers (AFT) president Albert Shanker (1994) editorialized that inclusion will have "the profoundest and most destructive effect on schooling." The Illinois Education Association (IEA), one of the two other teacher unions in Illinois, passed Resolution B-5, "Least Restrictive Environment" (IEA, 2008), regarding LRE and mainstreaming. While acknowledging the right of students to being educated in the LRE, the IEA's Resolution affirms that "the impact of ...a(n) inclusion program decisions is a mandatory subject of bargaining since these decisions impact the working conditions of members" (p. 47). This resolution speaks to the belief that inclusive practices are beyond what are considered standard working conditions by the state's teachers unions.

Lack of Vision? Lack of Respect?

While Illinois' history of inclusion is quite dismal, it was once a proud leader in the field of disability. The state was home to some of the most renowned scholars of the time, required compulsory education for all children, and designated funding for those children. In doing so, however, segregation was "institutionalized" across the state. The values and attitudes perpetuated by state funding encouraged and even required separation of children with cognitive disabilities. That legacy continues with separate buildings, separate curricula, and a relinquishing of responsibility of education to the state or to regional cooperatives. Furthermore, inclusive practices and inclusion are seen as constraints to good education.

Any school reform often gets stymied by the business as usual of education. Ending segregation in Illinois will mean systemic change at all levels: administrative, financial, and instruction. Judicial mandate has not been effective. Change requires a cultural shift in terms of beliefs and practices. Just as the segregation of African Americans continued long after such separation was deemed unlawful, changes in the beliefs and practices necessary for inclusion of students with disabilities, particularly severe disabilities, will likely take decades. This will not happen, however, unless there is both a vision of something more and a belief in the competence of those labeled with cognitive disabilities. That means respecting their rights to be active participants and members of the school community. The challenge to the educators as well as to all the people of Illinois is to have a vision for inclusive education.

References

AAIDD (2008). *The AAIDD definition.* Retrieved Oct. 29, 2008, from http://www. aamr.org/Policies/faq_intellectual_disability.shtml.

Baumgartner, B. (1955). *The Illinois plan for special education of exceptional children: A curriculum guide for teachers of the mentally retarded.* Springfield, IL: Superintendent of Public Instruction.

Beth B. v. Van Clay, 282 F.3d 493 (7th Cir. 2002).

Bogdan, R., & Kuglemass, J. (1984). Case studies of Main Street: A symbolic interactionist approach to special schooling. In L. Barton & S. Thomlinson (Eds.), *Special Education and Social Interests.* New York: Nichols.

Braddock, D., Hemp, R., & Rizzolo, M. K. (2008). *The State of the States in Developmental Disabilities.* Monograph of the American Association on Intellectual and Developmental Disabilities (2008 Edition).

Burton, T. (1976). *The trainable mentally retarded.* Columbus, OH: Merrill.

Center for Special Education Finance, Special Education Expenditure Project (2004). What Are We Spending on Special Education Services in the United States, 1999–2000? Retrieved Aug. 6, 2008, from http://csef.air.org/publications/ seep/national/AdvRpt1.PDF

Cohen, M. (1994) *Overcoming barriers to inclusion of children with disabilities in the local schools—A blueprint for change.* Springfield, IL: Illinois Council on Development Disabilities.

Constitution of Illinois (1970). Retrieved Sept. 30, 2008, from http://www.ilga.gov/ commission/lrb/con10.htm

Corey H. v. Board of Education, 995 F. Supp. 900 (N.D. Ill. 1998).

Danielson, L., & Bellamy, G. T. (1989). State variation in placement of children with handicaps in segregated environments. *Exceptional Children, 55,* 448–455.

Davis, S. (1992). *Report card to the nation on inclusion in education of students with mental retardation.* Arlington, TX: ARC.

Department of Public Welfare v. Haas, I5 Ill. 2d 204, 154 N.E.2d 265 (1958)

Designs for Change (1992). *Caught in the web II: The segregation of children with disabili-*

ties in Chicago and Illinois. Chicago: Designs for Change.

Eliot v. Board of Education, 63 Ill App 3d 299, 380 NE 2d 1137 (1st Dist. 1978).

Gold, M. (1980). "Did I say that?" Articles and commentary of the Try Another Way System. Champaign, IL: Research Press.

Hemp, R., Freagon, S., & Christensen-Leininger, R. (1991). Categorization and funding: Illinois disincentives to home school inclusion. Chicago: University of Illinois; DeKalb, IL: Northern Illinois University; Springfield, IL: Illinois Planning Council on Developmental Disabilities.

Illinois State Board of Education (2003). Illinois Professional Teaching Standards. Retrieved Oct. 25, 2009, from http://www.isbe.state.il.us/profprep/standards.htm

Illinois State Board of Education (2007). 2005–2006 Annual State Report on Special Education Performance. Retrieved Aug. 6, 2008, from http://www.isbe.state.il.us/spec-ed/pdfs/Annual_Report_2006.pdf

Illinois State Board of Education (2008). Illinois Public School Districts by County. Retrieved Aug. 8, 2008 from http://www.isbe/state.il.us/research/htmls/directories.htm

Illinois State Board of Education (2009). Directory of approved programs for the preparation of education personnel in Illinois institutions of higher education. Retrieved Apr. 29, 2009, from http://www.isbe.state.il.us/profprep/PDFs/ directory.pdf

Illinois Education Association (2008). Bylaws, Resolutions, and New Business. Retrieved Sept. 30, 2008, from http://www.ieanea.org/page32805632.aspx

Individuals with Disabilities Education Act, 20 U.S.C.A. §§ 1400–1487 (2006).

Kane, D., John, S., Bell, R., & Charlesworth, C. (1993). The identification of financial disincentives to educating children and youth with moderate to severe and multiple developmental disabilities in their home schools. Springfield, IL: Illinois Planning Council on Developmental Disabilities and the Illinois State Board of Education.

Kirk, S. (1953). What is special about special education: The child who is mentally handicapped. Exceptional Children, 19, 138–142.

Lieberman, G. (1993, Sept.). Inclusion in Illinois: Past, present and future. Springfield, IL: Illinois Council of Administrators of Special Education.

Mayorwitz, D., & Lapham, J. (2008). But we are a court of law. We're not in a legislature. Educational Policy, 22, 379-421.

National Council for Disabilities (1994). Inclusionary education for students with disabilities: Keeping the promise. Retrieved Sept. 24, 2008, from http://www.ncd.gov/newsroom/publications/1994/inclusion.htm

Oberti v. Board. of Education, 995 F.2d 1204 (3d Cir. 1993).

Pierce v. Board of Education of the City of Chicago, 69 Ill. 2d 89 (1977).

Project CHOICES (2007). FY 2007 Annual Report of Outcomes. Springfield, IL: Illinois State Board of Education.

Project CHOICES (2008). Evolution of Project CHOICES...Moving Forward. Retrieved Aug. 8, 2008 from http://www.projectchoices.org/aboutTimeline.aspx

Schalock, R. L., Luckasson, R., A., Shogren, K. A., Borthwick-Duffy, S., Bradley, V., Buntinx, W. H. E., Coulter, D. L., Craign, E. M, Gomez, S. C., Lachappelle, Y., Reeve, A., Snell, M. E., Spreat, S., Tasse, M. J., Thompson, J. R., Verdugo, M. A., Wehmeyer, M. L., Yeager, M. H. (2007). The renaming of mental retardation: Understanding the change to the term intellectual disability. Intellectual and Developmental Disabilities, 45(2), 116–124.

Scheerberger, R. (1983). *A History of Mental Retardation*. Baltimore: Brookes.

Shanker, A. (1994, 6 Jan.). Inclusion and ideology. *The New York Times*, p. E–7.

University of Illinois Opens Institute for Research on Exceptional Children. (1952, Oct.). *Exceptional Children*, Retrieved Aug. 8, 2008, from Education Research Complete database.

CHAPTER 5

The Inclusion of Students with Intellectual Disabilities in Michigan

BARBARA LEROY AND KRIM LACEY

Background

In Michigan, the public education of students with disabilities began with Public Act 198 of 1971, five years before U.S. Public Law 94-142 established a federal mandate. The Michigan law mandated that children with a wide range of disabilities from birth through age 25 be educated through the public school system. This mandate represented the most comprehensive program in the nation, and school districts proceeded to build state-of-the-art buildings and programs. Michigan was viewed as a leader in the field. It created intermediate school districts to develop education programs for students with more challenging disabilities and to support local school districts until they were prepared to educate their students in their home communities. This education mandate was coupled with the movement to deinstitutionalize children and adults with disabilities, and to bring those who lived at home into schools rather than be allowed to be part of the programs that were being run by local advocacy organizations. Strong administrative rules were promulgated addressing teacher and support staff competencies, eligibility requirements for students, caseload and class sizes, and procedural safeguards and timelines. To support these new programs, the State funded the training of special education teachers and ancillary support staff. Although considered best practice at the time, PA 198 led to the creation of a dual education system—one for special education and one for regular education.

In the 1980s, a national dialogue began to emerge that questioned the validity of educating students with disabilities in separate environments. The national Office of Special Education and Rehabilitation Services (OSERS) under Madeline Will called for a "regular education initiative" and shared general and special education responsibility for the education of students with disabilities (Will, 1986). In response to the OSERS' vision, the Michigan Department of Education and various Michigan advocacy organizations (e.g., the Michigan Developmental Disabilities Council, the Arc, and Michigan Protection and Advocacy) implemented several projects designed to identify "educational alternatives" for students with disabilities. However, the majority of all students with disabilities (66%) continued to be educated in separate classrooms and schools. Moreover, students with intellectual disabilities experienced a far higher degree of segregation, attending separate schools that were run through cross-district cooperative agreements administered by the intermediate school districts.

Data from the Michigan Department of Education (1986 Child Count) documented separate school segregation as follows: autism 62%; intellectual impairment 87%; multiple impairment 63%. These rates occurred at the time that the national rate for segregated school placement was reported to be 4.2% (Danielson & Bellamy, 1988). Michigan's rate of using segregated schools was 354% higher than the national average. If not being educated in separate schools, the vast majority of these students were in separate classrooms so that the combined percentages for segregation by disability were autism 94%, intellectual deficiency 92%, and multiple impairments 74%. Michigan was no longer a leader in best practice for students with disabilities.

The Inclusion Decade (1989–1999)

In 1989, Michigan applied for a systems change grant to facilitate inclusive education for students with intellectual disabilities, thus beginning an active decade in regular education placement for Michigan students (Peterson & LeRoy, 1994). Figure 1 illustrates the placement of students with intellectual disabilities from 1986 through 2001. As you can see from the figure, inclusive education placement for students with intellectual disabilities reached its peak in 1991, which was midway through the five-year systems change initiative. It maintained some momentum through the late 1990s but had in essence disappeared for students with intellectual disabilities by 1999. The facilitators of the inclusion decade are described below.

The systems change initiative was designed to provide intense statewide training and technical assistance to schools, policy analysis and development, leadership development, and related activities to facilitate the inclusion of students with intellectual disabilities into regular education classes in neighborhood schools. During the five-year initiative implementation, 3,722 students with disabilities, aged

3–26 years, were directly involved in the program (an additional 6,000 students moved into regular education as an indirect result of the training activities). These students represented all disability categories. They all had the unique distinction of having had no access to regular education classrooms or curricula prior to the initiative implementation. Eighty-two percent of Michigan's school districts participated in the Initiative. The goal and objectives of the Initiative included systemic change through the following areas of impact: (1) resource analysis and reallocation, (2) policy reform, (3) model implementation, (4) training and technical assistance to facilitate staff development and school reform, (5) family education and support, (6) materials development, and (7) university personnel preparation.

Figure 1: Placement of Students with Intellectual Disabilities

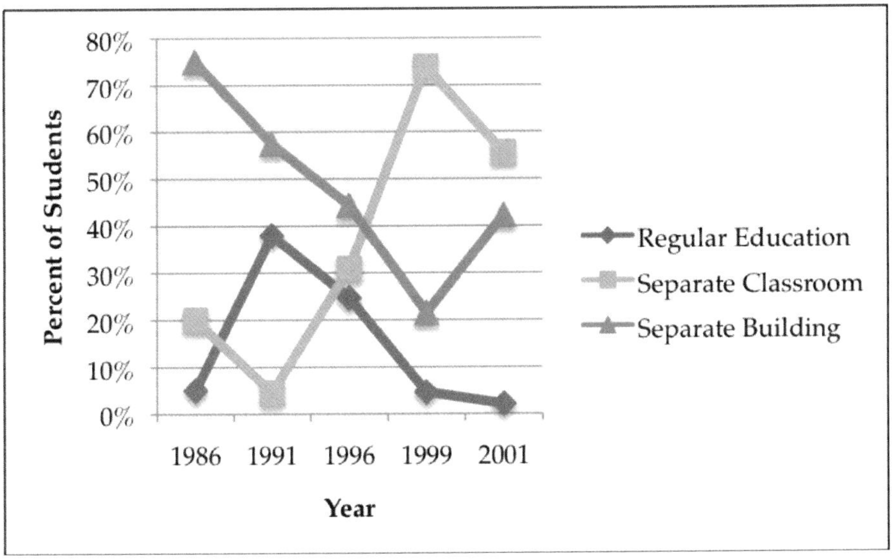

Why Was There Such Progress?

The short answer to this question is that there was tremendous synergy around the concept of inclusion—the timing was right. The reality is that many diverse stakeholders focused intense and sustained effort on the initiative. Each stakeholder group had a passionate interest and focus on one part of the system and the initiative pulled together the various parts into a collective whole. For some stakeholders, inclusion was a civil and legal rights issue, for some, it was administratively logical, for some, it was sound educational practice and a natural progression from deinstitutionalization, and for families, the inclusion of their children in their neighborhood schools felt just like coming home. Each of these perspectives is examined below in terms of its influence on the relative albeit short-term success of inclusive education for students with intellectual disabilities.

Civil and Legal Right

Following on the legal challenges to segregation from other states, the Michigan Protection and Advocacy Services, Inc. in conjunction with local attorneys, families, and advocates, mounted a sustained push for inclusive education. They made inclusive education one of their key priorities and supported individual cases in Michigan administrative hearings and in state and district courts. In addition, an analysis of the Administrative Hearing process from 1986 to 1993 was conducted. The study documented that school districts prevailed over 90% of the time with only a handful of hearing officers making all the decisions (Peterson & LeRoy, 1994). As a result of this study, relentless advocacy on the part of the MPAS, Inc. and intervention on the part of the federal department of education, the State was forced to expand its core of hearing officers, to provide a new training program for officers, and to create a viable mediation system. From the litigation side, disability attorneys identified and trained a core of potential expert witnesses and mentored them in the art of providing testimony. These actions coupled with the Inclusive Education Defense Fund (described below) pressured school districts to consider inclusive education placement versus legal action.

Administratively Logical

Four important administrative activities supported the inclusion movement: (1) the creation of a powerful and effective advisory council, (2) the alignment of IE systems change with general education school reform, (3) the establishment of State Board of Education policy, and (4) local administrator challenges to traditional methods of special education implementation and funding.

At the outset of the Inclusive Education Systems Change Initiative, the Michigan State Board of Education appointed a powerful advisory council to shape the vision, direction, implementation, and evaluation of the initiative. Membership on the council remained intact for five years with a 75% attendance rate at all meetings. Council members included representatives from the Parent Teacher Association, the Association of Secondary School Principals, the Local Education Agency Principals, the Association of Administrators of Special Education, the Association of Intermediate School Administrators, the Association of School Superintendents, the Middle Cities Schools Association, the State School Improvement Program, the two teacher unions, higher education, advocacy organizations, special and regular education parents and teachers, the Michigan Developmental Disabilities Council, and state early childhood and deaf/blind programs. The Council was chaired by the Michigan Department of Education associate superintendent who was also responsible for Michigan School Reform. The council addressed unique and far-reaching issues including:

- Department policies and position statements on inclusive education
- School improvement legislation
- Site-based training and technical assistance models
- Research and evaluation needs and designs
- Minority involvement
- Initiative marketing and publications
- Teacher unions
- The interface of inclusive education with early childhood programs
- Postsecondary/transition mandates and inclusive education
- Initiative sustainability and strategic planning
- Special education rule changes
- Administrator support for inclusive education implementation
- Proposed changes to teacher certification.

From the very beginning, the State emphasized that the inclusion of students with intellectual disabilities in regular education classrooms had to be conceptualized as a school reform activity, tightly aligned with the Michigan school improvement legislation (Public Act 25). The State was interested in making inclusion part of a larger initiative to improve instruction and social cohesion for all children. Therefore, all policy, training and technical assistance, and evaluation activities approached inclusion as a vehicle by which regular education classrooms could improve and extend their academic and social instructional methodologies and outcomes.

A systematic series of actions were implemented at the state level to address policies, barriers, and interagency collaboration. These actions included a State Department–led Committee on inclusive education, a series of administrative dialogues on inclusive education, a State Board of Education–directed Inclusive Education Recommendations Committee, and a Special Education Delivery System task force. The Committee on Inclusive Education developed a position statement on inclusive education that expanded its prior policy on least restrictive environment. Furthermore, the statement affirmed the State's commitment to increasing opportunities for inclusion in general education classrooms and to the integral involvement of parents in all processes. The position statement defined inclusive education as follows:

> The provision of educational services for students with disabilities, in schools where non-handicapped peers attend, in age-appropriate general education classes under the direct supervision of general education teachers, with special education support and assistance as determined appropriate through the individualized educational planning committee (IEPC). (Michigan State Board of Education, 1992)

The Administrative Dialogues provided a forum in which school administrators developed a linkage between school improvement and inclusive education; created a leadership vision among building principals; and shared their views on needed policy, rules, and staffing changes to support inclusion. Ad hoc task forces followed the forums to address specific issues to be forwarded to the Advisory Council and State Department of Education for action.

The State Board of Education Inclusive Education Recommendations Committee was charged with the development of specific recommendations for needed changes in policy, funding, and legislation to ensure the availability of an inclusive education option for students with disabilities in Michigan. Specifically, the committee addressed research and model programs, rules, collective bargaining, policy, finance, teacher preparation and staff development, and school improvement.

Following on the Recommendation Committee actions, a revision of the Administrative Rules for Special Education was implemented. This process included a field survey to 234 education-related organizations and 350 individuals, a task force to address the survey findings, and ultimately formal rule revision. The task force developed hundreds of recommendations for rule change comprised in a 150-page document.

Finally, as activities were proceeding at the state level, innovative local districts were testing new models and demonstrating how the proposed policies and rules could be implemented. Some districts recognized that there was an imbalance in how funding was allocated, suggesting that it favored segregation. In essence, this imbalance meant that intermediate school districts (which serve a county-wide area and historically were responsible for the education of students with more challenging disabilities) would fully fund their segregated programs and would not charge local districts for the placement of their children in these cross-district programs. Therefore, local districts had no financial incentive to keep the children in their home schools. Key districts moved to eliminate this barrier by having money follow the children to their local schools. Other districts conducted comprehensive studies of the cost issue, resulting in frequent discussions of inclusive education at local school boards.

Furthermore, many districts sought to establish a community vision for inclusion, by conducting forums for all stakeholders. One district put all community stakeholders, including the local media, on two school buses and took them all on a three-day trip to visit model inclusion programs in other states and Canadian provinces. They returned with a documentary that was shown on the local television station and was followed by community discussion groups. Innovative local administrators formed a support and training group and were instrumental in educating their peers on the vision, mechanisms, and outcomes of inclusion.

Sound Educational Practice

The deinstitutionalization movement ushered in new academic fields of study addressing community living and skill development for people with intellectual disabilities. Segregated school programs contributed knowledge on specific learning styles and methods for students with an array of disabilities and yet the skills learned in these separate environments did seem to generalize to community settings. Parents were observing that their children were clearly capable of learning and that they had many skills, and yet discrete skill mastery was not translating into desired post-school outcomes. People with disabilities were not true members of their communities, they did not have friends and natural supports outside of their immediate families, and they did not live on their own or have meaningful employment. They lived in a parallel universe to their typical peers.

Researchers, advocates, and families believed that in order for students with disabilities to be true community members they needed to be connected with their peers in natural age-appropriate settings— regular education classrooms and buildings. They also believed that the instructional methodology of segregated special education could be transported to a regular education classroom, to the benefit of both typical students and those with disabilities. Paralleling this desegregation movement for students with disabilities was the school reform movement in regular education, which was addressing, among other factors, the poor performance of a large number of students in typical classrooms. In aligning inclusive education with school reform, a bridge was built between the two silos of regular and special education.

The Michigan systems change initiative, from the outset, required that its model implementation sites create classrooms that employed promising and effective educational practices for all students. The initiative trained 15,000 teachers and support personnel in those practices and provided technical assistance to districts and classrooms to assure that the teachers were able to implement the practices with a degree of fidelity. Over the course of the five-year initiative project, staff logged more than one-half million miles on their cars assuring that classrooms continued to include students and to practice effective instruction. In addition, many universities took up the training mandate by offering summer training institutes for teachers. These institutes provided intense training in effective inclusion education practices.

Family Focus

The Inclusive Education systems change movement came a full generation after PA 198, which provided access to public school for children with disabilities. Twenty years later, this new generation of families was well educated as well as affluent and was not going to settle for segregation. There was intense interest on the part of the national and local media that reinforced families' beliefs and desires. Specifically in Michigan, local newspapers ran multiple series of articles on inclusive education models and success stories, local television stations filmed inclusion stories and covered school board meetings and testimonials.

As the systems change initiative began to create demonstration sites in the local school districts, families who pioneered inclusion for their children became active members of the initiative's training teams and keen supporters of each other. At the training events, they modeled collaborative planning and presented the process, activities, and outcomes of their children's inclusion in neighborhood schools. They also developed a book of stories that was distributed throughout the state.

Perhaps one of the most innovative and successful activities of families and advocates was the development of the Inclusive Education Network. This network was co-led by the Arc and the Michigan systems change initiative to provide a forum for monthly meetings between parents, advocates, and interested practitioners. The network developed a position statement calling for inclusive education as an integral part of school improvement for all students. Forty organizations signed in support of the position statement.

The network continued to meet for more than five years, monitoring the spread of inclusion, organizing and holding training programs, developing advocacy strategies for addressing emerging barriers, and funding an inclusive education defense fund. The defense fund provided families with money to cover attorney fees and expert witness expenses in situations in which they had to sue school districts for inclusive placements. The idea was that the families would reimburse the fund as they prevailed in hearing decisions and thus be able to obtain attorney fees from the districts. Eventually, the Children's Disability Law Collaborative was created to support ongoing advocacy, legal literacy, and policy reform, particularly for low-income families who could not afford private attorneys.

Why Did the Inclusive Education Progress for Students with Intellectual Disabilities Stop Short of Systemic Reform?

From the previous discussion of all the various elements that went into the inclusive education initiative it is hard to imagine why it unraveled and why the inclusion rate for students with intellectual disabilities fell from its peak of 24.7% to less than 10%. On the surface it appeared that the initiative was structurally, philosophically, and practically embedded in Michigan's education system to the extent that it should have had a full and vital life on its own. However, the movement could not sustain itself against the storms of change that were approaching across the field of education. The forces that reversed the tide of inclusion of students with intellectual disabilities are described below.

Federal Legislation

No Child Left Behind (U.S. Department of Education, 2001) unintentionally created a significant barrier to inclusion. The legislation created an environment in which schools and school personnel are fi-
nancially penalized if their students do not achieve annual yearly
progress (AYP) on standardized tests. In an attempt to maximize their
potential to reach AYP, principals and teachers have attempted to
eliminate any students who may not be achieving at the required levels. Although they used a variety of strategies, one obvious and easy
strategy was to discourage the inclusion of students with intellectual
disabilities. Teachers felt that having those students in their classes
was a luxury that they could no longer afford, given the pressure to
teach to the test standards and drill their students for test performance. The types of instruction and activities that constitute promising
practices and are most beneficial to the inclusion of students with intellectual disabilities (e.g., differentiated instruction, cooperative
learning groups, authentic and applied learning experiences) were no
longer encouraged. Although the NCLB did increase the overall
number of students with disabilities who participated in standardized
tests, the impact was not universal across all types of disabilities. Students with intellectual disabilities were less included after NCLB than
before.

State Leadership and Reporting Changes

The Michigan Department of Education and the Michigan Governor's
Council on Developmental Disabilities continued to fund technical
assistance to schools to support the inclusion of students with intellectual disabilities for a few years after the systems change initiative.
However, leadership change at the department and within the various education associations brought in new priorities, and the direct
funding of technical assistance to schools as well as the focus on policy and practice supports disappeared.

  Three key pieces of the inclusion equation that were moving forward under the systems change initiative were not seen through to
true reform. One, the State Department of Education failed to create
and mandate a neutral funding model for placement. Although some
districts did create and implement such a model in their local programs, the majority of intermediate school districts did not. The intermediate districts continued to pay for segregated placements first
and only then provided any remaining funds to local districts to sup-

port students with disabilities. If local districts wanted to place students with intellectual disabilities in regular education classrooms, they had to pay for that placement from their local special education and/or regular education funds.

Second, the Michigan State Board of Education failed to pass new standards for teacher certification or personnel preparation. The university teacher-training programs were able to block the unification of regular and special education teacher training. They continued to support special education certification based on disability categories and student teaching in segregated environments that were defined by those categories. Michigan teachers continued to be trained to educate students in segregated models of service delivery. General education teachers were required to take only one survey course in disabilities, with no curriculum emphasis on the concept of inclusiveness or on the methodology to implement inclusive education models.

Third, the federal and state agencies changed the data collection and reporting system so that students with intellectual disabilities were no longer separated into distinct groups by level of impairment (i.e., educable, trainable, or severe intellectual impairment). While the categorical distinctions were lost in this process, so too was the ability to truly track the placement of students with more challenging needs. This new categorization allowed schools to hide behind their aggregated data to imply that they were actually serving more students with intellectual disabilities in regular classrooms than was true. In addition, the state monitoring system now requires tallies and reports intermediate school district and local educational agency performance with regard to an inclusion target of 55%. Again, this type of aggregated percentage belies the true placement rates for specific groups of students.

Loss of Legal and Advocacy Support

By the end of the 1990s, the Inclusive Education Network and the Disability Law Collaborative had disbanded, leaving families with few advocacy options. In addition, the Michigan Protection and Advocacy Services changed their priorities, reducing their focus on inclusive education. They also decided that they could no longer support individual requests for assistance and stopped attending individual planning meetings and hearings. Finally, the number of private attorneys who were willing to represent individual families dwindled as they found it difficult to prevail.

Ironically, there are those who insist that IDEA itself is a major barrier to systems reform. The focus on an individualized education has hindered multiple attempts to file class action lawsuits on behalf of students who are educated in segregated environments. The hearing process and the courts have supported the notion that each child is unique and is not a member of a distinct class, although school systems have been able to create segregated classes by disability categories.

Finally, the recent Supreme Court decision with regard to *Arlington v. Murphy* (June 2006) also serves as a disincentive to parents who may have contemplated using litigation as a means of obtaining inclusive education for their children. In this case, the court decided that prevailing parents cannot recover expert witness fees. If parents have any hope of prevailing in a legal decision, they must have expert witnesses who can testify as to the appropriateness of the regular education classroom for their child. By not being able to recover the costs of such witnesses, they may be hesitant to proceed with such actions. This court decision will inadvertently reduce the number of children with intellectual disabilities in inclusive classrooms.

Loss of Direct Technical Assistance to Schools

Perhaps the most significant reason why true and lasting inclusive education did not occur is the loss of direct technical assistance to schools. Research that was conducted during the five years of federal support to inclusive education reform and the subsequent three years of state and DD Council support clearly demonstrated the importance of sustained support for change. During that period, approximately 20–30% of staff time was spent on personnel development (training) to create inclusive classrooms, while the remainder was spent on direct technical assistance in the classrooms (Peterson & LeRoy, 1994). The reduction in technical assistance exactly paralleled the reduction in the rate of inclusion, so that over time the school systems tended to revert to the mean rate that existed prior to the push for inclusion.

Interviews with building principals and teachers revealed that they believed in inclusion and had experienced the benefits for both typical students and those with intellectual disabilities. However, without the knowledge that "someone was watching" and the physical and emotional support for restructuring their classrooms, teachers just stop trying to make it work.

Further Storm Clouds on the Horizon

The most recent monitoring data from the Michigan Department of Education indicates that just 50.3% of students with disabilities are in regular education more than 80% of the school day, which is below the target of 55%. In terms of intermediate school districts, only 28% of Michigan school districts met the 55% target (Michigan Department of Education, 2007). Two disturbing facts belie these rates. One, this rate is higher than it was five years ago (44% in 2000), and it is lower than it was a decade ago (53% in 1995). In terms of a national ranking, Michigan continues to hover in the bottom one-third of states for inclusive placements. Two, this aggregated percentage disguises the situation for students with intellectual disabilities. As shown in Figure 1, the increase in overall inclusion has come at the cost of students with more challenging needs. As students with disabilities other than intellectual (e.g., speech and language impairments, health impairments, and visual impairments) have increased their rate of inclusion above the mean, students with intellectual disabilities have decreased their rate of inclusion to less than 10%. The current monitoring system (which reports only district- and ISD-aggregated rates) allows states and local school districts to falsely believe that they are making progress in inclusion for all students.

A second storm cloud is the data related to inclusive placement by age. As students age, their opportunity to be educated in regular education settings dramatically decreases, even if they started their educational experience in the regular classroom. According to the most recent Michigan special education data, 67.3% of elementary students with disabilities are educated in regular education settings, while the corresponding figures for secondary students and students over the age of 22 years are only 39.9% and 3.5% respectively (LeRoy & Lacey, 2007). As the curriculum becomes more demanding and peer relationships become more complex, it appears that inclusive education becomes less prominent.

Even more disconcerting than the findings on the overall rates of inclusion and age discrepancies is the disproportionate impact on students with disabilities from minority sectors, particularly those related to income and race. In a series of studies on the demography of inclusive education, we consistently found differential opportunities for inclusive education by district and student characteristics (LeRoy, 2005; Smith & Kozleski, 2005). At the district level, we examined what structural factors would predict inclusive education among

Michigan school districts. A model that included seven factors was able to explain 77% of the variance in placement rates. Factors included per capita income, racial composition, school size, population density, teacher salary, special education costs, and special education population. Among those factors, three in particular made a significant contribution to the placement rate. They were per capita income (27.2%), racial composition (17.2%), and special education costs (5.2%). Specifically, districts with high per capita income, homogeneous and predominantly white populations, and low individual special education student costs had higher inclusive education placement rates. Corroborating that study was a second analysis of Michigan districts, which found that wealthy districts were 2.7 times more likely to place students in inclusive education than poor districts. Similarly, white students were 1.52 times more likely to be placed in inclusive education than minority students.

Although wealthy districts are more likely to implement inclusive education, disparities still exist for students of color within these districts. In wealthy districts, Hispanic students were 3.5 times and black students were 2.1 times more likely to be educated in segregated settings than their white peers. Even in poor districts where few students have access to inclusive education, Hispanic students continued to be placed at significantly lower rates than the other students. They were twice as likely to be in segregated settings as other special education students, the majority of whom were black.

Recognizing that schools are middle-class communities in which the values of white, middle-class, college-educated citizens prevail, we examined the impact of multiple demographic characteristics on placement. We hypothesized that the more students appeared to differ from the dominant culture of the school, the more likely they were *not* to be in inclusive education settings. We found that student placement followed the predicted cultural pattern. We found that the additive effects of race, income, and disability drove inclusive education placement decisions in a way that minority/low-income students across all disability categories were significantly less likely to be included in regular education than white/middle-income students. Qualitative remarks from minority families confirmed our statistical findings. These families reported that they feel like outsiders in the school process. Minority families believed that their students' participation in inclusive education or other educational opportunities, such as vocational training, was a function of their income. They believed that because they were poor that teachers deemed them less worthy than other parents of these school offerings. Our studies at the Michigan district and student levels confirm what many minority families have always believed, which is that inclusive education is a middle-class option available primarily to white families. Families who fall outside of the normative culture and demography of the school environment have less status and, therefore, less opportunity to participate in the valued activities and options that the environment offers. Inclusive education becomes a reward associated with cultural status as opposed to an educational practice that every special education student receives.

Conclusion

Inclusive education for students with intellectual disabilities in Michigan made significant progress through a federally funded systems change initiative in the early 1990s. However, by the end of the decade, the gains had all but been reversed. While the overall rate of inclusion continued to increase for students with disabilities in general, regular education placement for students with intellectual disabilities was rapidly decreasing. When we further disaggregate the placement data, a picture of exclusion by district and student demographic characteristics emerges. Schools are complicated social institutions that are not immune to the worst of societal prejudices and behaviors. They use data to create their own realities and they employ effective educational practices as rewards rather than mandates.

References

Danielson, L., & Bellamy, T. (1988). *State variation in placement of children with handicaps in segregated environments.* Washington, DC: Special Education Programs, U.S. Office of Education.

LeRoy, B. (January/February 2005). School culture and inclusive education placement. *TASH Connections,* 24–26.

LeRoy, B., & Lacey, K. (2007). *Who's There II?* Detroit, MI: Developmental Disabilities Institute, Wayne State University.

Michigan Department of Education (1986). *Child Count.* Lansing: Author.

Michigan Department of Education (2007). *Child Count.* Lansing: Author.

Michigan State Board of Education (1992). *Inclusive Education Position Statement.* Lansing: Michigan Department of Education.

Peterson, J. M., & LeRoy, B. (1994). *Systems Change for Inclusive Education in Michigan Final Report.* Detroit, MI: Wayne State University.

Smith, A., & Kozleski, E. B. (2005). Witnessing Brown: Pursuit of an equity agenda in American education. *Remedial and Special Education, 26*(5), 270–280.

U.S. Department of Education. (2001). *No Child Left Behind (Elementary and Secondary Education Act)*. Washington, DC: Author.

Will, M. (1986). *Educating students with learning problems: A shared responsibility*. Washington, DC: U.S. Department of Education, Office of Special Education and Rehabilitative Services.

CHAPTER 6

Fighting Professional Opinions

Stories of Segregation by Three California Families

EMILY A. NUSBAUM

Introduction

The Individuals with Disabilities Education Act (IDEA), originally passed as the Education for all Handicapped Children Act of 1975 and reauthorized as recently as 2004, was written in order to give students with disabilities access to a free and appropriate public education in the least restrictive environment (LRE). Although the act uses ambiguous language (e.g., phrases such as "to the maximum extent appropriate"), few would argue against the idea that the intent of the law was to place responsibility for gaining access to inclusive educational settings on students and families, which for many has turned out to be the case. As early as 1988, the concept of LRE was critiqued for being flawed in its conception (Taylor, 1988). Others (Mlawer, 1998) have critiqued the lack of federal oversight of the responsibility of individual states to monitor and enforce LRE in the educational placement decisions for students with disabilities at the local level. This chapter will briefly examine both of these critiques and then use the stories of three families from the state of California to demonstrate the systematic denial of LRE, specifically for students with intellectual disabilities, and to highlight common themes that exist throughout all three of the stories.

There are almost 6.5 million students in the California public schools, approximately 635,000 of whom have identified disabilities (California Department of Education, 2004/05 data). Of these, approximately 39,000 receive services under the eligibility category "mental retardation" (from here on, referred to in this chapter as students with intellectual disabilities) (Office of Special Education and

Rehabilitation Services, 2005). Federal data also indicates that across 989 school districts in the state, 49% of students with identified disabilities spend at least 80% of their school day in general education settings. However, once this is disaggregated by eligibility category, time spent in general education settings decreases dramatically for students with certain disability labels. As Table 1 indicates, over 26,000 students with the label of intellectual disability are educated outside of general education settings for greater than 60% of the school day. The number of students with intellectual impairment who have access to general education environments for at least 80% of their school day is approximately equal to those educated in separate education facilities.

Table 1 Time spent outside of general education settings for students with intellectual disabilities

<21% of the school day	22–59% of the school day	>60% of the school day	Educated in separate facilities/ structures
3,055 students	4,754 students	26,198 students	3,404 students

As Table 1 clearly highlights, students with intellectual disabilities spend their educational time largely outside of general education settings (either in segregated classrooms with little opportunity for mainstreaming, or in separate facilities altogether). In addition to the fact that large numbers of students with intellectual disabilities in California are educated outside of general education, there is also tremendous variation from district to district (where you live *does* matter).

Critiquing the Least Restrictive Environment

In his 1988 seminal article, Steve Taylor identifies what he calls "pitfalls" in the conception of the LRE principle. First, Taylor identifies the inherent difficulty of arriving at a precise definition of LRE, since the phrase "least restrictive environment" is used in a range of ways, and to mean very different things, by school professionals and families. He concludes that the range of definitions ascribed to the term LRE is broad enough to encompass positions that reject separate school facilities and segregated classroom, as well as those who view a range of separate and segregated educational settings for students with identified disabilities as good and necessary. Further, Taylor identifies some major critiques of the conception of LRE, including the following: (a) the LRE principle legitimates (and codifies into law) restrictive educational settings; (b) LRE confuses segregation and inclusion with intensity of supports and services a student with a disability needs; (c) the LRE principle focuses attention on physical setting rather than services and supports; (d) the LRE principle supports the primacy placed on professional decision making, in terms of who gets to judge what is "appropriate" for a student with identified disabilities; and, finally, (e) the LRE is based in a "readiness model," which requires that students earn the right to move to less restrictive educational environments (1988). Evidence of Taylor's critiques of the LRE principle run throughout the stories of the three families told in this chapter.

Mlawer (1998) has argued that the LRE requirements stipulated by the IDEA are often ignored by school professionals and IEP teams, and that there is little federal oversight of the state-based responsibility to enforce and monitor LRE issues at the local, district level. Mlawer stated that one result of the abdication of oversight responsibility at federal and state levels is that responsibility for achieving LRE for students with identified disabilities is then placed on parents—who are often required to use, in one extreme, legal processes such as mediation and due process or, in the other, cajole and "make deals" with school professionals in the attempt to garner inclusive placements for their children in local or neighborhood schools. Finally, Mlawer argues that school teams and IEP professionals base placement decision largely on a range of factors other than the LRE principle and the decision-making process as outlined by IDEA. As early as 1989, the Department of Education articulated this same conclusion in their annual Report to Congress:

> It is reasonable to assume that the needs of students are broadly similar across States, and that random variation would be rather small in the summary data on the large numbers of students served by a State. Thus, the extent of variability suggests that factors in addition to the characteristics of students determine educational placements, and that the decision-making power vested in the IEP process has not been sufficient to overcome these factors. (p. 29)

The stories of the families in this chapter support Mlawer's argument, which can be summarized as follows:

IEPs should be written based on the unique education needs of a child.

Placement decisions are then based on an individual child's IEP.

Therefore, one would not expect much variation in placement rates in a state the size of California because the needs of a group of students as large as those who receive special education services in California could not vary that much.

There are, however, large variations across the state. Therefore, there must be factors other than the needs of individual children that are impacting placement decisions.

Stories from Three Families in California

The stories in this chapter are from three California families whose life histories vary along many lines. They are from different ethnic groups, socioeconomic classes, and educational levels. Their children range in age from five to thirty-two years and have attended schools in the largest urban districts in the state as well as in small suburban districts situated outside major urban centers. The children with disabilities in these three families have been educated primarily in segregated settings, and their families have fought for their right to be educated in less restrictive settings throughout the entirety of their children's school careers.

Although each family's story is obviously unique, they share many common experiences. All demonstrate the subtle and obvious efforts at coercion and intimidation on the part of school professionals to place students in increasingly restrictive educational settings, and that school professionals will go to great lengths and great costs in their attempts to do so. All of the stories contain continued references to the deficit-based frameworks on which school professionals base their argument that segregated educational settings are the best option for students with intellectual disabilities; in addition, the stories describe school teams that believe this disability label is a primary reason that these students *should* be educated in segregated and subpar classrooms and school settings. Further, school professionals seem to require that each of these students "prove" themselves and their readiness to be given access to inclusive school settings.

Conversely, the parents who shared their stories for this chapter had a vision for their children with disabilities. These visions were based on capacity-building, on believing in their children's strengths and abilities, and on the high expectations they had for their children's futures. And it was the vision that these parents had for their children's lives and the advocacy they pursued that makes the stories that are told here unique. Although many families have visions for their children that are situated in contrast to the dismal outcomes projected by school professionals for children with significant support needs, often including those with labels of intellectual disabilities, many families don't possess the knowledge that their children are entitled to an education outside segregated settings. Further, as these stories indicate, school professionals often couch their decisions about students and where they should be educated in specialized knowledge and vocabulary, and in "expert" decision making (Smith, 1999; Ware, 2002; Young & Mintz, 2008). Additionally, these stories show that often when given limited access to general education classrooms, students were "set up to fail" by not being provided sufficient, individualized, and age-appropriate supports; the eventual failure was then used as "evidence" by IEP teams to show that the students were not "ready" for full-time inclusive placements.

Joshua's Story

Joshua is five years old and currently attends a private preschool in which his younger sister is also enrolled. He and his family live in a major urban center in California. They are a white, middle-class family; Joshua's father is an attorney and his mother does not work outside the home. For two years Joshua attended a segregated preschool program in the public school district where he lives. Joshua's parents recall that when they were enrolling him in the school district at age three, there were just two spaces "available" at the only inclusive preschool program in the district, and that from very early on the school district seemed to indicate that there was no intention to educate Joshua in this, or any other, inclusive setting.

His parents, Rebecca and Michael, describe Joshua as an "inquisitive and interested child who is truly adept at interacting and engaging with the world around him." Joshua also does not communicate verbally and was identified soon after birth as having a rare genetic difference. Rebecca and Michael both recall that the initial information given to them by physicians about their son was that he would "never speak or communicate, would suffer from severe cognitive impairment and seizures, would have balance problems his whole life, and of course would never go to college, get married, or raise a family." Like many families of children with disabilities, Rebecca and Michael talked about the long process they went through to build a new vision and hope for Joshua's future.

Joshua's segregated preschool program did not offer him meaningful opportunities to interact with students without disabilities, nor any structured opportunities to interact with the other students with disabilities in his classroom. Many of the students in his segregated classroom did not communicate verbally, and few of them were supported in developing alternative methods of communicating beyond asking for various snack items. Joshua, Rebecca and Michael reported, simply gravitated to the many adults coming in and out of the classroom, who were the only individuals offering Joshua interaction and social opportunities.

Ironically, when Rebecca and Michael asked the IEP team for more opportunities for meaningful interaction with peers without disabilities, they were told by the school professionals that since Joshua wasn't "sufficiently" interacting with those peers in his classroom, there was "no need" to expand beyond those with whom he had the opportunity to communicate. This idea, that children and students with disabilities need to "prove themselves" in order to gain access to less-restrictive environments and peers without disabilities, is not uncommon and clearly goes against the intent (if not the letter) of federal legislation.

It was during Joshua's second year of preschool that Rebecca and Michael began the necessary lottery process to apply for a kindergarten space in an inclusive elementary school in the district—a process that parents of all prospective kindergarteners hoping to attend this particular school must follow. They said that the district immediately met them with hostility, and over the course of that academic year the family went through five IEP meetings and eventually filed an administrative complaint in order to begin a mediation and potential hearing process.

Rebecca and Michael remember that in the beginning of the school year they were contacted by a private law firm representing the school district in what they felt was an effort to intimidate them so they would not move toward mediation and the potential hearing. This law firm then filed a motion to dismiss Rebecca and Michael's complaint on technical grounds, forcing them to retain a special education attorney and begin the financial, personal, and emotional commitment required to enter legal action with a child's school district. Throughout all of the IEP meetings and two mediations, Joshua's parents recall the school district's attorney making repeated references to their son being "severely cognitively disabled." The attorney indicated that he would, therefore, require specific kinds of supports that would not allow him to benefit from general education settings and peers.

When asked how Joshua was doing in the private preschool that his sister attends, Rebecca and Michael described an open school community in which he is surrounded by 18 typically developing peers and is assisted by complete aide support. Joshua is invited to birthday parties, is sought out by his friends, and is beginning to develop relationships with other children for the first time in his life. Contrary to the school district's belief, they say, Joshua did not need a year-long transition to "get ready" to be in an inclusive classroom or to demonstrate that he could succeed in one. He simply needed school professionals who were committed to education and to the philosophy that every student deserves the opportunity to be a part of the school community and to learn with peers, no matter who they are. Joshua's family is currently preparing to move from the community where they live in order to find an elementary school that will educate their son in inclusive, general education settings.

Luis's Story

Luis is 14 years old and lives in the suburb of a medium-sized, northern California city. Luis is the younger of two sons, born to Mexican immigrants. His father provides janitorial services to the church that his family attends and his mother works as a parent-advocate for a local nonprofit organization. Luis was also born with Down syndrome. His mother, Maria, has spent 11 years advocating for his right to be given the opportunity to be included in a general education classroom. Despite her efforts, Luis was kept in a segregated class each school year between the ages of three and eleven. When Luis was in middle school, Maria fought to keep her son from being moved from a segregated classroom in the school district to a placement in a county-operated classroom for students with "severe disabilities."

Maria is also a parent-advocate at a regional parent-training and information center. For her, it is ironic that she works side by side with families every day to help them understand the school system so that their children can have access to mainstream settings, yet she has not been able to secure this for her own child.

Maria describes the school professionals' response to her request every year for Luis to have access to integrated, educational settings:

> As the years progressed it became more and more hard to advocate to keep him integrated. The professionals, teachers, and service providers always told me that because of his deficits and his abilities being so wide and far from his non-

disabled classmates it would be impossible for him to succeed in that environment (general education), with those expectations and his inability to keep up with the regular curriculum. He would not be successful in the regular classroom no matter. If I really insisted on having him there, he would not benefit from being there.

Maria goes on to describe the phrase repeated over and over again in IEP meetings each year, as she asked for opportunities for Luis to have access to general education settings. She says the phrase *"in my professional opinion he should be"* was used repeatedly by IEP team members to indicate that they, with their expertise, knew what was best for her son, without regard for her opinion or wishes.

When Luis reached middle school, Maria reported, he was allowed to participate only in art and physical education classes with peers without disabilities, and that the school district had "done a good job wearing me down from trying to convince them that my son deserved the opportunity and had the right to be in those places." She says that whenever she challenged their position about where Luis should be educated and the opportunities to which he should have access, school professionals would ask her, *"Does he have mental retardation? Yes? Then he is placed correctly."*

Maria was told time and time again that unless Luis was able to perform to the standards in his grade he could not have access to general education settings. Even further, when she asked why Luis was not mainstreamed into a photography class (as indicated by his IEP), the special day class teacher told her that she did not want to "risk" the good relationship she had with the photography teacher, and that if she were to have a bad experience with Luis because of his low abilities, then the door might be closed in the future for a "more able student who can benefit more."

As she prepared for his transition to high school, never having been successful at securing an inclusive placement or even well-supported mainstreaming opportunities for Luis throughout elementary or middle school, Maria was informed that at the high school level things were "done differently" and that based on their processes and policies they would place Luis according to his disability label. Again, the school professionals were prepared to make a judgment about Luis, Maria said, based on her son's label of intellectual disability. According to their standards, then, it means that Luis "can't learn" from a regular curriculum in regular classrooms and needs the life-skills program that is offered in the segregated, out-of-district classroom run by the County Office of Education (COE).

Two years ago, Maria received a letter from the director of special education in her local district, in response to her request that Luis not be moved out of the district into a segregated classroom operated by the COE (in many school districts in California, counties operate special education classrooms and centers to serve only students with identified disabilities). The letter begins,

> As a retarded adult Luis will face significant daily-living challenges... functional skills instruction will provide a safety net that prepares Luis for any eventuality and allows him to live a full adult life in the least restrictive environment. Additionally, the District sees this as its obligation to Luis, regardless of the work his family does in this area.

Maria described the subsequent transition into a segregated classroom within the school district as one full of misinformation, intimidation, and tactics designed to wear her down. She was first told Luis would attend a special day class in his home school, but when she went to register him there, the school told her that Luis had been un-enrolled since he would be moving to the county-operated classroom. Maria was then told that Luis would be assigned to a different high school and that she would receive information about it in the mail before the school year started. Just before the start of the school year, Maria was informed that Luis was assigned to a school that would require a two-hour bus ride each way; that she had no choice in the matter, as administrative decisions had been made; and that this was the "appropriate" placement for students like Luis, who had a label of intellectual disabilities.

At this point, Maria contacted numerous school board members about how the school district handled her son's high school placement, and within two weeks a "severely handicapped" classroom was opened at Luis's home school—a classroom that is currently staffed by an un-credentialed teacher, placed in the position at the last minute, without any opportunity for preparation.

When asked how she would summarize her long history advocating for Luis in the school system, Maria stated,

> My son is made to prove himself over and over again. To the school staff, teachers and "professionals," as they call themselves, my son is a second class citizen who could only visit the regular class if he can maintain behavior, if he can perform to the standards, if he can keep up to the same expectations that they have for non-disabled students. I have very painfully seen the lack of expectations that they have for him and other students with disabilities ... my son and other kids with disabilities are seen as a burden to teachers and to the system.

Julie's Story

Julie is a 32-year-old woman who currently lives with support in a rented apartment in an affluent California suburb. Julie runs her own puppet-show business, has a boyfriend, and serves on the board of a statewide disability rights organization. Julie is the only child of well-educated parents and has Down syndrome, diabetes, and is legally blind. Throughout her years in three different public school systems, Julie's educational placements included a segregated classroom with over 50% mainstreaming 50% of the time in a segregated classroom for core academic classes and 50% time in general education and in general education with resource specialist support.

Julie's parents, Joanne and John, believe ardently that if not for their strong advocacy role, one that they maintained through the entirety of her school career, Julie would not have had access to the amount of time in general education settings that she did. Julie's parents noted that the amount of time that Julie would have access to inclusive settings each year depended on the members of her IEP team and their own ideas and beliefs, as well as on Joanne and John's ability to convince a variety of people (e.g., special education teachers, general education teachers, and principals) each year that the best placement option for Julie must include as much access to general education settings as possible.

At three years of age, Julie was among the first group of students brought back into her small, affluent school district in southern California from segregated county programs. This school district had been chosen as one of several pilot districts assigned by the state to become early adopters of the principles that had become the provisions of P.L. 94-142 (predecessor to the IDEA) and, as such, was serving students with "severe handicaps" for the first time. Previously, such students had no access to academic curriculum content and were taught in highly segregated settings under the assumption that they could not learn basic academic skills such as reading.

Initially, at age three, Julie was assigned to an in-district segregated classroom for students with labels of severe disability. Joanne and John wanted Julie to be educated alongside peers without disabilities but felt that no one in the school district would respond to their request that her education be provided in this kind of setting. So Julie's parents paid for a preschool experience at a local church three days per week and additionally agreed to have her attend the in-district segregated classroom for the remaining two days, so that she could receive services such as occupational therapy, physical therapy, and speech therapy. It was at this point that they first became involved with the district-level Community Advisory Committee (CAC) and began to make efforts to know district-level administrators in order to share their belief in inclusive education for Julie and other students with disabilities (in California, school districts are required to have a CAC, which is made up primarily of parents, in order to advise boards of education about district policies and programs related to parents and their children with disabilities). Julie remained in this small, affluent school district for the remainder of elementary school, often in hybrid programs that were a mix of general education (with resource specialist support) and segregated classrooms.

Joanne remembers spending a great deal of her own time volunteering in the general education classrooms that Julie attended, and that ultimately it was the general education teacher and students who were most supportive of Julie. The special education staff and principal were much less receptive to providing Julie's educational services in general education. Joanne also notes that there were no other children with relatively significant support needs in general education at Julie's elementary school and that parents rarely advocated for their children to have access to inclusive settings. During this time, Joanne and John initiated training for parents through their involvement with the CAC.

Joanne and John recall that in middle school there were few opportunities for Julie to have access to general education settings and that it was more difficult for them to "win the argument" with school professionals and IEP team members about how and why this should happen. These professionals said, "it is too much to ask of the teachers." Joanne and John translated this as "We don't have to and we don't want to." Joanne reports that Julie's limited access to general education during middle school depended, again, on the interest and willingness of a few general education teachers, although to a lesser degree than in elementary school. Throughout this time, Julie had regular access to both English and chorus.

Julie attended a large, comprehensive high school in a different affluent suburb, now in northern California. Joanne and John recall that at this point, in the early 1990s, community-based instruction was a new educational tool for students with disabilities. Immediately, however, they submitted a statement to Julie's IEP team stating that they believed "that the high school campus is Julie's 'community' between 8am and 3pm." Further, they asked that every placement decision be put through the following filter: "Does it provide Julie with an opportunity to learn with and learn from students without disabilities and does it provide Julie access to a part of the general curriculum which is relevant to her?" Joanne reports that with continued reminders for the team to turn back to these questions, opposition was minimal for Julie to have access to a range of general education classes during high school. Still, Julie attended both math and reading in a segregated classroom.

Joanne reports that because she had access to general education classes in high school, Julie's favorite class became a key to her future vocation. The high school that Julie attended maintained a child-care program for teenage mothers who had come back to school after having their babies. Julie signed up for a class that allowed her to learn how to take care of young children, and during this time she was to develop her interest and skills in putting on puppet shows for the young children in the program.

It was also during this time that Julie demonstrated the seeds of advocacy that had been planted by her parents: she refused to ride the special education bus any more. Joanne and John report that the IEP team was afraid to teach Julie, as they would students without disabilities, to ride public transportation to high school. Joanne and John chose to do this on their own and Julie then began to ride public transportation with other students from her neighborhood.

Prior to Julie's graduation from high school, Joanne and John were required to make a choice about whether Julie would receive a diploma or a certificate of completion. They had to very carefully consider the option of Julie passing required courses that would have meant excruciating effort on her part. It would also have cost her participation in the more social aspects of high school, such as rallies, football games, and dances, since she was not allowed to receive a diploma completed with adaptations and modifications. As a result, they chose a certificate of completion and encouraged Julie to take as many general education classes as she would enjoy and from which she could acquire meaningful skills.

After graduation from high school, Julie attended classes at the local community college in her suburb. Again, through their advocacy and mobilization, Joanne and John worked with other families to get the transition program for students aged 18 through 22 to include places on the community college campus as well. They both recall that it took renewed advocacy efforts from them for the COE (who ran the transition program) and the college administrators to agree to allow Julie and other students to access courses at the community college level.

Joanne says that during this time their biggest adversaries were the staff of the Disabled Students' Program at the community college, whose response was similar to the resistance to inclusive education she saw during Julie's elementary school years. She remembers one of the staff members (whose job was to provide support services to community college students with identified disabilities) who at the time said to her, "How would SHE get anything out of that class?!" During her years at the community college, in which she earned 60 units, Julie had access to courses in music, music history, art, ceramics, dance, drama, and children's theater. This solidified Julie's interest and desire in owning her own puppet-show business, Julie's Puppets.

Joanne notes that as she moved from the high school campus and gained access to the courses she wanted to take at community college, Julie began to demonstrate a huge gain in self-confidence, self-esteem, and willingness to meet new people and go to new places. Joanne believes that this would never have happened without repeated and numerous opportunities to be educated with peers without disabilities throughout her educational career.

Conclusion

Although not unique, the stories of these three families demonstrate very explicitly some of the points that Taylor (1988) articulated in his early critique of the concept of LRE. The legal requirement that necessitates a continuum of increasingly restrictive educational settings perpetuates the running of separate education settings that serve only students with disabilities, such as segregated classrooms and the COEs in California. The mere existence of separate spaces—such as the county classrooms that Maria has fought to keep Luis out of since his transition to middle school—sends the message that general education settings can relinquish the responsibility for educating some students. Further, Mlawer's (1998) conclusion that factors other than the needs of individual students inform the placement decisions of educational teams also lends support to those points that Taylor identified in his critique. The focus on physical setting and on the conflation of segregation with the need for more intensive educational supports almost requires that students who are viewed as "more disabled" be educated outside of mainstream settings. As the stories of Joshua and Luis clearly indicate, school teams specifically link student disability label (intellectual disability) with intensity of support—thus the need for segregated education for these students. Somehow in this mixing up of what they view as intense support needs and segregation, school teams have forgotten another key component of federal legislation, which clearly states that disability type (label) cannot preclude involvement in general education settings. Despite the clear language of the law in this area, the stories contained in this chapter indicate that school teams actually rely on disability label as a reason to keep students with intellectual disabilities outside of general education.

The use of power given to "expert" (e.g., school professionals) decision making—another key component of Taylor's critique—was also evidenced through the experiences of these three families. As pointed out earlier in the chapter, these families are unique specifically because they chose to counter the deficit-based decisions of their children's IEP teams and to reject what the IEP teams communicated as the necessity of more and more restrictive settings for their children. If the stories of these three families demonstrates a common experience of the denial of access to inclusive classrooms for students with the label of intellectual impairment, then the experiences of the rest of the approximately 39,000 students in California who also have this disability label are likely similar. Fulcher (1989) also problematized the use of "expert" knowledge to make allegedly apolitical decisions about "appropriate" educational placement for students with disabilities; in doing so, he identified the very language of the federal legislation as revealing a tension between the rights of students with disabilities and a school's response to these students as judged by expert knowledge.

Finally, as Taylor (1988) identified two decades ago, the reliance on a continuum of educational placement options seems to also require that students with disabilities "prove" that they are "ready" to move to less restrictive educational settings. The stories of the families in these chapters demonstrate that many school teams, instead of using their "expert" knowledge to identify ways through which all students can access and gain from general education settings, use the power of professional knowledge to identify instances of student failure and then use these failures as a reason to deny access to less restrictive settings (an alternative practice would be to use professional knowledge to uncover *why* a student might not be succeeding and *how* they can be successful in inclusive settings). Further, in the experiences of the families featured in these chapters, school professionals specifically required that students demonstrate success according to normative ideas of achievement.

References

California Department of Education (2004/2005 data). Retrieved December 8, 2008, from http://dq.cde.ca.gov/dataquest

Department of Education (1989). Eleventh Annual Report to Congress on the Implementation of The Education of the Handicapped Act. Author: Washington, DC.

Fulcher, G. (1989). *Disabling policies? A comparative approach to education policy and disability.* London: Falmer Press.

Mlawer, M. (1998, Nov./Dec.). What's wrong with the Feds? *The Association for Persons with Severe Handicaps Newsletter,* 24–26.

Office of Special Education and Rehabilitation Services (2005). *U.S. Department of Education 27ᵗʰ Annual Report to Congress on the Implementation of the Individuals with Disabilities Education Act.* Washington, DC: Author.

Smith, P. (1999). Drawing new maps: A radical cartography of developmental disabilities. *Review of Educational Research, 69*(2), 117–114.

Taylor, S. (1988). Caught in the continuum: A critical analysis of the principle of the least restrictive environment. *The Journal of the Association for the Severely Handicapped, 13*(1).

Ware, L. (2002). A moral conversation on disability: Risking the personal in educational contexts. *Hypatia 17*(3), 143–172.

Young, K. & Mintz, E. (2008). A comparison: Difference, dependency, and stigmatization in special education and disability studies. In S. Gabel and S. Danforth (Eds.), *Disability and the Politics of Education* (pp. 499–511). New York: Peter Lang.

CHAPTER 7

"What Is This Inclusion Thing? Who Dumped These Kids on Me? How Am I Supposed to Do This?"

Tracing the Contours of Inclusion in Alabama

KAGENDO MUTUA AND JIM SIDERS

Many educators agree in principle with the moral and epistemological ideals espoused by inclusion. However, practices in schools across the country and specifically within the state of Alabama fall far short of this ideal. Students with intellectual and other developmental disabilities continue to receive their education largely in separate/segregated settings for the majority of the time while in school. A shift in placement is noted in the past decade, but instructional quality remains in question. In this chapter, we examine the case of including students with intellectual and other developmental disabilities in general education classrooms within the state of Alabama. We argue that within the public education context, inclusion is best understood within a rights discourse rather than simply as a moral virtue or epistemological issue, though, arguably, it is these latter two notions of inclusion that have driven public discourses and practices on inclusion. In the sections following, we first provide a brief discussion of inclusion as a rights discourse. We then follow it with a brief definition of intellectual disabilities (as applied in schools in the state of Alabama) and developmental disabilities. The impact of definitions on services is discussed from the standpoint of disability studies scholarship, drawing specifically from Oliver's (1990) and Linton's

(1998) critique of the role of labels and the politics of terminology. Next, we discuss the historical context of educating students with intellectual and developmental disabilities in Alabama, reviewing some of the historical events that have shaped education for all children in Alabama and focusing specially on how two major pieces of litigation filed in Alabama, namely *Lee v. Macon* (1967) and *Wyatt v. Stickney* (1971), shaped education of persons with disabilities in the state. This is followed by a discussion on the current inclusion practices in Alabama, drawing upon recent statewide data to offer an in-depth analysis of what that data tells us about inclusion of students with intellectual and developmental disabilities in Alabama. We end the chapter with some thoughts on practices within schools that lend hope for meaningful inclusion of students with intellectual and other developmental disabilities in schools across the state of Alabama and its implications for policy, practice, and research.

Inclusion as a Right, Not Just a Moral Ideal

Framed within the rights discourse, inclusion is viewed as a legal right of all students with disabilities (Stainback & Stainback, 1995). This right to education is indelibly etched in the equality clause of the *Fourteenth Amendment* to the Constitution (1868). In the Due Process Clause, all citizens are entitled to equal protection under the law. However, the interpretation of "equal protection" has not been clear-cut. When applied to education, the meaning of the equal protection clause has evolved over time, heavily influenced by the prevailing political climate, especially in regard to the education of members of non-white races. The legal challenges of the application, specifically equal protection within the practice of the separate-but-equal approach in education, resulted in the dismantling of the doctrine in the 1954 ruling of *Brown v. Board of Education* in Topeka, Kansas. The logic of the Brown ruling became the cornerstone of the arguments made by parents and advocates of children with disabilities when appealing for access to education, and ultimately when arguing for inclusion in general educational settings for children with disabilities (see, e.g., *Oberti v. Board of Education of the Borough of Clementon School District*, 3rd Circuit Court, 1993).

IDEA mandates call for students with disabilities, as much as possible, to be educated in the same settings as their non-disabled peers. The spirit of IDEA calls for placement in supportive integrated settings that are age-appropriate. From this standpoint, the least restrictive environment (LRE), as defined in IDEIA (2004) for all students with and without disabilities, is first and foremost the general education classroom within neighborhood schools, unless the needs of a student cannot be best met in that environment. In cases where the student's individualized education plan (IEP) team locates that optimal placement in another environment, an explanation as part of the student's IEP justifying such exclusion is warranted.

Spearheading litigation filed in the U.S. Supreme Court challenging the interpretation and application of least restriction as related to children with severe disabilities was the *Oberti v. Board of Education of the Borough of Clementon School District* (3rd Circuit Court, 1993). The decision by the court upheld the right of Rafael Oberti, a boy with Down syndrome, to receive his education in his neighborhood regular school with adequate and necessary supports. Further, the court placed the burden of proof for compliance with IDEA's mainstreaming requirements on the school district and the state, rather than on the family. The federal judge rendering his decision on the Oberti case stated, in words reminiscent of Judge Thurgood Marshall's "separate was not equal" ruling in *Brown v. Board of Education* (1954), that "inclusion is a right, not a special privilege for a select few," thereby setting a legal precedence for cases involving the inclusion of students with severe cognitive and developmental disabilities in general education classes. Further, the Oberti Court stated,

> that education law requires school systems to supplement and realign their resources to move beyond those systems, structures and practices which tend to result in unnecessary segregation of children with disabilities ... We emphasize that the Act does *not* require states to offer *the same* educational experience to a child with disabilities as is generally provided for nondisabled children ... To the contrary, states must address the unique needs of a disabled child, recognizing that that child may benefit differently from education in the regular classroom than other students ... In short, the fact that a child with disabilities will learn differently from his or her education within a regular classroom does not justify [their] exclusion from that environment ... Indeed the Act's strong presumption in favor of mainstreaming... would be turned on its head if parents had to prove that their child was worthy of being included, rather than the school district having to justify a decision to exclude the child from the regular classroom. (p. 6)

Some scholars have argued that in special education separate programming, its "paradox of differentiation and integration—[and] its tensions in practice and contradictions in policy" (Sailor & Roger, 2007, p. 7)—came about through our desire to foster differentiation. However, the pursuit of differentiation was carried out at the expense of integration, all the while believing that such differentiation would yield positive outcomes for students with intellectual and developmental disabilities. However, no such positive outcomes were realized (Sailor, 2002). Indeed, studies linked pull-out special education models and separate classroom placement with negative outcomes (Wang, Reynolds, & Wahlberg, 1987) and cited positive outcomes accruing from integrated educational practices (Ryndak & Fisher, 2003).

The realization that the early, highly specialized "diagnostic/prescriptive [special education] model characteristic of modern medicine [in which] disability was viewed as a pathology'" (Sailor & Roger, 2007) was not working spurred a paradigm shift in the 1980s. This model of service delivery to individuals with disabilities came to be known by its critics as the medical model of disability (see, e.g., Davis, 1995; Hahn, 1985; Marta, 1998). Within this medical model, persons with intellectual and other developmental disabilities were sequestered in segregated settings and were excluded from or given only minimal access to participating in their communities. In the case of school-age individuals with disabilities, the sequestering was manifested as placement in separate special education classrooms or facilities. During that period, the Regular Education Initiative (REI) was advanced by the U.S. Department of Education as reform policy intended to curtail the huge growth of categorical placements and practices within special education. REI was designed to increase the provision of special education services within the general education classrooms. By so doing, the REI would in effect limit the growing numbers of students identified as having a disability who were being pulled out of the general education classrooms and placed in separate special education classrooms.

However, REI was met with enormous resistance by many within special education communities (see, e.g., Lieberman, 1985; Kauffman, McGee, & Brigham, 2004) who vehemently refuted the research behind REI. School personnel and building-level leaders paid scant attention to the REI movement in Alabama. The educational culture in Alabama with respect to global professional initiatives tends to address issues in a top-down manner. There was limited, if any, systematic preparation to implement REI and similar policies. State department administrators attempted to implement these sweeping efforts but, typically, resources were either limited or nonexistent, and communication broke down in transmission from state to local education agencies. While there was no significant antagonism toward REI in Alabama, the initiative was not embraced either, particularly in local school settings.

Further, that paradigm shift moved special education services toward inclusion. When the President's Committee on Mental Retardation (PCMR) chose inclusion as its theme for their collaborative academies spanning 1995–1999 across all fifty states, they realized then that "there was no single formula for inclusion or definition of inclusion that fits every person with mental retardation" (U.S. Department of Health and Human Services, 1995, p. 2). However, literature suggests that effective inclusion is built around the individual, utilizing a unique array of individually tailored supports to promote self-determination and relationships with the objective of changing the environment and breaking down attitudinal barriers (Bradley, 1994; Sailor & Roger, 2007).

For some student with disabilities, inclusion has not worked well at all, especially for those with more significant intellectual and developmental disabilities. This is not to say that the failure of inclusion to work for this subpopulation has been because of problems inherent in those students themselves, but rather that the supports those students need to be successful in inclusive settings have not been adequately provided. Thus, for this subpopulation of students, even when inclusion is framed as a right, they have not been adequately included, though the special education programs are built on a rights discourse. However, proponents of inclusion as a moral imperative who argue that including persons with a disability is the right thing to do offer a more persuasive argument in support of inclusion of students with significant intellectual and developmental disabilities. Proponents of inclusion as a moral imperative further argue that the effects of exclusion are felt by the larger society and furthermore that "even partial exclusion is morally unacceptable" (Craig, n.d.). However, Craig (n.d.) observes that the views of this group are more likely to be ignored though "everybody benefits from inclusion. These inclusion advocates observe that though there are many children and young people who don't fit in (or feel as though they don't), inclusive schools should feel welcoming to all.

Defining Intellectual and Developmental Disabilities

In 1970, P.L. 91-517, the *Developmental Disabilities Services Facilities Construction Act* (referred hereafter as the DD Act) was enacted by Congress. The DD Act provided a definition of developmental disability. The DD Act was an amendment of previous legislation called

Mental Retardation and Facilities Construction Act of 1963 (P.L. 88-164), which was the first federal legislation that made defining the needs and subsequently developing a national framework for service delivery for persons with intellectual disabilities a national priority (Flexer, Simmons, Luft, & Baer, 2005). In 1970, the DD Act expanded the previous legislation "to benefit not only individuals who were mentally retarded but also disability groups whose impairments were developmental in nature and who had similar service needs" (Flexer et al., 2005, p. 33). Therefore, the change in the 1970 legislation was more than a name change. The tempo was set for understanding what services were needed to meet the needs of persons with developmental disabilities (of which intellectual disabilities was subsumed), as well as how they needed to be provided.

Unlike the definition of intellectual disabilities (or mental retardation) that is used in special education, the federal definition of "developmental disabilities" is a functional, rather than a clinical, one. Specifically, the current definition of developmental disabilities outlined in the 1978 amendments of the DD Act focuses on persons with substantial impairments rather than naming the specific categories of disabilities, as had been the case when the law was first enacted in 1970. Therefore, P.L. 95-602, *Rehabilitation, Comprehensive Services and Developmental Disability Amendments of 1978*, defined developmental disability as a severe, chronic disability of a person that

is attributable to a mental impairment, physical impairment, or combination of mental and physical impairments.

is manifested before the individual attains age 22.

is likely to continue indefinitely.

results in substantial functional limitations in three or more areas of major life activity:

self-care

receptive and expressive language

learning

mobility

self-direction

capacity for independent living

economic self-sufficiency;

reflects the person's need for a combination and sequence of special interdisci-

138   MUTUA & SIDERS

plinary or generic care, treatment, or other services which are of extended or life-long duration and are individually planned and coordinated.

On the other hand, IDEA defines intellectual disability as "significantly subaverage general intellectual functioning, existing concurrently with deficits in adaptive behavior and manifested during the developmental period, that adversely affects a child's educational performance" [34 *Code of Federal Regulations* §300.7(c)(6)]. This definition, originally put forth by Grossman in 1983, continues to function today as the federal definition, and as the definition that the state of Alabama uses in the identification and classification of students with intellectual disabilities in special education.

Writing from a disability studies perspective, Linton (1998) argues that the terms that have been used to label the characteristics that result from variations/differences in human sensory, physical, cognitive, or emotional functioning have been selected based upon their ease in arranging people in ways that are socially and economically convenient for society. Further, she argues that though disability is an arbitrary signifier, it is nonetheless used by the general population "to signify something material and concrete, a physical or psychological condition considered to have predominantly medical significance" (p. 10). In a similar vein, Oliver (1990) argues that conceptions of disability orient society's behavior toward persons with disabilities based upon the social meanings assigned to disability. As such, Oliver critiques the prevailing conception of disability that sees an individual with disability as a victim of his/her circumstance, thereby requiring compensatory individualized intervention, such as special education. By failing to see disability as a social construction, Oliver (1990) argues, "dominant definitions of disability pose problems for individual and group identity" (p. 30), thereby undermining collective efforts by disabled people to fight against the oppressions meted against them by an ableist society. Critiquing the labeling of children with disabilities and their education as "special," Linton argues that

> special can be understood only as a euphemistic formulation, obscuring the reality that neither the children nor the education are considered desirable and that they are not thought to "surpass what is common." (p. 15).

The Historical Context of Educating Students with Intellectual and Developmental Disabilities in Alabama

Generally speaking, despite the two-decade long opportunity to institutionalize inclusive practices, public schools in Alabama have been slow to change. For instance, reference to students with intellectual disabilities as "EMR" and "TMR" continue to be the jargon in schools staffed with seasoned teachers. Indeed the chapter authors have witnessed occasions when those antiquated labels and terms have been used by seasoned professionals during IEP meetings. While senior-level teachers continue to rely on unacceptable terminologies, they also frequently correlate with a preference toward segregated service models. However, we do not wish to appear to suggest that the blame for inadequate inclusive practices falls on special education personnel. Evidence in schools across the state indicates that, in general, there is poor reception accorded to co-teaching and co-planning by general education teachers, thereby further convincing special educators that utilizing stand-alone service models is the best answer.

Mirroring national trends, litigation in Alabama has impacted and shaped practices in special education. However, in Alabama, in order to have an adequate discourse on inclusion, one must address the issue of disproportionality in the representation of African Americans in special education. Specifically, the disproportional representation of African American males in categories of behavior disorders and mental retardation and their underrepresentation in gifted/talented and learning disabilities categories has greatly impacted inclusive delivery and its conceptualization within the state. In Alabama, a class-action suit, *Lee v. Macon*, was filed in 1963 concerning school desegregation in Macon County. Later, in 1967, all schools across the state joined in the lawsuit. Underlying this suit was the issue of equitable treatment of African American citizens of Alabama (Alabama Department of Education, 2008). Over three decades later in 2000, when the *Lee v. Macon* consent decree was signed, what began as a racial equity issue involving segregation in public schools in Alabama had evolved into an issue concerning disproportionality in the representation of African Americans within mental retardation and behavior disorder categories and their underrepresentation in learning disabilities and gifted/talented special education programs. The settlement of the consent decree, approved by the court on August 30, 2000, required that the state of Alabama undertake initiatives to provide teacher training, establish a program to improve reading achievement, and make changes to Alabama Administrative Code in the areas of pre-referral/referral intervention, evaluation procedures, and eligibility criteria. This emphasis on pre-referral intervention services resulted in substantial changes over the following six years of implementing the consent decree.

In order to fully understand the discourse of inclusion in Alabama, we have to factor in the role of disproportional representation of African Americans in special education. Further, to have a discussion about African Americans in education in Alabama, we feel that it is necessary to place that in the historical context of segregation in education in Alabama. According to O'Brien (1999), to fully grasp the discriminatory effects of segregation, one must place desegregation in its historical context. The history of desegregation of educational institutions in the South in the United States is dotted with practices that officially sanctioned and maintained the separation of races in all arenas of life, including education. Prior to the Civil War, African Americans received no formal education in many states in the South (O'Brien, 1999). Indeed, in many of those states, such as Alabama and Georgia, it was illegal to teach slaves to read or write (Joiner, Bonner, Shearouse, & Smith, 1979). According to Joiner and colleagues (1979), in the pre–Civil War South, the lack of education was experienced by not only African Americans but also poor whites.

The impetus for desegregation of schools is rooted in the Due Process Clause of the *Fourteenth Amendment* to the Constitution, in which all citizens are entitled to equal protection under the law. However, the interpretation of "equal protection" has not been as clear-cut as it may seem. The landmark case that stamped on the psyche of the American public that racial segregation was an acceptable practice, particularly in the South and also in some institutions in the North, was *Plessy v. Ferguson* (1896). The enormous influence of this landmark case was its legitimization of racial segregation through the deployment of the "separate but equal" doctrine, which *Brown v. Board of Education* (1954) later dismantled. It is, indeed, the "separate is not equal" doctrine that resulted from the *Brown v. Board of Education* ruling that spurred and still continues to inspire many inclusion advocates. In addition, the "separate is not equal" doctrine is the impetus of the enactment of P.L. 94-142, the *Education of All Handicapped Children's Act of 1975*.

Given these obvious connections between separatism and special education and overrepresentation of African Americans in special education, one can more clearly see the necessity for this historical framing. In addition, this historical context enriches the interpretations given to the current statistics on the racial distributions of children with disabilities in various special education categories in the state of Alabama that are presented in later sections in this chapter.

The Race Factor and Inclusion in Alabama

Since the implementation of the *Lee v. Macon Consent Degree* ruling (Alabama Department of Education, 2008), there has been a significant effort to remedy the disproportionality evidenced by the excessive number of African American learners placed in programs for students with emotional disturbance and/or intellectual disabilities. On the other end of the placement continuum, African Americans have been significantly underrepresented in programs for students with gifts and talents. An examination of the following five figures and tables must be made in the proper context.

Data available from the Alabama Department of Education spanning the years 2000 to 2005 show a distinct drop in the target black population, who were overrepresented in services for learners with intellectual disabilities and emotional disturbance. However, white students served in this type of program show almost a parallel decrease. What is missing from this picture is the depiction of the percentage of students classified as having intellectual disabilities. Interesting (and missing) analyses and data would emerge from an examination of how these trends would really look when black students, representing 38% of the total student population, are viewed in the context of overall, current placement trends for students with disabilities. This distortion is a concern when examining placements in classes for students with emotional disturbance, mental retardation, learning disabilities, and gifted ability. Figure 1 illustrates placement trends by race, thus highlighting the number of black students in the state identified as having an intellectual disability compared to their white counterparts between the years 2000 and 2005.

What is evident from the available data is that since the implementation of the *Lee v. Macon Consent Degree* (Alabama Department of Education, 2008), there have been significant reductions in racial disparities in the special education classification of intellectual disabilities (specifically learners diagnosed with mental retardation). Interestingly, the rate of placements, based on a census count, reveals that in 2000, despite representing only 38% of the total school population, black students were enrolled at a rate 2.5 times more than white students for services for learners with intellectual disabilities (mental retardation). The trend line in Figure 2 does reveal progress being made to narrow the census gap between black and white students, but proportionately many more black students continue to be identified and served as having intellectual disabilities than their white counterparts.

Figure 1: Service comparison Black and White students with Intellectual Disabilities

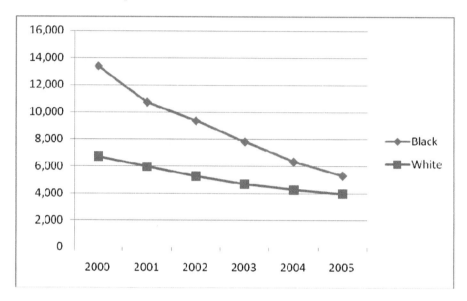

Mental Retardation

	2000	2001	2002	2003	2004	2005
Black	13,368	10,697	9,351	7,807	6,337	5,328
White	6,704	5,964	5,271	4,692	4,265	3,968

On the other hand, based upon placement trends, disparities have been minimized in the classifications of African Americans for emotional disturbance (ED) as illustrated in Figure 2. At the same time, the number of black students classified as gifted also has increased (see Figure 3). In the category of specific learning disabilities (SLD), trends show an increase in the number of African American students identified as such, as illustrated by Figure 4. Interestingly, an in-depth examination of Figure 3, which portrays the black and white student population identified with learning disabilities between the years 2000 and 2005, reveals that as the number of white students decreases in this category, the number of black students increases.

Figure 2: Service comparison Black and White students with Emotional Disturbance

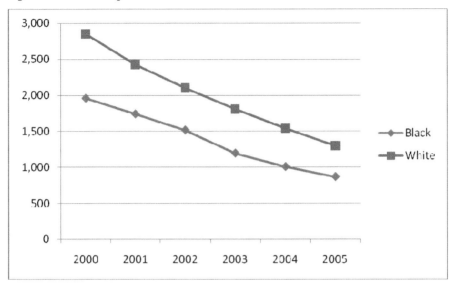

Emotional Disturbance

	2000	2001	2002	2003	2004	2005
Black	1,959	1,741	1,519	1,194	1,007	867
White	2,851	2,423	2,101	1,807	1,540	1,297

This identification trend is of importance to our discussion of inclusion. Students with measured IQ of 55 and above are typically served in general education. This practice, although not initially conceived as policy, emerged from comments made by M. Whetstone (2004), state director of special education, at a state conference.

When we examine those identification trends, it appears that more African Americans who previously had been identified as having intellectual disabilities and more often than not placed in segregated special education classrooms are currently included (at least partly) in general education classrooms. Two issues become apparent with this trend chart: (1) identification of black students appears to be shifting from having mental retardation to having learning disabilities, and (2) inclusion models appear to serve the purpose of removing white students from services for learners with learning disabilities. In the first instance, this movement toward an inclusive classroom model has promoted black students to a more socially de

Figure 3: Service comparison Black and White students with Gifts and Talents

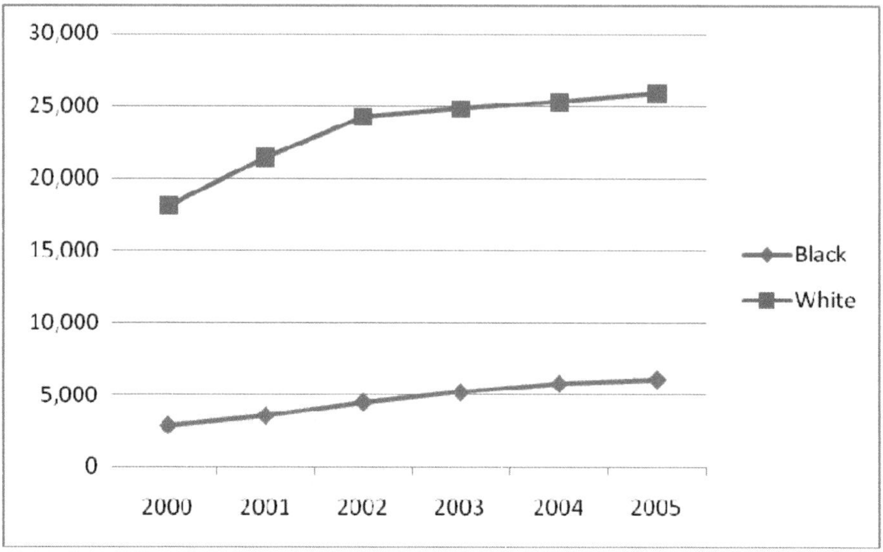

Gifted

	2000	2001	2002	2003	2004	2005
Black	2,870	3,549	4,480	5,164	5,751	6,030
White	18,076	21,414	24,217	24,809	25,282	25,881

sirable disability identity (from emotional disturbance and intellectu-aldisabilities to learning disabilities as seen in Figure 5). One could make an argument that inclusion is working and is benefiting black students by moving them up the Alabama model of Response to Intervention, called Tiered Intervention. Alabama Department of Education has referred to the system of inclusive education as Tier 1 and 2, maintaining education in the general classroom and depending on the instructor as the sole service provider.

They project 90% of all students to be served in the general classroom. In similar fashion, 5% of students with special needs should be maintained in the general classroom and are projected to be served with consultation and instructional /intervention prescriptions from a special educator during planning. The remaining 5% of students would be subject to special educator– delivered interventions made within the general classroom whenever possible. Theoretically, education is always provided in a general classroom; however, the question that begs to be asked is whether or not this is academic ad

Figure 4: Service comparison Black and White students with Learning Disabilities

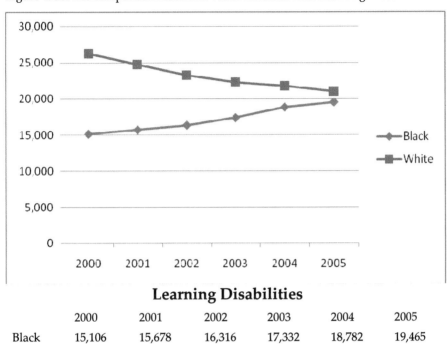

Learning Disabilities

	2000	2001	2002	2003	2004	2005
Black	15,106	15,678	16,316	17,332	18,782	19,465
White	26,232	24,727	23,238	22,261	21,738	21,007

vancement. Quite possibly the service in and of itself (this model of inclusion), simply by advocating for general classroom placements, is providing more appropriate attention in ways that will improve educational benefit to special needs learners. The general educator may begin to realize the positive impact of moreheterogeneous placements and the influence of this inclusive model on differentiating instruction to all learners, thereby fostering greater acceptance of special needs learners by the general population. Data justification from the state tends to focus on a census count of special needs learners placed in a variety of learning environments, which is one method of reviewing the impact of inclusion. Whether or not those learners are realizing academic gain unique to a history of service delivery out of the general classroom is a question currently with meager justification at best.

Figure 5: Service trends of Black students 2000–2005

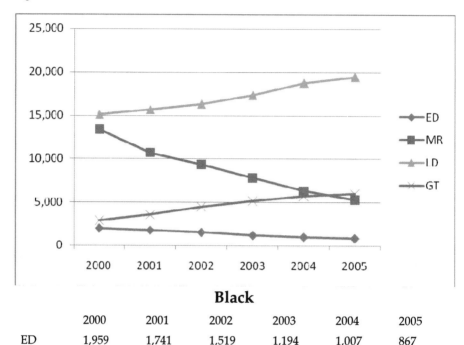

Black

	2000	2001	2002	2003	2004	2005
ED	1,959	1,741	1,519	1,194	1,007	867
MR	13,368	10,697	9,351	7,807	6,337	5,328
LD	15,106	15,678	16,316	17,332	18,782	19,465
GT	2,870	3,549	4,480	5,164	5,751	6,030

The settlement also required reevaluation of certain categories of minority students who had been identified as having intellectual disabilities. As a result, several hundred students who had been inappropriately classified as having intellectual disabilities were exited from special education. These students were provided with supplemental services to help them transition successfully into the general education programs and were carefully monitored during this process.

According to the Civil Rights Project of Harvard University (cited in ALDSE, 2008), African American males are less likely to receive early intervention, less likely to receive counseling and psychological supports, and more likely to be placed in restrictive environments. Indeed, corroborating these assertions, the Alabama State Department of Education's Special Education Services observed that while African American males living anywhere in the United States are twice as likely to be identified as mentally retarded compared to their white counterparts, living in Alabama, they are three times more likely to be identified as mentally retarded (Alabama Department of Education, 2008). What is evident in reviewing inclusion practices in Alabama is that race is strongly implicated in placement decisions and, therefore, cannot be abstracted from discourses on inclusion in the state.

In addition to *Lee v. Macon, Wyatt v. Stickney* (1971), another nationally significant suit, was filed in Alabama. The complaint ensued from the impact that personnel cutbacks due to budget cuts in the state government had on service delivery reductions. The complaint contended that a lack of program service and benefit to the recipients resulted from staff reductions. Defendants in the case revealed "rather conclusively" that treatment programs at Bryce Hospital in Tuscaloosa, Alabama, did not satisfy any of the following "three fundamental conditions for adequate and effective treatment [namely]: (1) Provision of a humane physical and psychological environment; (2) Sufficient and qualified staff to permit treatment delivery, and (3) individualized treatment plans" (p. 17) .

Historically Bryce Hospital was opened in 1851 as the Alabama Insane Hospital. Given the state of mental health care at the time, this facility provided model scientific, humane care and was nationally recognized. Today, unfortunately, Bryce Hospital is recovering from deplorable conditions that developed when residents swelled to over 5,000 patients in the late 1960s. At that time, the inadequacy of services led to the *Wyatt v. Stickney* complaint on behalf of a 15-year-old male placed in the facility who showed no signs of mental illness. Bryce Hospital has shrunk to approximately 250 residents at the present day. These lawsuits as well as others around the country speak to a larger underlying issue of the exclusion of persons with intellectual and other developmental disabilities through service models that embrace placement in segregated programs primarily due to one's disability.

Current Policies and Practices of Including Students with Intellectual and Developmental Disabilities in Schools in Alabama

Recent practices in schools across the nation appear to suggest that, of necessity, inclusion needs to be tied to a classroom-based model. This means that inclusion is tied to placement in a classroom with non-disabled peers, rather than being conceived broadly as providing instruction to all students in formats and contexts that are supportive of their unique learning needs. This conception of inclusion as a space rather than a practice or overarching philosophy of service provision is clearly problematic in the sense that schools to buy into the conception of inclusion as a place seldom pause to consider the overall inclusiveness of their entire educational practice. School districts have gradually come to embrace the fundamental value of inclusion and the life benefit delivered to exceptional students. What was initially considered to be a major achievement (e.g., providing campus access for learners with special needs) has finally realized acceptance. Inclusive education has currently come to mean least restrictive environment in the general classroom—until proven unacceptable—in Alabama and throughout the rest of United States. Such practices that link inclusion to a classroom (usually placement in general education classrooms) have continued to be embraced by schools that hold inclusion as a core value. Critics of this wholesale placement of students with intellectual and other developmental disabilities in the general education classroom argue that such practices create re-segregation within the general education classroom contexts (Giangreco & Doyle, 2002). Along this same vein, Sailor and Roger (2007), making a similar argument, observe,

> students with IEPs who cannot function in various components of the classroom curriculum often find themselves at tables, usually in the back of the classroom, with paraprofessionals who, in one-on-one approach, work with them on "something else." This practice not only segregates special education students within the general education classroom but also creates a distraction that has detrimental effect on general and special education students alike. (p. 8)

The state of Alabama, through a tiered model of service delivery (McCook, 2007), has attempted to address inclusion for learners of all types of ability, while simultaneously checking racial discrimination that has compromised educational equity. Underlying the tiered structure is the belief that the general classroom is the instructional environment of first resort. Moving all learners, regardless of skill, ability, or potential has been the impetus for program development efforts and educational improvements. Regarding the inclusion of special needs learners, communications from the Alabama Department of Education established an unpublished policy that any student with a measured IQ of 55 and above was to be served in the general classroom. While the arbitrary nature of this cut-off in determining who is included and who is not has been brought to question, much less discussion has focused on the racial elements of

this practice despite there being ample empirical evidence of the racial biases that IQ testing engenders. Although the mandate has been
refuted by state administrators, the concept has been a driving factor
in program placement decisions for the past half decade in the state of
Alabama. The instructional benefit resulting from this form of inclusion cannot be revealed in standardized assessment measures. Further confounding the comparison is the implementation of No Child
Left Behind caps on learner progress that determine who is exempt
from high-stakes assessments.

Through the use of a tiered model of support for students experiencing learning difficulties in the classroom, the state of Alabama has
undertaken proactive steps to limit the numbers of students identified
and placed in special education (McCook, 2007). This approach aligns
well with the *Lee v. Macon* consent decree (Alabama Department of
Education, 2008), which required that measures be put in place to assure that students were provided adequate instructional support in
the general education classroom in order to rule out poor teaching as
a confounding factor in the over-identification of black students as
having intellectual disabilities. This move has prompted not only the
accountability demands espoused by the No Child Left Behind legislation of 2000, but also those of IDEA 2004 that more emphatically
called for the use of evidence-based practices. The state of Alabama
turned to the tiered model of support, drawing upon empirical evidence as well as expert views supporting such an approach. For instance, the National Reading Panel (2000) stated that systematic, explicit reading instruction is essential for students to develop the skills
and processes to become fluent comprehenders of text. Further, students learn most effectively in small flexible groups (National Institute of Child Health and Human Development, 2000). On the other
hand, Marzano, Pickering, and Pollock (2001) found that students
need at least 24 successful practice sessions to gain mastery of a skill.
Literacy centers are designed to provide this much-needed practice.
Furthermore, teachers' regular use of formative assessments improves
their students' learning, especially if teachers have additional guid-
ance on using the assessment to design and to individualize instruction (National Mathematics Advisory Panel, 2008). For students who
have mathematical difficulties, explicit instruction using clear models
of proficient performance, many opportunities to verbalize their problem-solving strategies, and adequate practice and review should be a
part of the mathematics program (National Mathematics Advisory

Panel, 2008). Predicated upon the literature that demonstrates the support models that are proactive in nature, a three-tier model was developed by Alabama that provides supports to students within the general education classroom, thereby limiting the placement of students in special education classrooms.

Specifically, the Alabama's Response to Intervention (RtI) model utilizes three tiers of supports for students in school (McCook, 2007). Tier I interventions are geared to at least 80% of all students. Theoretically, decision making is completed by Grade Level Teams, Professional Learning Communities (PLC), and School Improvement Teams. This model of instructional intervention is a proactive approach to meeting unique learning needs and represents an attempt to replace a largely "crisis-managed" system that has been in place since (or before) the mandates of P.L. 94-142 over three decades ago. The unfortunate consequence of legislating instructional policy is the forced nature of change. When forcing change extends from top-down decisions and when the top resides in the federal government, the chances for a successful transformation become increasingly remote. There are pockets of success, however, in Alabama and progress has been made in the past five years toward this desired end. Some campuses (e.g., Oxford High School, Alba Middle School, and Homewood Elementary School) within districts have managed the leap to preventive teamed decisions. Relying on Professional Learning Communities requires that lead team members seek out professional development, understand effective research-based practices, and share interventions with one another. These Learning Communities sustain themselves with documentation, data-influenced decisions, and the all-important parity among all members. School Improvement Teams, the third arm of the model, generally and unfortunately, remains mired in the reactive mentality of schools past. With the advent of NCLB, high-stakes, test-driven recognition of poor-performing schools feeds into the reactive rather than proactive character of schools. Again, in theory, and in a growing number of school campuses, School Improvement Teams work internally to adopt contemporary practices, share among members, and support all faculty in the school to advance programming as a team. Outreach efforts by the authors and awareness from sister university school improvement efforts demonstrate that the transformation to Tiered intervention, particularly in levels 1 and 2 as described, is the exception rather than the rule.

Within Tier 2, interventions are targeted and provided to approximately 15% of the school population. Tier 2 supports are designed for students who are not responding to Tier 1. Again, decision making is done by Grade Level Teams, Professional Learning Communities (PLC), and School Improvement Teams. Tier 3 provides more intensive support to approximately 5% of the school population. Within Tier 3, decision making is done by the District/School Leadership Team and the Building-based Student Support Team (BBSST). BBSST is a pre-referral intervention mandated by the state in accord with the *Lee v. Macon* Consent Decree. The decree required that the state was to put into place strategies for supporting students in the general education classroom, thereby limiting those who were ultimately referred for special education evaluation, particularly African Americans who, according to the Alabama State Department of Education, were three times more likely to be identified as having an intellectual disability if residing in the state of Alabama (Alabama Department of Education, 2008).

Tier 3 supports are designed for students who are not responding to Tiers 1 or 2 and/or who are significantly behind. Decisions made within all tiers are geared at answering three fundamental questions:

What do we want students to learn?

How will we know if they've learned it?

What will we do if they don't?

The aforementioned mandates limit the review of educational placement census counts as an accurate assessment of the effectiveness of inclusion. In fact, efforts to instigate instructional change have occurred frequently enough in the past decade. However, measures of the impact of inclusion have been obscured by shifts in terminology and by the ensuing confusion accompanying the implementation of such change. Instructional intervention in the past 10 years may have occurred as a result of the use of teachers holding collaborative teaching credentials, who, for the most part, provided services to students in inclusive settings and sometimes utilized co-teaching models. Each of these intervention profiles or professionals has been so labeled in order to refine a special education delivery system that put a greater emphasis on the placement in the general classroom as a first-order option. However, frequent changes in terminologies/labels have seriously compromised the development of a deep understanding by the service providers of the intervention models espoused by

those frequently changing models. Inclusion as an educational model
of service provision to students with disabilities, including those with
intellectual and developmental disabilities, has not been immune to
the politics of meaning and interpretation.

While investigating the state regarding inclusion, a disconnect becomes increasingly clear. While a clear policy model is evident from
the vantage point of the Alabama Department of Education, much
confusion and anxiety tends to be present in the school buildings and
classrooms. The level of interpretation and implementation is desper-
ate for a champion of the cause, and building level leadership appears
to be in need of a clearer understanding of inclusive practice and policy. Discussion of model programs revealed a hiatus between strong
administrative leadership and exemplary implementation of inclusion. Unfortunately, key players in most situations continue to react
to inclusion after more than a decade of attempting to institute this
philosophy and model, rather than proactively advocating for the
benefit of inclusion for all learners. After talking with numerous
teachers, the sense that inclusion was "imposed" instead of "allowed"
permeated many reactions, particularly in university classroom discussions with practicing teachers.

Promising Practices

Identifying model-inclusive schools in Alabama is subject to a criteria
of success that may not be as readily apparent as state leaders desire.
Recent State Improvement Grants and the current State Professional
Development Improvement Grant (2008) have focused on the sophis-
tication of co-teaching relationships and the presence of collaborative
delivery at the building level. As previously reviewed, shifts in educational placements from more restrictive, pull-out services to general
classroom, inclusive delivery have been another basis to determine
the quality of inclusion. Standard evidence of effective and model inclusion programs remains to be defined. As fickle as defining quality
inclusion programming is, model inclusion programming is the exception rather than the rule.

Model elementary, middle school, and high school programs have
been identified by the Alabama Department of Education for pur-
poses of replication. Mountain Brook Intermediate School, in Bir-
mingham, has been identified as an outstanding elementary inclusion
program. The selection of this school was based on qualitative measures related to both the co-teaching instruction provided as well as

the administrative advocacy for delivery. Alba Middle School in Mobile was selected as a model middle school due to the comprehensive inclusion instruction delivered. Representatives of Alba Middle School have compiled empirical student performance measures to substantiate the value of their services. Strong administrative support of the inclusion model was another salient feature of the school evidence of success. Finally, qualitative, anecdotal comments from the student body have been used to establish the outstanding nature of the Alba Middle School instruction; for example, when special education faculty were called for a meeting over the public address system, students remarked that they were unaware the school had a special education program. Oxford High School in Anniston was selected as a top-performing high school inclusion program. Collaborative planning to diversify instruction and improve teaching practices for all students was the foundation for this school choice. Co-teaching models were also credited to the high school as reason to identify this school as a model site for inclusion programming. What is evident in Alabama, as in many other states, is that inclusion is quantitatively measured. The value of inclusion is most often predicated upon placement of students with disabilities in general education settings, not always upon the outcomes they achieve. However, placements in the general education contexts constitute the necessary first steps for students who have often operated from the margins.

Conclusion

Inclusive educational services have been associated with benefits for learners with and without disabilities throughout the nation. To that end, one must evaluate the influence this philosophy has had on educational benefit to learners under Individual Education Programs. Should the benefit be measured in terms of curriculum standards met? Should benefits be measured in terms of Average Yearly Progress? How about dropout rates (the graduation rate for Alabama in 2000 was 65.1%, putting it 39th when ranked against other states and Washington DC, and below the national average of 69.6% [Barton, 2005, p. 10])? Or should one look at employment rates? Alabama's public schools carry a dynamic that may not be as apparent in many other states—racial demographics. Segregationist policies that had been de jure practice in the past had not been completely removed from the general profile of school districts before peculiar patterns of placements began to emerge in special education services. Courts were solicited once again to sort out the Civil Rights of ethnically diverse populations germane to the state of Alabama, particularly as these rights were addressed/ignored in public schooling. However, the lack of data that specifically answers the question of the degree of integration of students with disabilities in the state limits the certainty of conclusions that can be drawn about the impact of inclusion in Alabama. Despite years of trying to build an inclusive public school system, overall this state has to be considered a work in progress.

Ironically, Alabama ranked 14th among all states and DC for the full inclusion of students with intellectual disabilities in general education classrooms in 2003–2004, with 14.82% of students with intellectual disabilities being fully included (Smith, 2007). An argument, then, can be made that populating classrooms and reporting shifts in placements into general classrooms and out of special education placements are insufficient to make a judgment as to the effectiveness of inclusion. The hard work that remains is that of demonstrating student benefit from inclusive practices. However, in many circumstances, students have found that another world exists other than the pull-out model of special education of the past.

References

Alabama Department of Education. (2008, April 5). Alabama success story, presentation at the Council for Exceptional Children International Convention & Expo in Boston, MA. Retrieved September 23, 2008, from http://www.alsde.edu/html/sections/documents.asp?section=65&sort=6&footer=sections

Barton, P. (2005). *One-third of a nation: Rising dropout rates and declining opportunities.* Princeton, NJ: Educational Testing Service.

Bradley, V. (1994). Evolution of a new service paradigm. In V. Bradley, J. Ashbaugh & B. Blaney (Eds.), *Creating individual supports for people with developmental disabilities.* Baltimore, MD: Paul H. Brookes Publishing.

Craig, G. (n.d.). Social justice. Retrieved from: http://www.isja.org.uk/articles_7_gcsj.html

Davis, L. (1995). *Enforcing normalcy: Disability, deafness, and the body.* London: Verso.

Developmental Disabilities Services Facilities Construction Act of 1970 (P.L. 91-517).

Education for All Handicapped Children Act of 1975, 20 U.S.C. §1401 et seq.

Flexer, R., Simmons, T., Luft, P. & Baer, R. (2005). *Transition planning for secondary students with disabilities* (2nd ed.). Upper Saddle River, NJ: Pearson.

Giangreco, M., & Doyle, M. (2002). Students with disabilities and paraprofessional supports: Benefits, balance, and band-aids. *Exceptional Children, 68,* 1–12.

Hahn, H. (1985). Towards a politics of disability. *Social Science Journal, 22,* 89.

Joiner, O., Bonner, J., Shearouse, H., & Smith, T. (1979) *A history of public education in Georgia.* Columbia, SC: The R. L. Bryan Company.

Kauffman, J., McGee, K., & Brigham, M. (2004). Enabling or disabling? Observations on changes in special education. *Phi Delta Kappan, 85,* 613–620.

Lee v. Macon County Bd., 267 F.Supp. 458, aff'd sub nom. Wallace v. United States, 389 U.S. 215 (1967).

Lieberman, L. (1985). Special education and regular education: A merger made in heaven?, *Exceptional Children, 51*, 513–516.

Linton, S. (1998). *Claiming disability: Knowledge and identity*. New York: New York University Press.

Marta, A. (1998). *Beyond ramps: Disability at the end of the social contract*. Monroe, ME: Common Courage Press.

Marzano, R., Pickering, D., & Pollock, J. (2001). *Classroom instruction that works: Research-based strategies for increasing student achievement*. Alexandria, VA: Association for Supervision and Curriculum Development.

McCook, J. (2007). Response to Intervention. A presentation to the Alabama Department of Education, Perdido Key, Alabama.

Mental Retardation and Facilities Construction Act of 1963 (P.L. 88-164)

National Mathematics Advisory Panel. (2008). Foundations for success: The final report of the National Mathematics Advisory Panel. Retrieved October 2, 2008 from http://www.ed.gov/about/bdscomm/list/mathpanel/report/final-report.pdf

National Institute of Child Health and Human Development. (2000). *Report of the National Reading Panel. Teaching children to read: An evidence-based assessment of the scientific research literature on reading and its implications for reading instruction* (NIH Publication No. 00-4769). Washington, DC: U.S. Government Printing Office.

Oberti v. Board of Education, 995 F.2d 1204 (3rd Cir. 1993)

O'Brien., M. (1999). Discriminatory effects: Desegregation litigation in higher education in Georgia. *William and Mary Bill of Rights Journal, 8*(1), 1–48.

Oliver, M. (1990). *The politics of disablement*. New York: St. Martin's Press.

Plessy v. Ferguson, 163 U.S. 537, 16 S. Ct. 1138, 41 L. Ed. 256 (1896).

President's Committee on Mental Retardation. (1995). *The journey to inclusion: A resource for state policy makers*. Washington, DC: U.S. Government Printing Office.

Rehabilitation, Comprehensive Services and Developmental Disability Amendments of 1978 (P.L. 95-602)

Ryndak, D., & Fisher, D. (Eds.). (2003). *The foundations of inclusive education: A compendium of articles on effective strategies to achieve inclusive education* (2nd ed.). Baltimore: TASH.

Sailor, W. (18 April 2002). Testimony before the Research Agenda Task Force of the President's Commission on Excellence in Special Education.

Sailor, W., & Roger, B. (2007). Rethinking inclusion: Schoolwide applications. In K. L. Frieberg, *Annual Editions (06–07): Educating Exceptional Children* (18th ed.) (pp. 7–13). Dubuque, IA: McGraw Hill.

Smith, P. (2007). Have we made any progress? Including students with intellectual disabilities in regular education classrooms. *Intellectual and Developmental Disabilities, 45*, 297–309.

Stainback, W., & Stainback, S. (1995). *Controversial Issues Confronting Special Education*. Needham Heights, MA: Allyn & Bacon.

State Professional Development Improvement Grant. (2008). Models of Collaboration and Co-Teaching. Professional development dvd produced by the Alabama Department of Education, Montgomery, Alabama.

Wang, M., Reynolds, M. & Wahlberg, H. (Eds.). (1987). *Handbook of special education:*

Research and practice (Vol. 1). Oxford: Pergamon Press.
Wyatt v. Stickney, 344 F.Supp. 387, 344 F.Supp. 3783 (M.D. Ala.1972), 334 F.Supp. 1341,
325 F.Supp.781 (M.D. Ala. 1971), 772 aff'd sub nom. Wyatt v. Aderholt, 503 F.2d,
1305 (5th Cir. 1974).

CHAPTER 8

Adding Urban Complexities into the Mix

Continued Resistance to the Inclusion of Students with Cognitive Impairments (*or* New York, New York: So Bad They Segregated It Twice)

DAVID CONNOR

Introduction

The inclusion of students with cognitive impairments (CI) has continuously troubled traditional notions of who belongs in a "regular" classroom. Even the Regular Education Initiative of the late 1980s limited its advocacy to students with mild[1] disabilities such as speech and language impairments, learning disabilities, and behavior disorders (Will, 1986). This conceptualization of inclusion still lingers in the minds of teachers, administrators, and scholars today, with many people believing that the students who most closely approximate "normalcy" are the best candidates for inclusive classrooms. Students with cognitive impairments have historically been relegated to segregated institutional settings (Stiker, 1999); although the inclusion movement has attempted to change this, they still remain one of the most marginalized groups of students within schools.

This chapter will focus on the specific context of urban education in relation to the challenges of inclusive education for students with intellectual disabilities. My preferred term of use for individuals with intellectual disabilities is cognitive impairment (CI). I acknowledge that in many sources cited within this chapter, the same phenomenon has historically been referred to as Mental Retardation (MR). Although I do not wish to condone the continued use of MR, I use a combination of the terminologies: CI/MR. This is done to provide a sense of cohesion and continuity and to lessen any distraction as we make a terminological shift in the field of education from "MR" to "CI."

Focusing on New York City, I use Kincheloe's twelve "unique features of urban education" (2007, pp. 5–8) to frame specific circumstances in which students and teachers operate; I do so to particularly highlight key issues relating to students with cognitive impairments and other disabilities. In addition, I discuss the findings of a recent independent report on New York City, *The Comprehensive Management Review and Evaluation of Special Education* (2005), by a team of Harvard-based expert consultants led by Thomas Hehir, former director of the U.S. Department of Education's Office of Special Education Programs from 1993 to 1999. Spotlighting District 75, the only separate superintendency in the United States for students with moderate and severe disabilities (children and youth with CI/MR fall into these categories), I examine the long-standing problematics of a segregated system and contemplate reasons for its continued existence. I begin by briefly discussing the historical relevance of people with CI and the construct of MR.

The (Un)Certainties of Classification

It is safe to say that there is great dissension among educators, scholars, doctors, and/or parents, as well as people with the classification of CI/MR, as to what a cognitive impairment means. For example, the influential philosopher John Rawls (2005) has endorsed a conception of personhood that excludes people labeled CI/MR. At a recent conference titled *Cognitive Disability: A Challenge to Moral Philosophy*, scholars grappled with Rawls's assertion by posing and answering contentious questions such as the following: What constitutes personhood? Who gets to decide? Is it a form of "social stillbirth" when the responsibilities of citizenship cannot be performed? (Silvers & Francis, 2008); What is lost in the denial of full citizenship? How does the concept of normal complicate notions of agency? (Bicklen, 2008); What happens when people are treated as non-persons? (Harris, 2008); Can we accord personhood without signs of intelligence? Should infants deemed profoundly cognitively disabled receive nurturance and live? (Singer, 2008); Are people labeled CI/MR owed justice? Are they equal subjects for justice? (Stark, 2008); Does moral personhood include a capacity for a sense of social justice? (Wong, 2008); Do "the gifted" impose restraints on the non-gifted in society (i.e., those deemed as having an "intelligence quotient" below 70)? Where do "we" place the threshold of incompetence? (Wilker, 2008); Who has the right to determine the moral status of another? What is a norm and why do we have them? (McMahon, 2008).

Space limitations do not permit a sufficiently complex discussion of the social construction of "mental retardation." However, it is worth noting that the label CI/MR is within the larger social construction of human intellect in general. Indeed, the establishment of intelligence tests was intricately connected with the scientific validation of racial hierarchies (Gould, 1996), and CI/MR has always been a label far more likely to be given to people of African descent (Hernstein & Murray, 1994: Stubblefield, 2008). The consensus that CI/MR "exists" because a person scores 70 or less on tests (lowered from 85 in 1969), although outdated to many, is still alive and functioning in the field of educational testing. Few school psychologists challenge the fallacy of IQ and continue to use it to justify decisions about labeling and placing students as CI/MR. The specter of IQ is so pervasive that even those who do not believe in these quantifications of ability use numbers to differentiate *within* the category of MR, that is, in subcategorizing into mild (70–55), moderate (55–40), and severe (below 40), representing 85%, 10%, and 3–5% respectively. Biklen calls attention to how unhelpful the term CI/MR is and how it serves to stigmatize people as bumbling and incompetent uneducable burdens (2008). He, instead, argues for an assumed competence, because if we do not then the "consequences are dire" in the form of self-fulfilling prophecies and perpetuating inequalities.

Hehir states, "Perhaps no group of disabled students has suffered more historically from negative societal attitudes than students with mental retardation" (2005, p. 3). For much of educational history, individuals with CI/MR did not attend schools but were likely to be institutionalized in places where they received no attention, nurturing, education, or stimulation but were housed naked en masse and intermittently hosed down. Over 100,000 individuals lived in institutions before Giraldo Rivera's infamous expose in 1972 of the state facility of Willowbrook in New York. In addition to being made to suffer emotional, physical, and sexual abuse of institutionalization, people with CI/MR have been subjected to medical experiments without consent, including being fed irradiated food at Harvard (Hehir, 2005, p. 6) and injected with the hepatitis virus (Harris, 2008). Children with CI/MR were often rejected from public schools altogether, and some states *required* local school districts to exclude students with CI/MR (Hehir & Gamm, 1999). As a result of their exclusion, a group of parents mobilized to advocate for legislation ensuring their children would be educated in public schools, resulting in the suit *Pennsylvania Association for Retarded Children v. Commonwealth of Pennsylvania* (1972). In a far-reaching decision, the court ordered that a free public education was to be provided for students with CI/MR. For many historians of disability and education, this ruling was the foundation on which the landmark PL.94-142, the Education for the Handicapped Act (EHA), rests, guaranteeing a public education for *all* students with disabilities.

Integral within the passage of this law was the concept of the Least Restrictive Environment (LRE) as the "appropriate" placement for students with disabilities, a placement that is selected from a continuum of possibilities. Unfortunately and paradoxically the determination of LRE for students on an individual basis helped create a segregated system of education that came to be known as "special education." Many disability studies scholars see LRE as a loophole that enabled educational institutions to segregate children with disabilities from the rest of the population (Linton, 1998; Russell, 1998). Noted disability studies scholar Harlan Hahn has remarked, "Particularly troubling to some is the negative phrasing of the concept of 'the least restrictive environment,' which was derived from court cases about incarceration rather than about discrimination based on race, ethnicity, or gender" (1997, p. 325). Environments more restrictive than general education tend to be in segregated facilities (such as wings or floors of larger buildings, in special schools, and in smaller spaces), which have fewer pupils per teacher. Many critics of special education have noticed both the academic and social shortcomings of these settings and claim that such marked segregation is unnecessary and not in the best interests of children with disabilities or, for that matter, all citizens (Brantlinger, 2006; Gallagher et al., 2004; Lipsky & Gardner, 1997; Semmel, Gottleib, & Robinson, 1979; Skrtic, 1991; Villa & Thousand, 1995). Hahn also questions the use of "appropriate" in legislative terminology, as it suggests conforming to a presumed standard of physical and mental competence before people are fully accepted in schools; he asserts, "Mastery of an unaccommodating and inhospitable environment is not an acceptable requirement for participation in a democratic society" (1997, p. 318).

LRE or MRE?

Generally speaking, CI/MR is a disability category that results in one of the most restrictive environment placements. The widespread overrepresentation of minority students in disability categories is also most likely with the label of CI/MR. As Parrish notes, "Only twelve states do not overrepresent blacks to an extensive degree in the MR disability category" (p. 15). Particularly troublesome is a continuation of the pervasive historical labeling of African Americans as CI/MR. Nationwide, it is more than 1.5 times more likely for a black child to be labeled MR than a white child. In some states the statistics are alarming: for example, in Connecticut it is 4.76 times more likely, Mississippi 4.31, South Carolina 4.3, North Carolina 4.08, and Nebraska 4.08 (Parrish, 2002). Fierros and Conroy (2002) found enormous variation in evaluation and placement of students in Connecticut, noticing that

> high minority districts of Bridgeport and New Haven had MR identification rates above 20 percent, while several dozen districts label fewer than 5 percent (Conroy, 1999). Interestingly, Hartford labels only 3.8 percent of their special education students as MR. These variations in districts serving high percentages of minority students raise questions about the labeling differences in Connecticut's larger urban school districts (pp. 63–64).

Based on their findings, the researchers determined that "black and Hispanic male students with MR in Connecticut were less likely to be educated in an inclusive setting than their white male counterparts" (p. 63).

Such restrictiveness has led some researchers to propose the notion of "double jeopardy," or punishing the most vulnerable students twice—"once for their MR label and once for the color of their skin" (p. 64). Others have noticed that increased access to the regular education classroom is primarily based on a student's race (Conroy, 1999; Harry & Klingner, 2005).

The overrepresentation of students of color categorized as CI/MR and in a restrictive environment reflects a trend in most urban centers. Fierros and Conroy (2002) found that 98.69% of students labeled CI/MR in Philadelphia spent more than 21% of their time outside of a regular classroom. Furthermore, although the overall percentage of black students enrolled is 64.55%, they constituted 71.27% of students labeled CI/MR. These figures reflect recent histories such as that of Chicago where, in the 1980s, the school system faced a class action suit to address "thousands of Chicago students (primarily African

Americans) [who] were misclassified in segregated classes for the mentally retarded" (Hehir, 2002, p. 246). Although pressure from the advocacy, research, and organizational-focused group Designs for Change resulted in 3,500 students formerly classified as Educable Mentally Handicapped (EMH) being either returned to regular classrooms or "re-diagnosed" as having some other disability, an additional 3,500 were not reclassified or able to change their placement.

The national level of restrictiveness for students labeled CI/MR with minority disproportionality indices reveals that 81.95% of students are restricted from general classrooms 20% of the time (Fierros & Conroy, 2002). Nationwide, New York State ranks 14th, with an above average record on restrictive placement for students labeled CI/MR at 87.69%. In terms of classification, when compared to European Americans, the likelihood of being labeled CI/MR translates to 1.8 times for American Indians, 0.66 times for Asian Americans, 1.72 times for Hispanic Americans, and 2.32 times for African Americans (Parrish, 2002, p. 23). As New York City contains approximately 42% of the population of the state, it is safe to say that given statistics on overrepresentation, it contains over half of the students labeled CI/MR. Fierros and Conroy cannot help but conclude that, nationwide, the indices of restrictive placement "suggest noncompliance with the IDEA requirement for placing students in the Least Restrictive Environment (LRE)" (2002, p. 51). This is no more blatantly clear than in the form of District 75, the citywide school subsystem for students with moderate and severe disabilities. Could it be that the complexities of providing special education services to approximately 115,000 students with disabilities in the country's largest metropolis led to a system-within-a-system in which those with moderate to severe disabilities were automatically placed? Before further discussing District 75, I believe it worthwhile to contemplate the context of urban schooling in general to illustrate the complexities involved.

Twelve Features of the Urban Cityscape

The realities of urban schools are captured well in the lifetime work of Jonathan Kozol, who speaks passionately, elegantly, and consistently about his outrage at the economic inequities within our nation and how they impact the lives of children (1987, 1991, 1995, 2000, 2005). His work captures complexities of the social and historical contexts of schools and the lives of children who attend them in New York City and other urban concentrations. Kozol's books accurately describe the historical tangle of economic extremes and racial segregation as a shameful paradox of the world's wealthiest country whose constitution claims that "all men are created equal" and yet we are born into a nation of "savage inequalities." His depictions of American life resonate with me today, as they did when I started my career in education, immediately becoming troubled by the widespread segregation of children according to disability *within* already existing social systems of segregation according to social class and race.

My twenty plus years as a professional educator in New York City have been spent in my own classroom and in the classrooms of others as well as in educating teachers working in city schools. I include this information because writing the following section makes me feel somewhat uneasy in case I portray "my city" as bleak, harsh, and unimaginable to some readers. And while they are the things I write about, it is also simultaneously filled with equal measures of resistance, hope, and beauty that may be similarly unimaginable to the same readers.

As Kincheloe writes, "In contemporary U.S. society, the use of the term *urban* itself has become in many quarters a signifier for poverty, nonwhite violence, narcotics, bad neighborhoods, and absence of family values, crumbling housing, and failing schools" (2007, p. 2). It is little wonder, in this context, that the term *urban education* conjures up images of a school filled with "at risk" students struggling to keep up academically, to be safe, and to "hold their own" in a highly competitive, overcrowded, and seemingly aggressive world. Kincheloe points out that one-third of all students in the United States attend 226 of the almost 16,000 school districts in the country. In other words, 31% of students go to 1.5% of school districts, all in large urban conurbations.

In terms of education research, comparatively little exists about urban education within special education and about how urban students experience schooling in relation to suburban counterparts (Artiles, 1997). Frequently, teachers in urban districts have either migrated from non-urban centers or are middle-class or both, bringing with them notions of middle class norms and expectations that they believe are "natural" and "right" (Delpit, 1995; McIntyre, 1997). Some mistakenly wish to "save" children from their environment. Thus, given the broader economic and racial arrangements of society, a "sociocultural chasm … has been produced between middle-class teacher-education students and the students they will teach if they do their student teaching or obtain positions in urban schools and poor communities" (Kincheloe, 2007, p. 3).

What is it, then, about urban education that makes it so unique? Kincheloe (2007) has identified twelve aspects of urban schools that help craft a realistic picture for those unfamiliar (or even those who are familiar) with the terrain. Using these twelve areas and given the historical lack of commitment toward integrating students labeled CI/MR, I contemplate each feature of urban education and ask in what ways might the complexities of an urban setting exacerbate the challenges of their inclusion into general education classes?

1. Urban schools operate in areas with high population density.

The concentration of people per square mile in urban settings often exceeds 1,000 individuals, most of whom spend the majority of their times in large, tall buildings. Home and school are usually in physical proximity, and schools often reflect the physical structures and social organizations of the neighborhoods in which they are located. Schools are frequently big, densely populated, and "manage" large numbers of individuals (some high schools have over 4,000 pupils).

For students with disabilities, such density poses challenges in terms of receiving an education that meets their individual needs when the demands of the class as a whole can be extremely taxing on teachers. Parents of students with disabilities sometimes are fearful that their children's needs will be eclipsed by those of the larger group, forcing their children to continually "get lost" in the curriculum or "fall through the cracks" and yet remain unnoticed by teachers.[2] Students with disabilities who are educated in segregated settings are frequently bussed to different neighborhoods and districts. Yet, despite the large numbers within highly dense urban populations, there exist networks of caring people who assiduously work so that students do become integral to school communities, regardless of integrated or segregated settings. Such teachers, paraprofessionals, principals, counselors, and service providers help students and parents negotiate the complex, rich, dynamic, and often fast-paced environment.

2. Urban schools are bigger, and urban school districts serve more students.

Directly related to population density and, therefore, overlapping with some of the issues listed above, larger enrollments of students also means that greater organization is needed in distributing services and resources to students with (and without) disabilities. Support services such as Response to Intervention (RtI) and Academic Intervention Services (AIS), along with "standard" services that include, among others, counseling, occupational therapy, and speech and language services, all must be managed by school administration.

Resources differ enormously between districts, and students in lower socioeconomic groups are more likely to receive services from new and/or inadequately educated providers. Obtaining requested services for students with disabilities may translate into a long and arduous process of navigating formidable bureaucracies. Once services are obtained on paper, receiving them may take time. For example, Hehir and colleagues' report noted that even student placements were delayed, with 92% of students citywide waiting over 60 days in September, the percentage declining to 54% by April of the same school year (2005, p. 65). Students with significant needs may attend school with these needs unmet (regardless of it being against the law). The sheer size of organizations such as the local Committee on Special Education can make parents feel alienated from the process of discussing the needs and placement of their children.

3. Urban schools function in areas marked by profound economic disparity.

In the sometimes unfettered growth of urban sprawl, city streets can vary enormously from block to block. High concentrations of poverty exist alongside other blocks representing a broad array of socioeconomic status (SES) groups, including working, middle, and upper classes, as well as the super rich. For some people, it is hard to believe that in the space of one block, all SES groups can be represented—especially if a neighborhood is "transitioning" either up or down the economic scale. Although a range of SES groups exist, urban communities contain a disproportionate number of poor people; four in five high-density poverty areas are in the 100 largest cities in the United States (Kincheloe, 2007). In some areas, it is commonplace that the number of students eligible for a free school lunch (an indicator of poverty) is 90% or above (ibid.). Within these areas there is a disproportionate number of minority students. It goes without saying that being raised in poverty significantly impacts an individual's future possibilities. Furthermore, the general infrastructure of poor neighborhoods is not strong, with comparatively fewer shops, banks, transportation options (try hailing a cab), and parks than in non-poor neighborhoods (Anyon, 1997). Conversely, in poorer neighborhoods, more liquor stores and places of worship are clearly evident, revealing ways in which large sections of the population respond to their economic circumstances.

Schools within different neighborhoods usually reflect the SES groups represented in those neighborhoods. In wealthier areas, schools are more likely to be newer and well equipped in terms of textbooks and technology. In poorer areas, schools are more likely to be in dilapidated buildings, possess fewer and older texts, and have outdated and/or less functional technology resources—and less access to them (Kincheloe, 2007). Because of the age of many buildings (some of them over 100 years old), physical access for wheelchair users is a problem. For example, when I worked in the office that oversaw all high schools in Manhattan, students who used wheelchairs could fully access only about 10% of the buildings, thus decreasing many of their options and choices. On another note, poor students do not access assistive technology as easily as their affluent counterparts, partly because their parents do not know they are eligible, are not informed of possibilities, and do not know how to make successful requests of the system. In keeping with parents, another example of the divide between "haves" and "have nots" can be seen in fund-raising for schools. While poorer schools may run raffles and social events to raise several hundreds of dollars, their affluent counterparts raise thousands. Ironically, it is the private schools in which many students with disabilities are educated at public expense that can raise millions of dollars (Cunningham, 2008).[3]

4. Urban Schools have a higher rate of ethnic, racial, and religious diversity.

As the hub of hope for many families who migrated, emigrated, or remain constantly in one place, urban areas are very diverse not only in economic terms but also in race, religion, ethnicity, social, linguistic, and religious backgrounds. As Kincheloe (2007) points out, two-thirds of urban students do not fall into America's norm of white and/or middle class.

Teachers, particularly those from more homogenized communities can experience culture shock at the amount of diversity in urban schools. Very few education programs teach disability as a form of diversity. Furthermore, few teach the complexities of multicultural understandings of disability, including how parents may perceive their own children and how that, in turn, influences where they think their child belongs. In addition, school situations can be complicated by perceptions of non-dominant groups that teachers from the dominant group may not care about the success of their students (Wilson, 2009).

5. Urban schools experience factionalized infighting on school boards over issues concerning resources and influence.
A characteristic of urban schools, also found in their suburban and rural counterparts, is the presence of competing priorities of people on school boards. However, interactions among school board members in urban settings have historically (and arguably) appeared contentious. In addition, there has been a shift away from policy-level concerns toward the urgency of day-to-day operations.

District positions on inclusive education vary enormously, and each district responds to both central initiatives and community requests. Parents have sometimes pushed to create inclusive opportunities for their children in schools where previously few or none have existed; conversely, parents have fought to keep segregated programs intact. The history of District 75 has reflected this push-and-pull factor (Belluck, 1996).

6. Urban schools are undermined by ineffective business operations.
When it comes to basic operations, many urban schools are not run as efficiently as their suburban or rural counterparts. Securing basic resources such as books, paper, and classroom computers may be difficult; sharing old, inadequate equipment such as photocopying machines and printers can be frustrating. Many teachers in the education classes I currently teach talk of "making do" with one or two outdated computers in their classrooms, although some do have access to computer labs and smart boards. That said, affluent schools operate daily with computer labs, rolling laptop carts, smart boards, an extensive selection of new texts, and well-stocked libraries. In addition, schools in high-poverty areas have significantly larger numbers of less-credentialed teachers and are more likely to have a higher number of positions staffed by long-term substitutes.

Ineffective business operations can impact all aspects of special education: obtaining basic or specialized equipment (e.g., leveled books or audio players), securing supplies (adaptive devices such as specialized scissors), hiring qualified professional staff (including teachers, paraprofessionals, and aides), securing services (e.g., occupational therapy, counseling), and ongoing transportation needed by students. In recent years, the chancellor of schools in New York City has made some inroads into streamlining the Kafkaesque levels of bureaucracy but much still remains to be done.

7. Urban schools are more likely to work with students who experience health problems.

Impoverished students, some of them homeless, do not primarily associate schools with academics but rather with being warm, fed, and having access to a bathroom. A large portion of the fifty million Americans who do not have health care (Moore, 2008) are children and youth who reside in urban areas. Incidence levels of lead poisoning, tuberculosis, asthma, and allergies are higher in urban areas. Like their rural and suburban counterparts, urban parents may or may not have the time or resources to take their children to doctors for preventative medicine or actual common ailments such as earache, toothache, or headaches.

Many disabilities—such as learning disabilities—can be attributable, in part, to environmental conditions, even though the federal definition actually precludes them. Students with high-incidence disabilities, including CI/MR, may also have conditions such as asthma, causing them to miss school when sick. In addition, older siblings are sometimes expected to stay home to help look after brothers and sisters who are sick and unable to attend school.

8. Urban schools experience higher student, teacher, and administrator mobility.

Like teachers preferring greater mobility, administrators are also inclined to move to schools with better conditions within the city or transfer out of the city to nearby suburbs such as those in Westchester and on Long Island. Higher salaries and better working conditions after "earning [their] wings" in urban conditions is commonplace. A high prevalence of exiting, transferring, or moving staff significantly impacts student achievement.

Suburban systems often woo the cream of urban teachers and administrators, including special educators, into middle-class and affluent communities. Professionals who recognize the pressures and

limitations of working in urban settings exchange positions to experience what they can achieve with far greater resources for students
with disabilities. Interestingly, teachers and administrators who do
make the leap describe an enormous shift in their own accountability
toward parents of students with disabilities who make far more demands including the crafting of appropriate IEP goals and how they
will be met.

9. Urban schools serve higher immigrant populations.
The economy and cultural vibrancy of cities—whether mega, big,
medium, or small—is fueled largely by immigrant populations who
have come to the United States for political, financial, and/or personal
reasons, following the American Dream. In addition, many urban
centers have high populations of African Americans who were invol-
untary immigrants for centuries and in many ways still do not experience equality in education, despite a major ruling in the form of
Brown v. Board of Education over fifty years ago (Blanchett, Brantlinger,
& Shealey, 2005; Ladson-Billings & Tate, 1995; Matsuda, Lawrence,
Delgado, & Crenshaw, 1993).

Parents of students with CI/MR often come from countries that
have limited if any inclusion. Parents may also be inclined to defer
decisions regarding their child to educational "authorities" (Harry &
Klingner, 2005; Kalyanpur & Harry, 2004), rather than make specific
requests such as a more or less restrictive environment.

10. Urban schools are characterized by linguistic diversity.
More urban students speak languages other than English in comparison to suburban/rural children. Over 200 languages and dialects are
spoken in New York City (Kincheloe, 2007). Oftentimes language has
primarily been perceived as a barrier/problem rather than an advantage, as can be seen in the former classification of Limited English
Proficient students (LEPs) used until the 1990s, now replaced by English Language Learners (ELLs). Effective teachers take time to learn
about the background and/or heritage of students, while being con-
scious of their own and how these may influence the process of teaching and learning (Banks, 2001; Nieto, 1995).

Official documents such as letters of notification of due process,
Individualized Education Programs (IEPs), and placement decisions
are legally required to be in the native language of parents. Although
the New York City Department of Education is able to provide stan-

dardized forms and letters (with space for insertions of dates, times, and signatures) in the major languages such as Spanish, Russian, Haitian Creole, and Mandarin, it cannot always do so for the majority of languages. Translators, although a legal requirement for meetings with parents, are not always available and/or provided. There is also a history of students whose primary language may or may not be English being erroneously placed in bilingual programs from which they rarely exit, a phenomenon akin to the "in-house" segregation of students with disabilities (Artiles, 1997; Figueroa & Newsome, 2006).

11. Urban schools experience unique transportation problems.

The majority of children in elementary and junior high school live in neighborhoods where they can either walk or take a short bus ride to school. The system encourages teenagers to compete for seats in specialized high schools around the city, such as those with a focus on math, science, visual or performing arts, and so on. For those who do not stay in local high schools, distances can be long, involving ninety minutes or more in each direction using several subways, buses, or even boats (Staten Island Ferry). The public transportation system is not always reliable: although buses are largely accessible, they can be slow; subways are virtually inaccessible and in rush hours may unexpectedly go express to ease congestion.

Students with moderate to severe disabilities are usually picked up and dropped off by school buses. Coordinating this sometimes means either long waits for the bus to come or long commutes on the bus to pick up or drop off other children, or both. The sheer numbers of students who require transportation poses logistical problems associated with safety and time management. Students with CI/MR who are placed in an out-of-neighborhood setting are more likely to begin school late and end early because of scheduling demands of the bus company. In New York City, transportation of students away from their neighborhood to segregated schools costs up to 14% of the special education budget (Hehir et al., 2005, p. 11).

12. Urban schools employ teachers who are less likely to live in the poor communities surrounding the schools than teachers in suburban and rural systems.

The teaching profession remains largely composed of white, middle-class females (Delpit, 1995, 2001), who usually do not live in neighborhoods of the children and families they serve. A general cultural dissonance exists in terms of class, social, economical, racial, and historical experiences. Teacher beliefs about the purpose of school impacts how students, in turn, come to perceive school. If teachers believe children live in a deficit subculture (that some students do not or cannot do x, y, and z like middle-class students), they sometimes cultivate a desire to "save" them. However, if parents feel this divide, then teacher-parent relationships may be poor, strained, or nonexistent. Of course, not all teachers see students from deficit-based lenses and instead employ multiple perspectives. Yet many teachers do so initially, they themselves having been subjected to a culture that is shaped by middle-class norms that include expected levels of academics, behavior, and social skills.

Parents who do not have cultural capital akin to teachers and other professionals in education are often stymied in their requests to have their children placed in inclusive settings (Valle & Aponte, 2002). Teachers can easily use their influence to suggest an evaluation or push for another placement outside of their own classroom.

The Complexities of Context

In crafting these dozen issues that must be considered when contemplating the context of urban education, Kincheloe (2007) calls attention to many of the complexities that are simultaneously in play. It is also a great irony that teacher education programs in urban areas do not always explicitly teach these issues. Instead, they often serve as "teacher factories," focused on rapidly certifying people who enter these professional conditions with a 50% likelihood of exiting within five years. Noting the functional focus of urban educator programs, Kincheloe writes,

> Too infrequently are teachers in university, student teaching, or in-service professional education encouraged to confront why they think as they do about themselves as teachers, especially in relation to the social, political, economic, and historical world around them. Mainstream teacher education provides little insight into the forces that shape identity and consciousness. Becoming educated as a critical practitioner necessitates personal transformation. (2007, p. 12)

Given the marginalization of people with disabilities in society, teachers-to-be usually arrive with a medicalized, deficit-based perception of disability. Segregated special education teacher programs tend to reinforce this. Few are inclusive in composition, and even those that claim to be integrated or inclusive actually prove otherwise (Young, 2008). Future educators are not sufficiently challenged in terms of inclusive practices. Educators who elect to teach students labeled CI/MR in New York City begin their work in a system that is still essentially segregated. In the next section, we look at the phenomenon of this self-contained district.

District 75: One of a Kind

"Is that legal?" asked an incredulous mother of a son with Down syndrome, when I described District 75, "To have a segregated system?" It is a reasonable response and reflects what many of you reading this book might think. For public school educators in New York City, District 75 is a familiar part of the education land-scape, responsible for 13% of all students labeled disabled. Having a separate district for students with disabilities has been a political hot potato for some time, yet, despite substantial criticism, several administration regimes, and citywide reorganizations, District 75 has so far been largely resilient to any substantial changes.

In some respects, District 75 is quite low key, seldom "on the radar." In many ways it is as if New York City has tacitly agreed to "let sleeping dogs lie." The official web-page(http://schools.nyc.gov/Of-fices/District75/default.htm), like that of most district organizations, presents a body of information that includes the following: a mission statement, a brief overview with statistics, a professional development calendar, common terms, funding formulas, and useful websites. In terms of informa-tion about inclusion, it has a grid comparing inclusive practices, collaborative team teaching, and mainstreaming; a definition of inclusion (from Utah!); FAQs for parents; several models of inclu-sive practices; a success story from a student's point of view, *A Day in the Life of Being in Inclusion;* and a parent's perspective: *Why I Want Inclusion for My Child: Inclusion Is Possible for All Students.* On the surface, it looks as if District 75 supports inclusion as a po-tentially valid option for all or most students.

Things that are "off the radar" do not elude the media entirely, and District 75 appears in local news in a variety of ways, many of them with familiar longtime themes of what I have grouped as taxation, inspiration, and segregation. In the first theme of taxa-tion, newspapers regularly highlight the fight of parents who seek to avoid District 75 services and have their children with disabili-ties placed in private schools at public expense. Schemo and Medina (2007) report, "As of 2005, more than 88,000 disabled students were educated in private settings at taxpayer expense, an increase of 34 percent over a decade" (p. 1). In New York City, over 7,000 pupils with moderate to severe disabilities fall into this category. Parents fear the conditions and services in public schools, whereas a lawyer from the New York City Department of Education claims, "When people realize they can't get something for free at the government's expense, you see more and more people take advantage" (p. 1). It is worth noting that many of the parents who are successful in gaining private services at public expense are middle class or affluent, and usually European American. Almost 80% of students in District 75 settings are African American or Latino (see Table 1).

The second theme relevant to District 75 found in newspapers is inspiration, a subject all too associated with the portrayal of people with disabilities. In the article *Learning All about Miracles*, with the subheading *An Untold Story of Love and Dedication That Will Touch the Heart of Every New Yorker* (Evans, 2005), stories are told of hospital-based teachers ("invisible angels") who give bedside instruction to severely ill and dying children. Another article, *Exhibit A for Mainstreaming: A Boy with Brain Damage, Happy in a Regular School* (Medina, 2003), tells the tale of Malcolm, whose mother pointedly fought for him not to be segregated in a District 75 school. In a third example, a principal of a District 75 school is one of seven publiclycelebrated city workers in the *New York Times'* "Up from Obscurity" section (Stamler, 2000). He is feted for developing innovative programs that allow preschoolers with disabilities to go to mainstream schools. Although these stories are worth sharing, they all convey the heavy-handed but often unseen *rhetorics* of disability portrayal: self-sacrificing miracle workers steeped in sentimentality, the exhibition of a "damaged" individual held up to a medicalized gaze of non-disabled people, and the lauding of an undoubtedly honorable principal who is cast as the exception to the rule for doing what all principals should do.

		American Indian	Asian American	Hispanic American	African American	European American	
Manhattan	Male	19	82	1,096	912	145	2,254
	Female	8	33	472	368	72	953
	All	27	115	1,568	1,280	217	3,207
Bronx	Male	35	78	2,047	1,429	131	3,720
	Female	12	32	729	504	59	1,336
	All	47	110	2,776	1,933	190	5,056
Brooklyn	Male	38	148	1,137	2,809	667	4,799
	Female	17	85	431	986	256	1,775
	All	55	233	1,568	3,795	923	6,574
Queens	Male	33	438	1,031	1,734	756	3,992
	Female	6	198	446	571	313	1,534
	All	39	636	1,477	2,305	1,069	5,526
Staten Island	Male	5	43	212	310	593	1,163
	Female	1	17	80	99	198	395
	All	174	1,154	7,681	9,722	3,190	21,921

Table 1 District 75 Citywide Population Disaggregated by Race
Source: http://schools.nyc.gov/AboutUs/DOEData/Stats/Register/JFormbyDistricts/default.htm, retrieved October 3, 2008.

The third theme associated with District 75 is a concern about segregation. This can surface in quirky ways, such as *Disabled Return to Old School but Segregation Is Charged* (Barnes, 1999). In this particular instance, under pressure from the New York–based Hispanic community organization United We Stand, a public elementary school agreed to move students with moderate and severe disabilities back into their original school. However, when this occurred, they objected to the self-imposed segregation of disabled Hasidic children in another program within the building (... perhaps an example of "only in New York"). In *State's Special Ed Pupils Too Segregated—Report,* Gendar (2003) describes how New York State has been charged with supporting too many segregated programs, with students having twice the likelihood of being isolated in segregated schools when compared to other states (Gendar, 2003). In addition, Gandar points out that "special education students made up 8% of the student population ... but accounted for 23% of the public school budget" (p. 1). In New York City suburbs, restrictive placements have been successfully challenged in court; take, for instance, the case in Central Islip where 1,000 students receiving special education services were paid $725,000 and were charged to "ensure that over the next five years, fewer students would be designated as needing special education and fewer would be educated outside regular schools or classrooms"—this in a district where 22% of students had been placed in special education (Kelley, 2000).

Segregation can reach far beyond classroom walls and school buildings. For example, the article *School Achievement Reports Often Exclude the Disabled* (Schemo, 2004) calls attention to nationwide exclusion of students in official school progress reports. Schemo cites District 75 as giving "only fragments of the information the federal law requires for accountability, reporting schools 'in good standing' despite dismal results" (p. 10). Many states find ways to circumvent reporting specific information from special schools and do not issue report cards that are required of non-special schools. Schemo explains, "Like California, states generally contend that these [segregated settings for students with moderate and severe disabilities] are not schools, but programs, and thus are exempt from the federal law, an argument largely accepted by officials in Washington" (ibid.). Alarmingly, in District 75 it has been noted that "many of the district's schools exclude more than half their students from state standardized tests and do not report how they do on the special achievement tests. Nor do they report how many graduate or drop out" (ibid.). The State Education Department has requested that District 75 improve its public reporting. Resistance to public disclosure has been noted by many lawyers, who believe that the reticence to report school results "is too pervasive to be accidental ... and the information being withheld was crucial for parents and advocates" (ibid.). In another example of distancing parents of students with disabilities, the city claims that it wants to hear from all parents and teachers about the quality of schools—except this does not include segregated schools for students with disabilities (Einhorn, 2007).

Issues reported in the media do not go unnoticed by the State Education Department, administrators of New York City Department of Education, and members of the general public. With 22,000 students in 350 schools and settings, District 75 is an anomaly: a special education system within a special education system. As such, its "twice removed" status appears to have helped it weather the storms of the last few decades that have urged a more inclusive approach for students with disabilities. However, the extensive independent report of the state of special education in New York City (Hehir et al., 2005) forced District 75 into the limelight. In the next section, I highlight findings from that report.

Critical Feedback from the Independent Report

Background on the Big Apple

In New York City, students with disabilities constitute 11.1% (137,930) of a school population that exceeds 1.1 million children and youth. Within this number, 4.6% (6,341) are categorized as CI/MR compared to 14.11% (7,765) in Chicago and 5.71% (4,380) in Los Angeles (Hehir et al., 2005). The report claims that special education is still overwhelmingly perceived as a place rather than a service. The placement of students with CI/MR verifies this notion, with only one in twenty students (5.03%) placed in general education classes for 80% or more of their school day. Another 1.03% are placed out of general education classes for 21–60% of their school day, but 61.91% are placed in segregated settings for more than 60% of their time in school. Furthermore, 27.69% are placed in special public day schools, 3.63% in private day schools, 0.47% in private residential facilities, and 0.24% in home or hospital instruction. District 75 contains 13% of students with disabilities in New York City, including more than 50%

labeled CI/MR.

Enrollment in high schools for students with disabilities ranges from 0% to 38.3% (p. 67), indicating restricted access to some institutions and overpopulation of others. The number of students with disabilities who drop out of school is high, regardless of the source; the report gives 45% as the drop-out rate, compared to 32% in the state and 25% in the nation. However, parental groups such as Advocates for Children state the rate as much higher; only 11.84% of students with disabilities graduate with a non-IEP diploma (Losen, 2005).

Maintaining Levels of Segregation

The report found that segregation throughout city schools, for the most part, was still largely unquestioned, an everyday practice of doing business:

> The historic perception in NYC of special education as a place rather than a service perpetuates the need for special education classrooms. Specifically, large numbers of students with disabilities are being educated in special education classes and programs. In particular, we found that District 75, which provides placements mainly for students with emotional disturbances (ED) and students with significant cognitive disabilities, operates separately for the most part from the rest of the Department in a manner that may be inconsistent with IDEA's LRE requirements. At the same time, we also found that several models operating within NYC public schools, including one District 75 model, support the move towards more inclusive special educations services: however, these models are both underutilized and perceived as separate "placements." (p. 24)

In pointing out *one* example of District 75, Hehir and colleagues validate the efforts of a few people in the face of such resistance, finding "the needle in the haystack" of the inclusive practices existing for students with moderate and severe disabilities. Compared to other large cities, the report adds, New York City has a greater percentage of students with disabilities who are educated in separate special education classes. For example, 40.61% of students with disabilities in NYC are in general education buildings but spend more than 60% of their time outside of the general education class in segregated facilities, compared to 29.06% in Chicago, 33.38% in Los Angeles, 27.01% in New York State, and 18.53% in the nation. In addition, 9.4% of students with disabilities are educated outside of the general school in a public/private separate facility or in a residential/hospital setting, a larger percentage than Chicago at 6.46%, Los Angeles at 8.42%, New York State at 7.2%, and the national average of 3.9% (p. 70). Sadly, and given historical trends, perhaps unsurprisingly, African American students were less likely to be in inclusive settings (44%) than European Americans (64%).

Organizational and school practices do not encourage or support much more than nominal gestures of inclusion. The report states, "our analysis of students' IEPs found no mention of either 'Team Teaching' or 'Inclusionary'" (p. 66). This is because the Department of Education prohibits the phrase "Inclusive Setting" on Individual Educational Programs. Many of the placements are not necessarily planned with the parents' desire in mind but are rather determined by space available in an overcrowded system. Placement was found to be driven by vacant "seats" in sites with a "rigidly defined service delivery model" (p. 14). Furthermore, the report found that virtually no children or youth were served for 20–60% of their school day in special education settings, indicating that the continuum of services is not linear in shape but rather resembles a bar-bell with two main options weighing each end—placement in segregated special classes with a modicum of inclusion *or* in general education with a modicum of special education support services. This skewed offering is partly responsible for the continuing "practice of moving children with high incidence disabilities out of their school to receive special education services" (p. 15). Conversely, moving a student out of a District 75 placement to a less restrictive environment is, therefore, "especially problematic and uncommon" (p. 73). Altogether, there is very little evidence of movement, with just 4% of students with disabilities transferring from of District 75 settings. For example, in 2003, only 25 out of 2,775 (0.54%) students labeled CI/MR moved to a non-District 75 setting (0.54%).

Separate Operations

In much of their study of special education in New York City, Hehir and colleagues point out that orchestrators of recent reorganizations had not sufficiently challenged District 75's existence as a separate entity, allowing it to continue as a citywide district for children with moderate and severe disabilities. Currently consisting of 56 school organizations and 360 satellites, District 75 assigns a principal to each organization. However, the physical settings of the space allotted to District 75 are in separate edifices, wings of buildings, top floors, or basements (as well as in hospitals and homes). The pervasive segregation in classes and schools is mirrored within organizational structures, leading Hehir and colleagues to conclude,

We found that District 75 for the most part operates separately from the Central Office and the other Regions. We feel that the current structure leads to abdication of responsibility at the school level for students with ED and significant cognitive/physical disabilities. (p. 71)

Although students enrolled in District 75 inclusion classes receive their education in a general education classroom within a community school, District 75 still has primary responsibility for them (i.e., they remain on their register), and students cannot receive services from non-District 75 service providers at the school. Thus, as one principal explains, "The child is still on our register, so ultimately whatever the IEP requires is a District 75 requirement" (p. 75). Principals of general education schools are, therefore, absolved from accountability for children with moderate to severe disabilities.

Because the District 75 programs placed in community schools are still run as separate entities, the disconnected services and untrained teachers that Hehir and colleagues observed can easily remain unnoticed and, therefore, unaddressed. Regional operations and initiatives oftentimes exclude District 75 staff members, leaving "a strong disconnect" (p. 34) in professional areas as diverse as staff development and attending impartial hearings. Poor or nonexistent relationships between organizations are sometimes exacerbated by new and/or uninformed principals without the requisite background knowledge of students with disabilities. These conditions prove to be a very frustrating experience for many parents, who feel uninformed and shuffled around (p. 73).

Attitudes

Attitudes of administrators, teachers, and paraprofessionals greatly contribute to the success or failure of students in inclusive settings. The report noted that many staff members had an unquestioned acceptance of disability hierarchy. For example, one educator stated of students, "[If] they're mentally retarded, they're only in self-contained [classrooms]," and one high-ranking regional administrator explained that the inclusion of the few students with CI/MR is a result of "pushback from parents" (p. 70).

The prevalence of segregated classes is, in some part, due to general educators' belief that special educators possess high levels of specialized knowledge. One administrator said children and youth who attend District 75 programs "have a greater need for either a small class, more intense staffing ratio, or specific interventions that are related to other disabilities—the more physically challenged, the more cognitively challenged who really cannot participate in general education" (p. 72) and, to bolster this argument, adds that non-special educators feel "ill-equipped" (ibid.). It is with great irony that the report points out that teachers working in District 75 appeared unaware of differentiated instruction (p. 80), given that IEPs require individualized instruction.

Recommendations Made

Although recommendations contained in the report were plentiful, only a few will be highlighted here because of space limitations. One of the most powerful aspects of the report is Hehir and colleagues' critique of the medical model of disability (a first for me to read within a major special education document pertaining to policy) and how problematic it is that the Department of Education operations appear firmly based upon this limiting concept. They explain,

> Under this model, children with disabilities are assumed to have a "condition" that is intrinsic to the child and that will respond to "treatments" ... this model is associated with categorical placement systems in which children with similar disability types are removed from regular classes to have specialized services by category of disability. (p.12)

They also stress how damaging this can be, stating that "the provision of the medical model may give the inappropriate impression that the disability is being addressed when in some cases these practices may actually exacerbate the impact of the disability" (p. 14). Segregated settings do not appear to best serve the overwhelming majority of students within them, leaving Hehir and colleagues to conclude, "This practice of moving large numbers of students with disabilities out of their home schools to receive special education services is not only educationally questionable but is costly and unnecessary" (p. 13).

The report notes that 90% of children with disabilities in New York City have one or more of the following five conditions: learning disabilities, speech and language impairments, mild to moderate "emotional disturbance," mild to moderate CI/MR, and attention deficit disorder/attention deficit hyperactivity disorder (classified as health impairments). Because these are high-incidence disabilities, in these cases "the LRE would most often be in the general education classroom" (p. 95). Hehir and colleagues urge schools to develop more options through small but promising inclusive practices already in existence, such as collaborative team teaching, coordinated use of paraprofessionals, utilization of "inclusion coaches," and more fluid arrangements. If the Department of Education is genuine about wanting to shift from seeing special education as a service, not a place, then more leadership is needed by central operations because researchers "found that insufficient support is being provided to the schools to enable them [schools] to make the philosophical, organizational, and programmatic changes necessary to realize this goal" (p. 69).

Ultimately, the 2005 report recommended that "District 75, over the next five years, should transition from a separate region to become a support system for low incidence disabilities, with the goal of serving all students with low incidence disabilities on a Regional level" (p. 97). This solution has been proposed before, dividing parents of students served by District 75 who see it either as a restrictive institution with outdated practices or as a safe haven for society's most vulnerable children.

Conclusion

In the inclusion of students labeled CI/MR, New York State ranks 28th out of 50 states, plus Washington DC and Puerto Rico. It reflects miniscule but sustained integration. The percentage of students with CI/MR included more than 79% of the time has grown from 6.86% in 1992–1993 to 7.34% in 1997–1998, to 8.35% in 2002–2003 (Smith, 2007). It is fair to say that New York City reflects this "growth" that reveals an overall increase of 1.5% in a decade, confirming Smith's observation that a snail's pace is simply not acceptable if substantial change is to occur within our lifetime.

In recalling one of his earliest graduate-level special education courses, Hehir realized, "The conditions evident in the state schools were not the result of mental retardation alone but, rather, the way society responded to mental retardation" (2002, p. 2). Although children with CI/MR have been removed from lifelong institutionalization and do attend public schools, the type of school, quality of education, and accepted level of marginalization needs to be challenged. Perhaps best described as "cautiously optimistic," Hehir believes progress made "through innovation within a values-based context of optimism propelled by strong law based on constitutional principles of equal rights that has occurred for children and adults with mental retardation is the result of the conversation of three forces" (p. 8). The three forces he alludes to are attitudes, care, and new approaches, with particular emphasis on the first, because "attitudes toward disability have a major impact on education these children receive" (p. 8). Without these components, there may very well exist the continuation of widespread resistance to, and large-scale poor, inadequate, and even destructive attempts at, inclusive practices for students labeled CI/MR. One special educator has dishearteningly referred to his professional experience of witnessing "the debauchery of the implementation of inclusive practices in the New York City public school system" (Valentino, 2007, p. 132).

Lest this picture become too pessimistic, I end by asking what can be done about the state of inclusive education in New York City, particularly for students with CI/MR. I agree with Kincheloe's (2007) belief that first an acknowledgment of the problems is needed to keep hope alive, build resilience, encourage possibilities, and move toward change. He advocates that

> we focus attention on the sociocultural context of each school, examine student backgrounds, the positions of empowerment and disempowerment from which they operate, the knowledge they bring to the classroom, they language that they speak, and the ways in which all of these dynamics shape learning and teaching. (p. 4)

In focusing on who children and youth are and where they come from, and working with their families, deficit-driven perceptions learned within the traditional special education paradigm of thinking can shift to the assumed competence. This focus also recognizes the reality of high-stakes testing but can also see the unethical aspects of it, such as how a lock-step standardized curriculum creates school failures that can have profound influence on the life-long identities of individuals (Brantlinger, 2004; Varenne & McDermott, 1998). Without the fear of appearing naive, Hehir has advocated that "it is important to instill a love of learning in all children, including those with disabilities," because "assuming that the entire education of any child with a disability be 'functional' is unduly limiting, deadly boring, and at its root ableist" (p. 73).

Smith (2007) has pointed out the need for inclusive education to be cast as best practice, including a complex interrelationship among legal, moral, procedural, and philosophical understandings. Emphasizing the LRE within law has been a major barrier to inclusion (Connor & Ferri, 2007), suggesting that students with disabilities would be better served by having inclusion defined within IDEIA. Until then, teachers working in urban areas, including those who are charged with implementing inclusive practices, will work at a challenging task within a difficult situation. As Kincheloe (2007) states,

> Urban teachers have no choice—they must work with what they have. Until more well-to-do citizens assume their civic responsibility to help the fiscal condition of inner cities, urban teachers in poor schools will have to operate in a hostile social environment. (p. 15)

Finally, Hehir and colleagues' report on special education *has* made an impact. A "more porous" relationship between the Department of Education and District 75 is currently being cultivated (Gonen, 2008). And although there is no immediate plan to abolish District 75 altogether, there is movement toward dissolving some of its existing boundaries. The deputy school chancellor now emphasizes the message that "all principals are expected to support all students with disabilities" (ibid.). Meanwhile, newspaper articles sporting alarmist headlines (*District Shakeup May Fail Special Ed Kids*) describe the plan to decrease automatic placements of students with moderate and severe disabilities into District 75 schools (Gonen, 2008). As expected, the articles juxtapose parents of children with disabilities who fear the inadequacy of traditional schools with those who claim that their children are treated as second-class citizens within segregated settings.

To be continued …

Notes

1   The categories of "mild," "moderate," and "severe" are highly subjective subcategories of disability that often oversimplify the actual, lived, reality of people with disabilities as they experience different contexts. It is not my intention to reify these concepts, but these terms are integral to understanding ways in which inclusive practices (or lack of) have been structured in New York City.

2   A former graduate student of mine works in a self-contained class in a special school with students labeled CI/MR, LD, ED, and autism. She states, "Almost 100% of the parents I have met believe this to be the best environment for their children." Parents believe it is a safer environment, as there have been no problems with "… weapons and the smaller population allows for a much stricter and personalized behavior regulation in the school" (Mayer, personal communication, 2008).

3   I occasionally work with schools which serve children of parents with political connections and "clout," where one-night fundraisers raise millions of dollars.

References

Anyon, J. (1997). *Ghetto schooling: A political economy of urban educational reform.* New York: Teachers College Press.

Artiles, A. (1997). Learning disabilities empirical research on ethnic minority students: An analysis of 22 years of studies published in selected refereed journals. *Learning Disabilities Research and Practice, 12*(2), 82–91.

Banks, J. (2001). Citizenship education and diversity: Implications for teacher education. *Journal of Teacher Education, 52*(1), 5–16.

Barnes, J. (1999, March 29). Disabled return to old school but segregation is charged. *New York Times*, p. 8.

Belluck, P. (1996, Nov. 6). A plan to revamp special education. *New York Times*, p. A1.

Biklen, D. (2008, September). *Presuming competence: Why 'mental retardation' is an unhelpful idea.* Paper presented at the conference in Cognitive Disability: A Challenge to Moral Philosophy. New York.

Blanchett, W., Brantlinger, E., & Shealey, M. (2005). Brown 50 Years Later—Exclusion, Segregation, and Inclusion: Guest Editors' Introduction. *Remedial and Special Education, 26*(2), 66–69.

Brantlinger, E. (2004). Confounding the needs and confronting the norms: An extension of Reid and Valle's essay. *Journal of Learning Disabilities, 37*(6), 490–499.

——— (Ed.). (2006). *Who benefits from special education? Remediating (fixing) other people's children.* Mahwah, NJ: Lawrence Erlbaum.

Connor, D., & Ferri, B. (2007). The conflict within: Resistance to inclusion and other paradoxes within special education. *Disability & Society, 22*(1), 63–77.

Conroy, J.(1999). *Connecticut's special education labeling and displacement practices: Analysis of the ISSIS data base. Unpublished report, Center for Outcome Analysis,* Rosemont, PA.

Cunningham, B. (2008). Personal communication.

Delpit, L. (1995). *Other people's children: Cultural conflict in the classroom.* New York: New Press.

——— (2001). "Skin-Deep" Learning. In P. Rodis, S. Garrod & M. L. Boscardin (Eds.), *Learning Disabilities & Life Stories* (pp. 157–164). Needham Heights, MA: Allyn & Bacon.

Education of All Handicapped Children Act (1975). P.L. 94–142.

Einhorn, E. (2007, May 15). Disabled in survey snub. *Daily News* (New York), p. 14.

Evans, H. (2005, April 10). Learning all about miracles: An untold story of love and dedication that will touch the heart of every New Yorker. *The Daily News* (New York), p. 28.

Fierros, E., & Conroy, J. (2002). Double jeopardy: An exploration of restrictiveness and race in special education. In D. J. Losen & G. Orfield (Eds.), *Racial Inequity in Special Education.* Cambridge, MA: Harvard Education Press.

Figueroa, R., & Newsome, P. (2006). The diagnosis of LD in English learners: Is it nondiscriminatory? *Journal of Learning Disabilities, 39*(3), 206–214.

Gallagher, D., Heshusius, L., Iano, R., & Skrtic, T. (2004). *Challenging orthodoxy in special education: Dissenting voices.* Denver, CO: Love.

Gendar, A. (2003, March 19). State's special ed. pupils too segregated—report. *Daily News* (New York), p. 1.

Gonen, Y. (2008). District shake up may fail special-ed kids. *New York Post.* Retrieved on September 15 from http://www.nypost.com/seven/08032008/news/retgional news/district_shakeup_may_fail_specialed_kid122818.htm

Gould, S. (1996). *The mismeasure of man*. New York: W. W. Norton and Company.

Hahn, H. (1997). New trends in disability studies: Implications for educational policy. In D. K. Lipsky & A. Gardner (Eds.), *Inclusion and school reform: Transforming America's classrooms*. (pp. 315–328). Baltimore, MD: Paul Brookes.

Harris, J. (2008, September). *A developmental perspective on the emergence of moral personhood*. Paper presented at the conference in Cognitive Disability: A Challenge to Moral Philosophy, New York.

Harry, B., & Klingner, J. (2005). *Why are so many minority students in special education? Understanding Race & Disability in Schools*. New York: Teachers College Press.

Hehir, T. (2002). IDEA and disproportionality: Federal enforcement, effective advocacy, and strategies for change. In D. J. Losen & G. Orfield (Eds.), *Racial inequity in special education* (pp. 219–238). Cambridge, MA: Harvard Education Press.

——— (2005). *New directions in special education: Eliminating ableism in policy and practice*. Cambridge, MA: Harvard Education Press.

Hehir, T., & Gamm, S. (1999). Special education: From legislation to collaboration. In J. Heubert (Ed.), *Law and school reform* (pp. 205–227). New Haven, CT: Yale University Press.

Hehir, T., Figueroa, R., Gamm, S., Katzman, L., Gruner, A., Karger, J., & Hernandez, J. (2005). *Comprehension management review and evaluation of special education submitted to the New York City Department of Education*. Cambridge, MA: Harvard School of Education.

Hernstein, R., & Murray, C. (1994). *The bell curve: Intelligence and class structure in American life*. New York: Simon & Schuster.

Kalyanpur, M., & Harry, B. (2004). Impact of the social construction of LD on culturally diverse families: A response to Reid and Valle. *Journal of Learning Disabilities*, 37(6), 530–533.

Kelley, T. (2000, December 1). Metro briefing. *New York Times*, p. 8.

Kincheloe, J. (2007). Why a book on urban education? In S. Steinberg & J. Kincheloe (Eds.), *19 urban questions: Teaching in the city* (pp. 1–27). New York: Peter Lang.

Kozol, J. (1987). *Rachel and her children: Homeless families in America*. New York: Crown.

——— (1991). *Savage inequalities: Children in America's schools*. New York: Crown Publishers.

——— (1995). *Amazing Grace: The lives of children and the conscience of a nation*. New York: Harper Perennial.

——— (2000). *Ordinary resurrections: Children in the years of hope*. New York: Crown.

——— (2005). *The shame of the nation: The restoration of apartheid schooling in America*. New York: Crown.

Ladson-Billings, G., & Tate, W. (1995). Toward a critical race theory of education. *Teachers College Record*, 97(1), 47–68.

Linton, S. (1998). *Claiming disability*. New York University: New York University Press.

Lipsky, D., & Gardner, A. (1997). *Inclusion and school reform: Transforming America's classrooms*. Baltimore, MD: Paul H. Brookes.

Losen, D. (2005, March 20). Behind the group out rate. *Gotham Gazette*, retrieved October 3 from http://www.gothamgazette.com/article/fea/20060320/202/

1792

Matsuda, M., Lawrence, C., Delgado, R., & Crenshaw, K. (1993). *Critical race theory, assaultative speech, and the first amendment.* Boulder, CO: Westview Press.

McIntyre, A. (1997). Constructing the image of a white teacher. *Teachers College Record, 98*(4), 653–681.

McMahon, J. (2008, September). *Cognitive disability, cognitive enhancement and moral status.* Paper presented at the conference in Cognitive Disability: A Challenge to Moral Philosophy, New York.

Medina, J. (2003, February 12). Exhibit A for mainstreaming: A boy with brain damage, happy in a regular school. *New York Times,* p. B1.

Moore, M. (Producer/Director) (2008). *Sicko* [Motion picture]. United States. Dog Eat Dog Pictures.

Nieto, S. (1995). From brown heroes and holidays to assimilationist agendas: reconsidering the critiques of multicultural education. In C. Sleeter, (Ed.), *Multicultural education, critical pedagogy, and the politics of difference* (pp. 191–220). Albany, NY: SUNY Press.

Parrish, T. (2002). Racial disparities in the identification, funding, and provision of special education. In D. J. Losen & G. Orfield (Eds.), *Racial inequality in special education* (pp. 15–37). Cambridge, MA: Harvard Education Press.

Pennsylvania Association for Retarded Children v. Commonwealth of Pennsylvania, 343 F. Supp.279 (E.D. Pa., 1972).

Rawls, J. (2005). *A theory of justice.* Boston, MA: Harvard University Press.

Russell, M. (1998). *Beyond ramps: Disability at the end of the social contract.* Monroe, ME: Common Courage.

Schemo, D. (2004, October 7). School achievement reports often exclude the disabled. *The New York Times,* p. A1.

Schemo, D., & Medina, J. (2007, October 27). Disabilities fight grows as taxes pay for tuition. *The New York Times,* p. A1.

Semmel, M., Gottleib, J., & Robinson, N. (1979). Mainstreaming: Perspectives on educating handicapped children in the public schools. In D. C. Berliner (Ed.), *Review of Research in Education* (Vol. 7, pp. 223–279). Washington, DC: American Education Research Education.

Silvers, A., & Francis, L. (2008, September). *Rethinking 'conceptions of the good' in light of intellectual disabilities.* Paper presented at the conference in Cognitive Disability: A Challenge to Moral Philosophy, New York.

Singer, P. (2008, September). *Speciesim and moral status.* Paper presented at the conference in Cognitive Disability: A Challenge to Moral Philosophy, New York.

Skrtic, T. (1991). *Behind special education: A critical analysis of professional culture and school organization.* Denver, CO: Love.

Smith, P. (2007). Have we made any progress? Including students with intellectual disabilities in regular education classrooms. *Intellectual and Developmental Disabilities, 45*(5), 297-309.

Stamler, B. (2000, March 12). New Yorkers & co.: Up from obscurity. *New York Times,* p. 4.

Stark, C. (2008, September). *Reasons, persons, and capabilities.* Paper presented at the conference in Cognitive Disability: A Challenge to Moral Philosophy, New York.

Stiker, H. (1999). *A history of disability.* Ann Arbor, MI: Love Publishing House.

Stubblefield, A. (2008, September). *The entanglement of race and cognitive disability.* Paper presented at the conference in Cognitive Disability: A Challenge to Moral Philosophy,

Valentino, J. (2007). How can we transgress the field of disabilities in urban education? In S. R. Steinberg & J. L. Kincheloe (Eds.), *19 urban questions: Teaching in the city* (pp. 209–218). New York: Peter Lang.

Valle, J., & Aponte, E. (2002). IDEA and collaboration: A Bakhtinian perspective on parent and professional discourse. *Journal of Learning Disabilities, 35*(5), 469-479.

Varenne, H., & McDermott, R. (1998). *Successful failure.* Boulder, CO: Westview Press.

Villa, R., & Thousand, J. (1995). *Creating an inclusive school.* Alexandria, VA: Council for Supervision and Curriculum Development.

Wilker, D. (2008, September). *Paternalism and the moderately intellectually disabled.* Paper presented at the conference in Cognitive Disability: A Challenge to Moral Philosophy, New York.

Will, M. (1986). Educating children with learning problems: A shared responsibility. *Exceptional Children, 52,* 411–415.

Wilson, E. (2009). *Alternatively certified teacher and technology agency/structure dialectic integration of technology mediated instructions to improve literacy by creating comic books in a special education learning community* [dissertation]. New York, Graduate Center of the City University of New York.

Wong, S. (2008, September). *Duties of justice to citizens with cognitive disabilities.* Paper presented at the conference in Cognitive Disability: A Challenge to Moral Philosophy, New York.

Young, K. (2008). Physical and social organization of space in a combined credential program: Implications for inclusion. *Journal of Inclusive Education, 12*(5-6), 477-495.

CHAPTER 9

The Story(s) of the States

What Does It All Mean?

The authors of the preceding five chapters have looked at the place of students with intellectual disabilities in general education classrooms across five very different locations within the United States: Alabama, California, Illinois, Michigan, and New York City. They have told varying stories about inclusion and exclusion, in terms of how they chose to enter the conversation, how they understand the meaning of intellectual disabilities, what frameworks they used to explore meaning and importance, and who they looked to for answers to questions that they posed.

In this chapter, I will explore the meanings of what has gone on in individual places around the country in terms of including students with intellectual and developmental disabilities in general education classrooms. What are the common themes? Why has one state been successful where another has seen limited or declining numbers? What works and what doesn't? I will work to uncover the meaning of these stories—at research, policy, and practice levels.

Looking at the Numbers

First, let's revisit the rankings of the particular states that authors in this text have explored for the inclusion of students with intellectual disabilities in general education classrooms and compare these to others around the country. In the table, I've chosen to include New York State in order to compare apples to apples. But it should be pointed out that there is some difference between the percentages of students with intellectual disabilities who are fully included in the *state* of New York and in the *city* of New York. In 2003–2004, while New York State had 7.81% of students with intellectual disabilities included in general education classrooms for 79% of the time or more, Connor (citing Hehir et al., 2005) notes that in New York City 5.03% of students with intellectual disabilities were included in general education classrooms for 80% or more of the time. Were New York City to be ranked alongside states, it would be ranked 45th for the inclusion of students with intellectual disabilities in general education classrooms.

Table 1 Percentage of Students with Intellectual Disabilities (Mental Retardation) Included in Regular Education Classrooms More Than 79% of the Time in Select States

Rank Order, 2003–2004	State	Percentage, 2003–2004
14.	Alabama	4.82
35.	California	7.88
36.	New York (state	7.81
43.	Michigan	5.41
47.	Illinois	4.05
	U.S. Total	11.66

Note. Data for "Percentage, 2003–2004", is from the 27th *annual report to Congress on the implementation of the Individuals with Disabilities Education Act, Part 2,* by the Office of Special Education and Rehabilitative Services, Table 2–2c, p. 186, and reflects the percentage of students with intellectual disabilities (mental retardation) who were outside of regular classes less than 21% of the time in the fall of 2003. U.S. totals noted in the table reflect data for the 50 states, Washington DC, and Bureau of Indian Affairs schools. Ranking of the states is by the author.

That said, looking at the places in which inclusion is explored, there is one that is ranked in the top third of states; the balance of the five are in the bottom third of all states. Four are below the national average. Most of the places explored in this book, then, are not doing particularly well in the full inclusion of students with intellectual disabilities, when compared to other places around the United States.

Issues of Definition and Labeling

The various authors in this text have clearly struggled with how people with so-called intellectual and developmental disabilities have been and continue to be labeled and defined by our society. Owen and Gabel (this volume) point out that the current label used by the

Illinois Department of Education is that of cognitive disability, although the definition remains the same as when the label was mental retardation—the words have changed, but not the meaning. They point out the ways in which labels have changed historically even as they continued to reference perceived differences in intellectual functioning and adaptive behavior as though these were objective, fixed, and immutable.

Mutua and Siders (this volume) place the descriptor "intellectual disabilities" within the larger and more functional definition of developmental disabilities used to describe a variety of disability labels. The label of intellectual disabilities as used in Alabama, they argue, is still a clinical definition and is based on sorting strategies that meet the needs of the dominating, hegemonic culture—strategies that are designed to prevent people with disabilities from denying that the location for difference resides within them rather than within cultural constructs of normalcy. Special education, for clinicians who control it as proxies for the dominating normate culture, becomes a means of ensuring normative privilege—thus ensuring that students with disabilities are segregated outside of general education classrooms.

Connor (this volume) notes that there is substantial confusion in the literature regarding ways in which people with intellectual disabilities are referred, reflecting changes in cultural mores and thinking. He, too, hints that these are merely changes in words rather than in the underlying understandings of people, which are not seen as mutable.

Generally, then, it would be safe to say that the authors in this volume would critique current special education understandings of students with intellectual disabilities as rising from medical models of difference and disability, ones that do substantive harm to the students and whose descriptive language lacks any particular benefit or merit to people with disabilities and their allies. Any benefit that is accrued can be said to be tied to those who perceive themselves as residing within normative educational and social landscapes.

LRE as a Tool of Segregation

The Individuals with Disabilities Education Improvement Act (IDEIA), throughout its history and several reauthorizations, has made consistent reference to a least restrictive environment (LRE) as the appropriate placement for students with Individual Educational Plans (IEP's). Founded on principles inherent in the seminal *Brown v.*

Board of Education Supreme Court decision, the concept of an LRE is central to the IDEIA, and an important idea for those seeking to ensure that students with intellectual disabilities are educated in general education classrooms. Unfortunately, current congressional special education policy is described as preferring inclusion rather than requiring it (Howard, 2004).

The LRE construct, of course, implies a continuum of possible environments (from least to most restrictive) in which individuals or groups of students might receive services and supports (Taylor, 2004). Taylor and others have long argued that the LRE construct and the notion of a continuum impose negative outcomes on people with disabilities, especially those with the most significant disabilities, including intellectual disabilities (Taylor, Racino, Knoll, & Lutfiyya, 1987). Their argument, relevant even today, points out the problems of the continuum model:

People labeled as having significant disabilities end up in the most restrictive settings.

These most restrictive settings do not enable people to move to less restrictive settings.

The settings that are most restrictive are not needed.

Bottlenecks are inevitable on the continuum, preventing movement.

The continuum means that, when people change or grow, they must leave their homes in order to move to less restrictive environments.

Resources tend to be concentrated in environments that are most restrictive.

Services and supports should not be restrictive.

The model of the continuum focuses on facilities, rather than supports.

They argue for environments that eliminate restriction, rather than a least restrictive environment; the best approach eliminates the continuum, creating instead nonrestrictive environments (Taylor, Racino, Knoll, & Lutfiyya, 1987).

Although the phrasing of Least Restrictive Environment indicates a positive impact on particular students, with almost inarguable benefits (how can one disagree with placement in an environment deemed to be the least restrictive for a particular student?), use of the LRE construct by professionals has served as a tool to segregate rather than include.

The teacher's union in Illinois, Owen and Gabel (this volume) point out, affirmed that inclusive settings are outside the bounds of typical, normal working conditions, thus ensuring that LREs will remain de facto segregated settings. This is in alignment with the work and advocacy of the national educator union, the American Federation of Teachers (AFT), which has long held that inclusion has a negative impact on teacher working conditions (1994), and its former president, Al Shanker (1994), was a stalwart and leading opponent of inclusion. They note that stakeholders in the state were very effective at systematically segregating students with intellectual disabilities from their peers without disability labels. The segregation of general education and special education teacher preparation programs, they point out, had (and continues to have) a powerful impact on the segregation of students with intellectual (as well as other) disabilities. Although court decisions in Illinois appear to have been progressive in some respects, favoring inclusion, they have done little to change current funding streams and policy disincentives, placing the onus of responsibility for ensuring the LRE as an inclusive option on teacher preparation and then primarily in the field of special education.

LeRoy and Lacey (this volume) describe how Michigan established one of the earliest special education systems in the country. Although progressive at the time, educational policy established a two-track education system that inherently segregated students with disabilities. During what LeRoy and Lacey describe as Michigan's inclusion decade, state educational policy was widened to include a broader definition of LRE, creating more inclusive opportunities for students.

Discussing the outline of inclusion for students with intellectual disabilities in California, Mintz (this volume) notes that the IDEA places (whether intentionally or not) the responsibility for creating inclusive opportunities within the LRE squarely on the shoulders of students with disabilities and their families. In what may be the most powerful and pointed condemnation of the LRE notion in this volume, she goes on to describe ways in which professionals in California use the concept of the LRE to systematically exclude students with intellectual disabilities from general education environments. As she points out, following Mlawer (1998), the variability of placement for students with intellectual disabilities indicates that the notion of an LRE is deeply broken.

In Alabama, as Mutua and Siders (this volume) point out, LRE is interpreted differently depending on disability labels. For students with more significant disabilities, such as those said to have intellectual and developmental disabilities, segregated settings are more likely to be the norm rather than the exception.

Looking at the particular case of New York City, Connor (this volume) follows other disability studies scholars in seeing the LRE mandate of IDEA as a loophole that allows and creates opportunities for segregation, rather than preventing it. He points out that the concept of LRE created a second system of education—separate and certainly not equal—and that LRE is founded on systems of incarceration rather than freedom. He goes on to describe ways in which students with minority status in urban environments are especially at risk of being placed in restrictive environments.

As Mintz points out in her chapter (this volume), Taylor (2004) outlines seven flaws that are inherent in the concept of LRE. Taylor asserts that the idea of an LRE, which was once a progressive approach, has become outmoded, one that is in conflict with current disability studies and sociocultural understandings of services, supports, and disability.

The concept of LRE, inherent and fundamental to special education law, policy, and practice in the United States, is deeply flawed, as it denies students with intellectual disabilities and their families civil and human rights as well as social justice; it is counter to any notion of progressive morality. It's utility is in ensuring that students with intellectual disabilities remain segregated from normative culture, in both educational and other communities.

Continued Domination of Professional Discourse and Influence

Professional, medicalized discourse continues to have a stranglehold on the lives of people with intellectual and developmental disabilities and their families (Smith, 1999; 2001; 2006). The kind of power and control wielded by professionals is described by a number of the authors in this text; for example, Owen and Gabel (this volume) refer to the "deference" shown to educators in Illinois when making decisions about placement, deference that allows professionals who believe that segregated education may be in the best interests of students to place them in segregated settings, even if students clearly benefit from learning in inclusive environments. As a result, they note, power imbalances are created and maintained between school personnel and the families of students with intellectual disabilities. Court cases in Illinois describe inclusion as restrictive and constraining on schools and the work of educators.

Connor (this volume), in his exploration of inclusion in New York

City, notes that the construct of IQ as a taxonomic tool used to sort
people with intellectual disabilities, both to label them and to rank
them among the labeled as a means to determine the "severity" of
their disability, remains a powerful force in the hands of professionals, especially psychologists. He points to the way that such determi-
nations creates reified understandings of people with intellectual disabilities that are stigmatizing and oppressive. And he notes that
special education teacher preparation programs, for the most part,
tend to reinforce these medicalized stories of disability, ensuring that
educators play out their role of fixing "broken" people. The resulting
creation of separate and certainly not-equal special education systems
is perhaps best exemplified around the United States by New York
City's District 75.

LeRoy and Lacey (this volume) describe ways in which inclusion
initiatives of the 1990s in Michigan could not possibly withstand the
storm of standards-based curriculum and accountability changes that
arrived at the end of the decade—changes that, I've argued here in
previous chapters, are a function of neoliberal economic forces and
are founded in conservatizing educational epistemologies. These epistemologies are created by the kinds of medical-model approaches to
learning endemic to much of separate-and-not-equal special education. LeRoy and Lacey also point out the same kind of findings that
Connor outlined, noting that inclusion is something to which middle
and upper class families have access and is not available to families
from lower socioeconomic classes.

In exploring ways in which inclusion plays out in California,
Mintz (this volume) points to ways in which IDEA itself is designed
to support the work of segregating professionals and to place responsibility for creating inclusive environments on families and students.
She describes the kind of subtle (and not so) means by which professionals coerce and intimidate families, forcing students into separate
and poor-quality learning environments, using expert discourse held
only by professionals.

Mutua and Siders (this volume), exploring the place of students
with intellectual disabilities in Alabama general education settings,
use a disability studies approach to critique professionalized and
medicalized understandings of intellectual and developmental disabilities that enhance the privilege of dominating hegemony of normate culture at the expense of people who are given labels. Classroom-level decisions by educational professionals deny access to

general education settings for students with intellectual (and other) disabilities.

Intentional or Unintentional: NCLB as a Barrier to Inclusion

Authors here have pointed out, in several ways and instances, the impact of the so-called No Child Left Behind Act on the inclusion of students with disabilities, including those with intellectual disabilities. For example, LeRoy and Lacey (this volume) indicate that NCLB unintentionally creates barriers to the inclusion of students with disabilities in Michigan. This impacts students with intellectual disabilities, specifically through the notion of Annual Yearly Progress (AYP), which forces schools to meet standardized achievement benchmarks annually. LeRoy and Lacey indicate that administrators avoid placing students who will likely not contribute to meeting AYP goals (such as students with intellectual disabilities) in general education contexts, thus eliminating previous gains in increasing the level of inclusion in various schools and districts.

Mutua and Siders (this volume) point toward NCLB as a reason why Alabama has moved toward adoption of a Response to Intervention (RTI) approach using a three-tier model to determine levels and intensity of intervention. Although designed to reduce the number of students labeled as having disabilities and in need of an IEP and to implement appropriate degrees of intervention depending on student need, RTI has been critiqued as representing traditional special education approaches dressed up in new language (Ferri, 2008).

Is the impact of NCLB on the inclusion of students with disabilities in general education really unintentional, as has been suggested? I would argue not, in the same way that the roots of special education as an essentially eugenicist ideology remain an important part of current special education policy and practice, despite the fact that most educators of the twenty-first century would publicly disavow any relationship or agreement with eugenicist thinking. In fact, I would argue that NCLB is itself a twenty-first-century representation of eugenicist pseudoscience in its use of standards-based, Cartesian, modernist representation of what (literally) counts as learning and how it can be measured. The measuring of learning is a distinctly eugenicist construct and has long been used as a way to sort people. NCLB ratchets this approach up a notch by sorting schools, not just individuals.

And NCLB goes one step further. In addition to identifying

schools that are not meeting standards for practice, instead of providing those schools with appropriate financial and other resources to begin to address problems, it quite intentionally withholds those resources and gives families the opportunity to go to other schools described as successful—ensuring that failing schools will never be anything but failing and that they will, in fact, ultimately disappear. The same process that allows eugenicist thinking to remain active in twenty-first-century special education—a kind of intentional forgetting or ignoring—I would argue, is active in how NCLB proceeds to enact eugenicist ideologies in schools today (Smith, 2008).

Race and Intellectual Disability

In a general way, special education law and practice in the United States is founded on judicial decisions that were initially focused on issues related to race. Most important of these decisions, as has been pointed out in several places in this text, is the famous *Brown v. Board of Education of Topeka* (1954). In that case (a unanimous decision), the Supreme Court said, "where a State has undertaken to provide an opportunity for an education in its public schools, such an opportunity is a right which must be made available to all on equal terms" (p. 493). It is manifestly ironic, then, that race continues to play such a powerful and negative role in issues related to education, particularly as they play out in matters of inclusion and segregation, and even more particularly for students with intellectual disabilities.

LeRoy and Lacey (this volume) report on research that demonstrates that inclusion is a function of race in Michigan, and in the United States—students of color with disability labels remain predominantly in highly segregated educational settings, while their richer, white peers have many more opportunities to be educated in general education classrooms. And, they say, among students of color with disabilities, Hispanic students are the most likely to be placed in segregated special education settings. Inclusion is a matter of race and class.

Mutua and Siders (this volume) point to ways in which the history of Alabama, as with that of much of the South, is based on the segregation of students of color—a history that continues to be played out in the overrepresentation of students labeled as having intellectual disabilities in special education. Although there appears to be some recent progress in reducing the number of African American students who are labeled as having intellectual disabilities, they note that, in some sense, disability labels are merely being shifted for them, from that of intellectual disability to labels of learning disabilities. In addition, male students are at much greater risk of receiving a label of intellectual disability in Alabama than elsewhere in the United States.

Connor (this volume) also points out the overrepresentation of students of color with labels of intellectual disabilities, particularly in urban settings, and that they are less likely to be included in general education settings. These issues are played out in urban districts, characterized by huge disparities in socioeconomic status, large numbers of racially and ethnically diverse students, greater numbers of immigrants, and more linguistic diversity.

That the United States is, at its roots, a culture founded on racist ideologies, is clear (Smith, 2004). With origins in eugenicist pseudo-science, special education continues to play out the segregation of students of color through taxonomic sorting processes. Resolving these issues will require systemic dismantling of current educational policy and practice.

Impact of Court Decisions

With the passage of P.L. 94-142 (now reauthorized numerous times and referred to as IDEIA), families and students with intellectual disabilities have legal rights before the law. Yet over time, court decisions have not always or systematically enabled the inclusion of students with intellectual disabilities.

Owen and Gabel (this volume) outline the history of Illinois state law and judicial decision that have resulted in reliance on segregated settings for students with intellectual and other disabilities. They report that, although there was much hope surrounding the outcome of the so-called *Corey H. v. Board of Education* decision (1998), little positive change has resulted in the inclusion of students with disabilities in Illinois. They also contrast two decisions that fall on opposite sides of LRE: *Oberti v. Board of Education* in New Jersey (1993) and *Beth B. v. Van Clay* in Illinois (2002). Regrettably, the *Beth B.* decision upholds the right of classroom-level professionals to decide the nature of a particular student's LRE, usually pointing toward increased exclusion.

LeRoy and Lacey (this volume) have pointed out that cases involving special education in the judicial system have not, generally speaking, advanced the cause of inclusion in significant ways. This is, to a great degree, because federal special education legislation focuses on individualized educational planning and supports. Because the courts see each child as an individual, different from every other, they cannot be regarded as being members of sets or classes of children, so that court cases cannot necessarily be applied in general ways. This allows schools to continue to segregate students with disabilities, ironically applying the notion that students with particular disabilities fall into separate and distinct groups, thus allowing districts to provide instruction in classrooms designed for distinct disability labels. In addition, recent federal decisions prevent families from recovering fees for expert witnesses when they prevail in judicial decisions, in effect creating a further disincentive for families to bring special education issues to court.

Mutua and Siders (this volume) also refer to the promise of the *Oberti* decision for Alabama—a promise that does not seem to have been fully realized. More applicable to the state of Alabama are decisions such as *Lee v. Macon* (1967), which eventually (after more than 30 years) resulted in judicial support for ending the overrepresentation of African Americans labeled as having intellectual disabilities.

Teacher Preparation Issues

What are the issues of teacher preparation for inclusion in the five locations around the country that these authors found? In Illinois, Owen and Gabel (this volume) found that teacher preparation programs support and ensure the segregation of students with intellectual disabilities. Since the early 1950s, when researchers and practitioners began looking at best practices for teaching students with intellectual disabilities in Illinois, there has been a deep-seated emphasis on exclusion and segregation. Special educators continue to learn in teacher preparation programs that are separate from the learning experiences of general educators. Although the *Corey H.* decision (1998) held promise for a systematic restructuring of teacher education in Illinois, structural and essential change was not forthcoming. Although changes were made in the highly categorical nature of teacher certification, and the number of standards related to teaching students with disabilities for general educators increased, the essential separation between general and special educator preparation remains in place.

LeRoy and Lacey (this volume) also outline the gradual development of a dual education system in Michigan, one that, in spite of beginning in a progressive environment, has failed to keep up with best practices surrounding inclusion. There appears to have been substantial progress in creating professional development and teacher education opportunities that support inclusion during what the authors call "the inclusion decade" of the 1990s. However, because Michigan's Board of Education did not overhaul state certification requirements, teacher preparation programs successfully fought the integration of general and special education preparation programs, and they remain highly segregated enterprises throughout the state. General education preservice educators are required to take only one course in special education (this is, it should be pointed out, the norm around the country).

Connor (this volume) describes teacher preparation programs in urban settings like the one he explores as being "teacher factories," places designed to crank out many educators quickly (and who will most likely burn out rapidly as well and leave the world of teaching). Such preparation programs avoid looking at the kind of complex environments that exist in urban environments, creating educators who lack the skills, experience, and knowledge they need both to be successful there and to effect the kind of change necessary to create inclusive opportunities. Instead, he points out, they continue the kind of medicalized, segregated settings that prevent the possibility for inclusion.

Inclusion Blips

Some of the states outlined in this text have had what Owen and Gabel (this volume) describe as small blips of inclusion on the radar screen of education, historical moments in which, for a variety of reasons, various elements came together in such a way as to allow students with intellectual disabilities to have increased access to general education classrooms. Where and when did these blips occur, and why?

One began in Illinois in the 1980s. Owen and Gabel describe Project CHOICES, which supported a small number of schools to develop inclusive opportunities. While the number of schools involved has grown to a miniscule 41, the project has developed a variety of resources that it shares around the state. Active sites use a team approach involving a variety of stakeholders—a model that has been successful in other places on other systems change initiatives as well (Aichroth et al., 2002).

A project with substantially greater impact was the one that came to fruition during the 1990s, a period described by LeRoy and Lacey (this volume) as Michigan's Inclusion Decade. A substantial statewide systems change initiative, again involving multiple stakeholders from a variety of policy and practice arenas, resulted in substantive change around Michigan. Regrettably, neither the project nor policy initiatives resulted in sustained change beyond the decade.

Mutua and Siders (this volume) also outline some occasional, discrete successes in the inclusion arena within Alabama. They cite a variety of model schools and districts that are being used by the state Department of Education as exemplars of inclusive opportunities. Unfortunately, these examples are few and far between and there is a sense from many classroom teachers that, even when schools begin to look at inclusion as a viable way of doing things, systems change efforts seem to be top-down rather than involving the input of multiple stakeholders.

What Does It All Mean?

So what can we say from the chapters here that look at how inclusion plays out (or does not, mostly) in these several varied locations in the United States? Well, briefly put, we can say the following:

*   The labels and names that we use to describe students with intellectual disabilities become self-fulfilling prophecies, ensuring that they will be placed in segregated settings, away from their peers without disabilities.
*   The notion of Least Restrictive Environment is outmoded and functions now as a loophole for professionals to continue placing students with intellectual disabilities in segregated settings.
*   Professional discourse remains dominant in schools, ensuring that students with intellectual disabilities and their families (who are, after all, the real experts in their lives and needs) remain outside the normative boundaries of educational (and other) communities.
*   The so-called No Child Left Behind Act, besides its many other problems, serves as a barrier to the inclusion of students with disabilities (whether they have intellectual disabilities or not), in a way that is intentional, in the same sense that eugenics is a kind of intentional forgetting of the normative.
*   Students with intellectual disabilities, who also have ethnic or racial minority status, experience a kind of double jeopardy—they are more likely to be labeled as having intellectual disabilities and

more likely to receive their education in segregated settings than their peers who are white and middle or upper class.

- Teacher preparation in the United States, far from working to resolve these and other issues, serves to maintain the status quo of the segregation of students with intellectual (and other) disabilities.

- Although some states have had some success in increasing opportunities for the inclusion of students with intellectual disabilities in general education environments, these successes have been generally small, temporary, and not systemic.

As I began preparing to write and edit this volume, I asked a variety of researchers that I respected from around the country to consider contributing. Some said yes; some, legitimately, had other projects or issues with which they were dealing. I remember one in particular, though, who responded in a way that really surprised me. He is a researcher and teacher educator who has worked for a long time in the field of inclusive education—I knew he would have much to add to the topics under discussion here. What he said, though, was that he didn't see the need for the kind of exploration that I and other authors in this text have undertaken. He had so many new inclusive educators to teach, he said, that he didn't have time to look at whether inclusion was happening and, if so, what long-term trajectory it was following.

I remain deeply disturbed by the apparent complacency of that kind of thinking, so apparent among researchers, practitioners, policymakers, educators, and even advocates. Inclusion for students with intellectual disabilities in general education is not happening the way that it should be, or could be. The rights of families and students continue to be violated and denied every day, every week, every year. It's not good enough. It's got to change.

References

Aichroth, S., Carpenter, J., Daniels, K., Grassette, P., Kelly, D., Murray, A., Rice, J., Rivard, B., Smith, C., Smith, P., & Topper, K. (2002). Creating a new system of supports: The Vermont self-determination project. *Rural Special Education Quarterly, 21*(2), 16–28.

American Federation of Teachers (1994). Resolution on inclusion of students with disabilities. Adopted by the American Federation of Teachers at its 1994 National Convention in Anaheim, California. Retrieved on May 9, 2009 from http://www.aft.org/about/resolutions/1994/inclusion.htm

Beth B. v. Van Clay. 282 F.3d 493 (7th Cir. 2002).

Brown v. Board of Education of Topeka. 347 U.S. 483 (Supreme Court 1954).

Corey H. v. Board of Education. 995 F. Supp. 900 (N.D. Ill. 1998).

Ferri, B. (2008). RTI: How [traditional] special education tries to get its groove back. 8th Annual Disability Studies in Education Conference, New York City, NY.

Hehir, T., Figueroa, R., Gamm, S., Katzman, L., Gruner, A., Karger, J., & Hernandez, J. (2005). *Comprehensive management review and evaluation of special education submitted to the New York City Department of Education*. Cambridge, MA: Harvard School of Education.

Howard, P. (2004). The least restrictive environment: How to tell? *Journal of Law & Education, 33*, 167–180.

Lee v. Macon County Bd., 267 F.Supp. 458, aff'd sub nom. *Wallace v. United States*, 389 U.S. 215 (1967).

Mlawer, M. (1998, Nov./Dec.). What's wrong with the Feds? *The Association for Persons with Severe Handicaps Newsletter*, 24–26.

Oberti v. Board of Education. 995 F.2d 1204 (3d Cir. 1993).

Office of Special Education and Rehabilitative Services (2007). *27th annual report to Congress on the implementation of the Individuals with Disabilities Education Act*. Washington, DC: Author.

Shanker, A. (1994). Full inclusion is neither free or appropriate. *Educational Leadership, 52*(4), 18–21.

Smith, P. (1999). Drawing new maps: A radical cartography of developmental disabilities. *Review of Educational Research, 69*(2), 117–144.

——— (2001). MAN.i.f.e.s.t.o.: A Poetics of D(EVIL)op(MENTAL) Dis(ABILITY). *Taboo: The Journal of Education and Culture, 5*(1), 27–36.

——— (2004). Whiteness, normal theory, and disability studies. *Disability Studies Quarterly, 2* (2).

——— (2006). Split------ting the rock of {speci [ES]al} e.ducat.ion: flowers of lang[ue]age in >DIS<ability studies. In S. Danforth and S. Gabel (Eds.), *Vital Questions in Disability Studies in Education*, (pp. 31–58). New York: Peter Lang.

——— (2008). Cartographies of eugenics and special education: A history of the (ab)normal. In S. Gabel & S. Danforth (Eds.), *Disability and the politics of education: An international reader*. New York: Peter Lang.

Taylor, S. (2004). Caught in the continuum: A critical analysis of the principle of the least restrictive environment. *Research and Practice for Persons with Severe Disabilities, 29*, 218–230.

Taylor, S., Racino, J., Knoll, J., & Lutfiyya, Z. (1987). *The nonrestrictive environment: On community integration for people with the most severe disabilities*. Syracuse, NY: Human Policy Press.

CHAPTER 10

Preparing Educators for Inclusion

What We're Doing Right, What We're Doing Wrong

PHIL SMITH

There are probably over 1,000 teacher education programs in the United States (National Council on Teacher Quality, 2004). Many of them train special educators. I work at one. In fact, the university I work at bills itself as the largest producer of educational personnel in the country. It was the first state teachers college in the United States to train special educators. It is home to the first school building especially designed and equipped for the training of special educators in the United States and includes the largest department of special education in the country (I do not really see these as good things, but they are what they are).

When I look around at the teacher education practices in which this department of special education engages—in fact, the practices of the university's entire College of Education, including departments of Leadership and Counseling and Teacher Education—it becomes evident that the kinds of things we do on a daily basis come nowhere close to modeling the ways that special educators, general educators, educational leaders, and school counselors should be working to include students with intellectual (and/or other) disabilities in general education classrooms. Almost no one is co-teaching. Differentiated instruction and Universal Design for Learning are mentioned only in special education classes. A definition of ableism is rarely mentioned, in any class, special or otherwise. When I ask my special education students how many of my colleagues talk about inclusion in their classes, they tell me there are two: me and one other colleague. There is almost no collaboration among the different departments within the college in terms of working with students with disabilities, understanding ableism, and exploring best practices for including students with a variety of learning or cultural differences.

We may be the biggest. But the university at which I work is no-where close to being the best in terms of exploring and implementing inclusive practices. We don't even model what we preach. That's pretty damning, at least from my perspective. When I try to bring up these issues within the department and the college, I'm looked on as a troublemaker, a rabble-rouser, a radical. Roadblocks and hurdles seem to spring up overnight whenever these concerns are raised. I keep asking myself questions—What the heck is going on? Why is it like this, here and elsewhere around the country? Why aren't we do-ing what we know to be the right thing to do?

Relatively little is known, formally, about the effectiveness of teacher preparation practices designed to prepare educators to create and function in inclusive classrooms for students with intellectual or other disabilities (Nevin, Cohen, Salazar, & Marshall, 2007). School partnerships with teacher preparation programs are limited, which affects the ability of teacher educators to work collaboratively with schools to find out what, in fact, does work (Griffin, Jones, & Kilgore, 2007). Typically around the country, preservice general educators re-ceive only a single 2–3-credit course in special education; this class is often a survey course with insufficient time to go into details about instructional strategies and methods (Agran & Alper, 2000). And states do little to ensure that teacher preparation programs provide appropriate training to future special educators (National Council on Teacher Quality, 2007).

In an important review of the literature on teacher preparation, re-searchers found that the impact of training in pedagogy, student-teaching experiences, and the receipt of a master's degree on increases in student academic achievement is weak at best (Department of Edu-cation, 2002). Teacher certification programs, as currently structured, appear to have little impact on the effectiveness of educators. What does seem to matter is teacher experience, general cognitive ability, and content knowledge. Rather than having a positive impact, most teacher certification programs merely place a set of hurdles and ob-stacles in the way of those seeking to become educators (Department of Education, 2002). Other researchers have made similar findings (Walsh, 2001). In addition, teachers who become certified through al-ternative certification programs perform just as well on state qualifi-cation examinations as do those who complete traditional teacher preparation programs through colleges and universities (Department of Education, 2006; National Council on Teacher Quality, 2004).

What are the implications of this research? The work that teacher educators do in methods courses, supervising student teaching, and the like has only a negligible positive effect on the quality of teaching. Traditional teacher preparation programs, as currently structured, are an ineffective means for preparing educators, whether general or special.

So what is to be done? What teacher preparation practices will we need to develop in order to ensure that both general and special educators are adequately trained to work in inclusive schools? How will teacher education programs need to change and restructure in order to ensure that all educators have the skills they need to work with all students?

Education for Inclusion:
What's Not Working in Teacher Preparation

In current practice, teacher preparation and certification programs reinforce the segregation of special education, by ensuring that general education teachers and special education teachers are trained separately, using separate curriculum and criteria (National Council on Disability, 1994; Titone, 2005; Ware, 2005). General educators don't get enough training and experience to be able to implement the kinds of teaching strategies necessary to teach diverse learners (Smith and Routel, 2008), especially those with significant disabilities (Agran & Alper, 2000).

We know that experience working with students with disabilities is a powerful factor in developing positive attitudes toward them: "direct contact for an extended period of time is one of the most effective ways to change attitudes" (Scott, Jellison, Chappell, & Standridge, 2007, p. 51). And coursework can have a positive impact as well: preservice educators who took a single survey course on special education and students with disabilities had less hostility toward students with disabilities and less anxiety about working with them than educators who did not take such a course (Shippen, Crites, Houchins, Ramsey, & Simon, 2005). Coursework plus preservice experience in inclusive schools has a positive effect on teachers' knowledge of special education and inclusion (Hardin, 2005: Singh, 2006). When given an opportunity to collaborate with special educators in inclusive classrooms, preservice general educators developed increasingly positive attitudes toward students with disabilities (Henning & Mitchell, 2002).

Yet neither general nor special education preparation programs, whether inservice or preservice, appear to provide future teachers with sufficient experience and training to work successfully and collaboratively in inclusive classrooms (Austin, 2001; Buell, Hallam, Gamel-McCormick, & Scheer, 1999; DeSimone & Parmar, 2006; Elhoweris & Alsheikh, 2004; Kamens, Loprete, & Slostad, 2003; Kerns, 1996; Short & Martin, 2005; Singh, 2007; Smith & Routel, 2008; Snyder, Garriott, & Aylor, 2001; Titone, 2005). Nor do general educators receive sufficient training and experience to work cooperatively with parents of children with disabilities and to see parents as experts on the needs and goals of their children (Yssel, Engelbrecht, Oswald, Eloff, & Swart, 2007).

The preparation of general educators with adequate and appropriate knowledge and experience about how to educate students with disabilities in general education classrooms is critical to the success of inclusion (Kleinhammer-Trammill, 2003). But new teachers say that although they had some training in working with students with disabilities, it wasn't enough (National Comprehensive Center for Teacher Quality, 2008). General educators clearly want and need increased experience and knowledge regarding how to teach students with intellectual (as well as other) disabilities in general education classrooms (Ammah & Hodge, 2006; Brownell & Pajares, 1999; DeSimone & Parmar, 2006; Nevin, Cohen, Salazar, & Marshall, 2007; Short & Martin, 2005; Silverman, 2007; Singh, 2007).

The use of paraprofessionals in supporting students with disabilities in general education classrooms has a number of negative impacts on student learning, social experiences, and teachers and should be avoided (Broer, Doyle, & Giangreco, 2005; Giangreco & Broer, 2005; 2007; Giangreco & Doyle, 2007; Giangreco, Halvorson, Doyle, & Broer, 2004; Giangreco, Smith, & Pinckney, 2006; Giangreco, Yuan, McKenzie, Cameron, & Fialka, 2005). Unfortunately, these issues are compounded—with clear teacher preparation implications—by educators' lack of knowledge or experience in working with and supervising educational paraprofessionals (DeSimone & Parmar, 2006; Giangreco & Doyle, 2004; Kerns, 1996; Mastropieri, 2001).

Professional Development and Educational Leadership: Essential Elements for Inclusion

Understanding the professional development and training needs of educational leaders—principals, superintendents, and other district and school administrators—is essential to creating inclusive schools. Educational administrators are a critical element in the development and implementation of inclusive policies and practices (Kamens, Loprete, & Slostad, 2003). Unfortunately, educational leadership programs don't provide future administrators with adequate knowledge about the meaning of inclusion, who it can benefit, necessary supports and educational practices, and the kinds of leadership models and processes needed to ensure the success of inclusion (Barnett & Monda-Amaya, 1998; Brownell & Pajares, 1999; Praisner, 2003; Salisbury, 2006). Principals want more opportunities to learn about collaborative decision-making and service delivery models (Foley, 2001).

New Skill Sets and Experiences for Inclusive Educators: What Teacher Preparation Programs Need to Do

Some argue that training educators to work in inclusive classrooms is simply not possible (Mock & Kauffman, 2002). Yet, clearly, teacher education programs must ensure that teachers have what they need—skills and experiences—so that they can provide instruction to students with disabilities in general education classrooms (National Council on Disability, 1995; Pierson & Howell, 2006). And they must work hard to evaluate preservice educator attitudes toward students with disabilities and toward inclusion and make sure that those attitudes and values are positive (Silverman, 2007). In particular, teacher educators need to develop and enhance "critically reflective thinking skills [i.e. the deliberate scrutiny of one's beliefs and actions, along with other perspectives, regarding teaching behavior and the moral, ethical, and social justice aspects of teaching] ..." (Silverman, 2007, p. 48)—qualities essential to nourishing inclusive settings, processes, and interactions.

General educators need increased coursework and experiences regarding inclusion, both preservice and inservice (Buell, Hallam, Gamel-McCormick, & Scheer, 1999; DeSimone & Parmar, 2006; Elhoweris & Alsheikh, 2004; Shippen, Crites, Houchins, Ramsey, & Simon, 2005). This must be beyond the typical 2–3-credit survey course that most general educators around the United States get currently (Agran & Alper, 2000; Hardin, 2005; Kamens, Loprete, & Slostad, 2003).

An essential theme throughout inclusion and teacher preparation literature is related to collaboration (Nevin, 2000; Thousand & Villa, 2000; Titone, 2005). Both general and special educators need training

and practice in co-teaching, consultation, and collaboration in inclusive settings (Bradley & Monda-Amaya, 2005; DeSimone & Parmar,
2006; Downing & Peckham-Hardin, 2007; Henning & Mitchell, 2002;
Kamens, 2007; Shippen, Crites, Houchins, Ramsey, & Simon, 2005;
Short & Martin, 2005; Silverman, 2007; Thompson, 2007). Developing
opportunities for preservice general and special educators to collaborate in inclusive classrooms is one avenue for them to gain experience
in this area, and a way for them to begin to construct for themselves
the meaning of what inclusion can look like (Henning & Mitchell,
2002; Kamens, 2007). Opportunities for ongoing discussion and reflection about preservice co-teaching experiences can have an affirmative
impact on developing positive attitudes and useful strategies for en-
couraging inclusive processes (Kamens, 2007).

Positive relationships between teachers are an essential element
for successful collaboration (Henning & Mitchell, 2002). But, as
McCormick, Noonan, Ogata, and Heck (2001) point out,

> we must not assume that because prospective teachers are adults themselves
> they know how to work, communicate, and collaborate with other adults ... Ad-
> ditionally, they need to learn (a) how to talk to, listen to, and respect one another
> while finding areas of agreement; (b) how to discuss and evaluate options with-
> out taking a value position; (c) how to follow through on responsibilities in a
> timely fashion; and (d) how to engender trust. (p. 130)

Although these seem like simple skills, working successfully with
other professionals is in reality complex, difficult, and emotion-laden
work, often undervalued in teacher education programs. The success
or failure of inclusion is largely dependent on the desire and skills
necessary for professionals to work collaboratively; put another way,
the success of inclusion is about what grownups do, not about what
students do (Ferguson, Meyer, Jeanchild, & Juniper, 1992). These
skills are essential to teacher collaboration, and thus to the success of
inclusive classrooms and schools.

Overreliance on the use of paraprofessionals in general education
classrooms, seen as a way to support the inclusion of students with
disabilities, in reality has substantial negative effects on inclusion, in
both academic and social domains (Giangreco & Broer, 2007; Giangreco & Doyle, 2007). Until schools understand this and reduce or
eliminate their use, at minimum, educators will need more experience
and training in how to work with educational paraprofessionals (De-
Simone & Parmar, 2006; Kerns, 1996). Increasing experience and training in how to use paraprofessionals can mitigate problems rooted in
their overuse.

Educators must also have adequate training and experiential learning opportunities to know how to work cooperatively with parents of children with disabilities, to see parents as having knowledge and expertise about their children (Yssel, Engelbrecht, Oswald, Eloff, & Swart, 2007). Too often, "the sense of belonging and shared ownership that is inherent in the philosophy of inclusive education has yet to be experienced by many ... parents" (Yssel et al., 2007, p. 363). Empowering parents in real ways can create the trust and communication necessary to create collaboratively designed and implemented inclusive opportunities.

All educators need training in how to provide appropriate accommodations (Kamens, Loprete, & Slostad, 2003; Downing & Peckham-Hardin, 2007). They also need experience and training in using technology to enhance learning for students with disabilities (Downing & Peckham-Hardin, 2007). They need specific skills and strategies related to developing three areas essential for the success of inclusion: social competence, self-determination, and reading (Agran & Alper, 2000). Teacher educators and teacher education programs must model the kinds of educational strategies and attitudes that are essential for the success of inclusive approaches to education (Nevin, Cohen, Salazar, & Marshall, 2007).

Preservice and inservice training and experience in educational strategies and tools in inclusive settings need to be ongoing and not one-shot workshops in order to generate the kinds of positive attitudes and adequate levels of experience in implementing the inclusion of students with disabilities (Kamens, Loprete, & Slostad, 2003; Reusen, Shoho, & Barker, 2001; Yssel, Engelbrecht, Oswald, Eloff, & Swart, 2007). This will mean that, over time, experiences and instruction related to inclusion must be imbedded strategically in a broad variety of coursework and inservice activities (Hardin, 2005; Titone, 2005).

To meet the needs of all educators and administrators, university teacher education programs should also explore alternative options for delivery of training—going to schools and other local venues rather than providing educational opportunities only on campus (Short & Martin, 2005). When schools and universities work together collaboratively, they can enhance those preservice educators skills that are needed to make inclusion happen and enhance positive attitudes and values (Sprague & Pennell, 2000).

Given the huge disparity in educational outcomes between students (with and without disabilities) in poor urban school districts and those in richer suburban environments, it would seem obvious that we need highly skilled educators to work in poor urban schools. Yet there remains a huge need for special educators in those schools. And although many students in urban settings are diverse, with minority status, most educators (special or otherwise) are white, and female (National Collaborative on Diversity in the Teaching Force, 2004; Torres, Santos, Peck, & Cortes, 2004). Recruiting and preparing special educators to work in inclusive urban settings must be given a high priority.

An important theme running through this book is the inseparability of disability and diversity understood more globally. That is, although ableism is not typically an area explored by critical educators, it remains as important to a socially just culture (and a socially just education system) as issues of racism, classism, sexism, ageism, heterosexism, and the like. So educators, including (but most especially not limited to) special educators, need to understand issues related to ableism and how that gets played out in schools. An understanding of ableism through its exploration within teacher education is a critical component of multicultural education writ large and must be an integral part of coursework and experiences looking at the social foundations of education, at minimum.

Training Educational Leaders: What Needs to Be Done

One project found seven themes related to leadership issues in schools that were successful in including students with disabilities. These themes include the following:

Challenge all students and their teachers to high standards

Build an inclusive and collaborative community of learning

Foster a school culture of innovation and creativity

Engage stakeholders in school leadership

Promote professional development

Hire staff who reinforce school values and vision

Use data for decision-making and school improvement planning (Bartholomay, Wallace, & Mason, 2001, p. 1)

To ensure the implementation of these goals, educational leadership programs need to ensure that administrators, perhaps especially school principals, have adequate training and preparation in order to know how to define inclusion, its benefit for all students, and the kinds of supports and leadership styles they need to develop, person-ally and institutionally (Barnett & Monda-Amaya, 1998; Brownell & Pajares, 1999; Praisner, 2003; Reusuen, Shoho, & Barker, 2001). Doing so will require that

> preparation programs will not only have to reconceptualize how they think about educational leadership, but correspondingly, they must reorganize the way that they prepare others to do so. In other words, they need to prepare future educational leaders to reculture schools, but in the process, they must also reculture themselves. (Doyle, 2003, p. 12)

Because collaborative decision-making models and a commitment to inclusion that is founded in philosophy appear to be important elements in schools that successfully include students with disabili-ties, administrators will need training and experience that help them foster these approaches (Doyle, 2003; Foley, 2001; Salisbury, 2006).

Administrators need successful experiences in seeing inclusion happen in positive ways. Administrators who spent more than 10% of coursework and other experiences learning about special education and inclusion had more positive attitudes about inclusion (Praisner, 2003). In addition to coursework, experiential learning, perhaps in the form of internships, may be helpful in developing these positive atti-tudes.

Administrators need a clear understanding of the time it takes for educators to collaborate successfully and of the kinds of support needed, both from educator peers and administrators, to successfully implement inclusive schools (Kamens, Loprete, & Slostad, 2003). Edu-cational leadership programs will want to provide experiences and coursework that address these concerns.

Educational leaders need the same kinds of experiences as those that educators need to understand, both theoretically and practically, the role of ableism within our culture as well as within the social insti-tution of education. Leaders must become knowledgeable and experi-enced cultural activists with a broad understanding of issues related to race, class, gender, sexual orientation—and disability (among a host of others). Multicultural education is as much about ableism as it is about any of a host of other isms, and educational leaders need deep and personal learning in this area.

Restructuring Teacher Education Programs for Inclusive Education

Researchers and teacher educators are convinced that teacher prepa-ration programs must change and restructure, in some cases radically, in order for them to adequately prepare future and inservice educators to work effectively in inclusive schools (Brownell & Pajares, 1999; Elhoweris & Alsheikh, 2004; Everington, Hamill, & Lubic, 1996; Griffin, Jones, & Kilgore, 2007; Laarhoven et al., 2006; Nevin, Cohen, Salazar, & Marshall, 2007; Walsh, 2001). Program foci should include extensive field experience, knowledge of and expertise in collaboration, continuous reevaluation, and attention to issues of diversity and inclusion (Brownell, Ross, Colon, & McCallum, 2005).

In one university that successfully restructured its general and special education programs, administrative support was essential and team teaching was an important element (Everington, Hamill, & Lubic, 1996). In another, general and special education faculty together developed a set of common values and designed a program that was cohort based, used a block approach to coursework and experience, and allowed (but didn't require) dual licensure through a fifth-year program (Ford, Pugach, & Otis-Wilborn, 2001).

Teacher certification programs around the country need to be drastically streamlined and reorganized. Giving increased responsibility for teacher education and training to local school districts may be a more efficient and effective model (Walsh, 2001). Developing programs that place inclusion in a variety of courses and experiences, rather than a single survey course, seems an essential ingredient (Kamens, Loprete, & Slostad, 2003).

Reliance on a dual general and special education binary in teacher preparation is clearly outmoded and does a disservice to all educators. Special and general educators, at minimum, must model the kinds of collaborative work necessary to support and sustain inclusive approaches (Titone, 2005).

Use of professional development schools may be one venue for restructuring both teacher education programs and the wider school community. They have clear benefits for university faculty, inservice educators, university students learning to be teachers, as well as K–12 students themselves—it is a win-win approach for all stakeholders. Although often peripheral to the work that goes on in professional schools, special education can play an integral and important role in developing understanding of what inclusion means, how it can work, and the kinds of roles educators must assume in order for it to be successful (Voltz, 2001).

Teacher preparation programs must also move farther away from a medical model approach. Such a model often leaves educators with the notion that students with disabilities are discrete groups whose learning needs can be addressed only by specific and very different teaching strategies (Titone, 2005). Given this understanding, general and special education teacher preparation must clearly move toward programs that are founded in disability studies approaches.

Putting Disability Studies and Critical Theory at the Foundation

What will teacher preparation programs founded in disability studies approaches look like? First, they will be places where educators begin to explore their own ideas, values, and thinking about inclusion, and to see these in cultural contexts. They will also be places where pre- and inservice educators explore the wants, needs, and dreams of people with disabilities, to understand how they will meet those in their classrooms. All of this will require a substantive shift in the culture of teacher education programs themselves (Titone, 2005).

Kincheloe (2003; 2004) argues that teacher education programs must be places where educators develop a critical ontology. He describes this as a process by which they begin "to confront why they think as they do about themselves as teachers—especially in relation to the social, cultural, political, economic, and historical world around them" (2003; p. 47). This kind of critical self-reflection—too often absent in teacher preparation—provides educators an opportunity to explore the meaning of ableism in their thinking and understanding of themselves as well as discover the implications of sexual orientation, gender, class, and race. It offers a chance to look at the meaning of disability and normality and the ways in which they are constituted (Smith, 2004). Perhaps most importantly, it provides an opportunity for educators to seek ways out of the binaries that such traps place us in, both personally and as institutions.

Kincheloe (2004) goes on to argue that teacher education must cultivate educators with an understanding of how they can create a progressive, just, egalitarian, and democratic society through critical and analytical approaches—approaches that are in clear opposition to current ways of seeing processes of teaching and learning. This will mean that they need skills and knowledge about policy, power, and politics, helping themselves and others move beyond a vision of educators as deskilled automatons. And they'll need to understand and expose the negative embrace of current positivist, Cartesian approaches to science and knowledge in education, simplifying rather than complexifying human life and culture. From the perspective of disability studies, this allows educators to see the negative impact of much of what we regard as special education practice and look at ways of moving beyond those.

According to Henry Giroux (2004), public schools have the potential—and so are under attack—to "become democratic public spheres instilling in students the skills, knowledge, and values necessary for them to be critical citizens capable of making power accountable and knowledge an intense object of dialogue and engagement" (p. 12). Later, he comments that

> education can help us imagine a world in which violence can be minimized, and reject the disparagement, exclusion, and abuse of those deemed others in a social order in which one's worth is often measured through the privileged categories of gender, class, citizenship, and language [to this list I would, of course, add ability]. (p. 18)

These are precisely the kinds of schools and the kind of education needed to eliminate prejudice, segregation, and stigma—all essential conditions for the exclusion of students with intellectual and other disabilities.

Unfortunately, says Giroux,

> schools now serve to promote a culture of conformity, consumerism, and deception, on the one hand, and to punish those deemed marginalized by virtue of class and color, on the other. No longer addressed as critical educators and responsible intellectuals, teachers are now largely reduced to deskilled technicians, depoliticized professionals, paramilitary police forces, hawkers for corporate goods, or grant writers. (2006, p. 170)

Educators need to have the means and the language to talk back to those kinds of practices:

> In teacher education programs, ... two important critical pedagogical principles need to inform the curriculum: a critical understanding of dominant ideologies, and exposure to and development of effective counterhegemonic discourses to resist and transform such oppressive practices. (Bartolomé, 2007, p. 280)

These elements must be reflectively explored and explicitly taught in order for them to become future habits of mind for critical educators.

If, as seems clear, the forces of globalization and neoliberalist market economics are undermining public schooling and its attempts to include students with disabilities in educational communities (see chapters 2 and 9 for a more extended discussion), then teacher preparation programs at the very least will need to work actively to ensure that future and inservice educators understand these forces.

From a disability studies perspective, teacher education will need to undergo substantial transformation. Young and Mintz (2008) point out that

> special education and disabilities studies have different goals for the same students—special education works to remediate students so they may live independently in the future and disability studies explores societal constraints that keep students from accessing social and academic experiences now and in the future. (p. 500)

In one sense, then, special education locates brokenness in individuals and seeks to fix that. Disability studies sees oppression and prejudice in sociocultural contexts and seeks to address those concerns.

Teacher preparation programs designed to train educators from a disability studies perspective would seek to explore the source of ableism in cultural contexts and to understand specifically how ableist cultural processes and practices are played out within schools. From a praxic (as opposed to a simply theoretical) perspective, such teacher education programs would focus on changing schools to eliminate ableism and the accompanying segregative practices.

Continued use of special education practices in the United States and around the world has resulted in a dual system of education (Lim, Thaver, & Poon, 2008). To avoid this, disability studies offers education a way to look at "the external factors such as cultural, social, political and economic conditions that contribute toward how people with disabilities are treated" (Lim, Thaver, & Poon, 2008, p. 589). Preservice and inservice educators would be invited to look at ways that they reenact ableism and disabling processes in schools and to create ways for including students with disabilities into civic and educational communities.

Certainly, any teacher education program that includes a disability studies approach will need to be interdisciplinary. It must also eliminate any vestiges of the dual education process in which special and general educators learn in separate, exclusionary silos. Embracing inclusive practices and removing behaviorist understandings of people in the work of teacher educators is essential for transforming visionary teacher education (Ware, 2005).

A truly inclusive teacher education process will interrogate, rather than reinscribe, difference, exclusion, and inclusion. Rice (2006) asserts that there are three essentials for recreating teacher education from a disability studies perspective: "engaging a critical pedagogy of disability, educating disabled citizens and allies, and redefining professional knowledge" (p. 25). To do this, she argues, requires an interdisciplinary approach, drawing from a diverse set of academic fields. Ferri (2006) argues that we need a "pedagogy of disruption" (p. 299) that confronts ableism in educators and ourselves—it is precisely in those intellectual places of cognitive dissonance that real learning and change occurs. I couldn't agree more.

Teacher education in the United States—including at the university at which I teach—will require a substantive transformation. We know what to do to make that happen. The fact that institutions of higher education continue to resist such transformation is a damning indictment of the utility of teacher education to meet the real needs of students in general and of those labeled as having disabilities in particular. Until teacher education programs do so, any claims they make about working toward social justice are a kind of falsifying rhetoric designed to maintain the status quo.

References

Agran, M., & Alper, D. (2000). Curriculum and instruction in general education: Implications for service delivery and teacher preparation. *Journal of the Association for Persons with Severe Handicaps, 25,* 167–174.

Ammah, J., & Hodge, S. (2006). Secondary physical education teachers' beliefs and practices in teaching students with severe disabilities: A descriptive analysis. *The High School Journal, 89,* 40–54.

Austin, V. (2001). Teacher's beliefs about co-teaching. *Remedial and Special Education, 22,* 245-255.

Barnett, C., & Monda-Amaya, L. (1998). Principals' knowledge of and attitudes toward inclusion. *Remedial and Special Education, 19,* 181–92.

Bartholomay, T., Wallace, T., & Mason, C. (2001). *The leadership factor: A key to effective inclusive high schools.* Minneapolis, MN: University of Minnesota Institute on Community Integration.

Bartolomé, L. (2007). Critical pedagogy and teacher education: Radicalizing prospective teachers. In P. McLaren J. Kincheloe (Eds.) *Critical pedagogy: Where are we now?* (pp. 263–286). New York: Peter Lang.

Bradley, J., & Monda-Amaya, L. (2005). Conflict resolution: Preparing preservice special educators to work in collaborative settings. *Teacher Education and Special Education, 28,* 171–184.

Broer, S., Doyle, M., & Giangreco, M. (2005). Perspectives of students with intellectual disabilities about their experiences with paraprofessional support. *Exceptional Children, 71,* 415–430.

Brownell, M., & Pajares, F. (1999). Teacher efficacy and perceived success in mainstreaming students with learning and behavior problems. *Teacher Education and Special Education, 22,* 154–64.

Brownell, M., Ross, D., Colon, E., & McCallum, C. (2005). Critical features of special education teacher preparation: A comparison with general teacher education. *The*

Journal of Special Education. 38, 242–253.

Buell, M., Hallam, R., Gamel-McCormick, M., & Scheer, S. (1999). A survey of general and special education teachers' perceptions and inservice needs concerning inclusion. *International Journal of Disability, Development, and Education, 46,* 143–156.

Department of Education (2002). *Meeting the highly qualified teacher's challenge: The Secretary's second annual report on teacher quality.* Washington, DC: Author.

Department of Education (2006). *The Secretary's fifth annual report on teacher quality.* Washington, DC: Author.

DeSimone, J., & Parmar, R. (2006). Issues and challenges for middle school mathematics teachers in inclusion classrooms. *School Science and Mathematics, 106,* 338–348.

Downing, J., & Peckham-Hardin, K. (2007). Inclusive education: What makes it a good education for students with moderate to severe disabilities? *Research and Practice for Persons with Severe Disabilities, 32,* 16–30.

Doyle, L. (2003). Inclusion: The unifying thread for fragmented metaphors. Annual Meeting of the American Association of Educational Research, Chicago, IL.

Elhoweris, H., & Alsheikh, N. (2004). Teacher's attitudes towards inclusion. Paper presented at the New York State Federation of the Council for Exceptional Children, Albany, NY

Everington, C., Hamill, L., & Lubic, B. (1996). Restructuring teacher preparation programs for inclusion: The change process in one university. *Contemporary Education, 68,* 52–56.

Ferguson, D., Meyer, G., Jeanchild, L., & Juniper, L. (1992). Figuring out what to do with the grownups: How teachers make inclusion "work" for students with disabilities. *Journal of the Association of People with Severe Handicaps, 17,* 218–226.

Ferri, B. (2006). Teaching to trouble. In S. Danforth & S. Gabel (Eds.), *Vital questions facing disability studies in education* (pp. 290–306). New York: Peter Lang.

Foley, R. (2001). Professional development needs of secondary school principals of collaborative-based service delivery models. *The High School Journal, 84,* 10–23.

Ford, A., Pugach, M., & Otis-Wilborn, A. (2001). Preparing general educators to work well with students who have disabilities: What's reasonable at the preservice level? *Learning Disability Quarterly, 24,* 275–285.

Giangreco, M., & Broer, S. (2005). Questionable utilization of paraprofessionals in inclusive schools: Are we addressing symptoms or causes? *Focus on Autism and Other Developmental Disabilities, 20,* 10–26.

Giangreco, M., & Broer, S. (2007). School-based screening to determine overreliance on paraprofessionals. *Focus on Autism and Other Developmental Disabilities, 22,* 149–158.

Giangreco, M., & Doyle, M. (2004). Directing paraprofessional work. In C. Kennedy & E. Horn (Eds.) *Including students with severe disabilities* (pp. 185–204). Boston: Allyn & Bacon.

——— (2007). Teacher assistants in inclusive schools. In L. Florian (Ed.) *The Sage handbook of special education* (pp. 429–439). London: Sage.

Giangreco, M., Halvorson, A., Doyle, M., & Broer, S. (2004). Alternatives to overreliance on paraprofessionals in inclusive schools. *Journal of Special Education Leadership, 17,* 82–90.

Giangreco, M., Smith, C., & Pinckney, E. (2006). Addressing the paraprofessional dilemma in an inclusive school: A program description. *Research & Practice for Persons with Severe Disabilities, 31,* 215–229.

Giangreco, M., Yuan, S., McKenzie, B., Cameron, P., & Fialka, J. (2005). "Be careful what you wish for…": Five reasons to be concerned about the assignment of individual paraprofessionals. *Teaching Exceptional Children, 37,* 28–34.

Giroux, H. (2004). What might education mean after Abu Ghraib? Revisiting Adorno's Politics of Education. *Comparative Studies of South Asia, Africa and the Middle East, 24,* 3–22.

Griffin, C., Jones, H., & Kilgore, K. (2007). The unintended side effects of including students with learning disabilities for teacher educators. *Learning Disabilities, 14,* 195–204.

Hardin, B. (2005). Physical education teachers' reflections on preparation for inclusion. *The Physical Educator, 62,* 44–56.

Henning, M., & Mitchell, L. (2002). Preparing for inclusion. *Child Study Journal, 32,* 19–29.

Kamens, M. (2007). Learning about co-teaching: A collaborative student teaching experience for preservice teachers. *Teacher Education and Special Education, 30,* 155–166.

Kamens, M., Loprete, S., & Slostad, F. (2003). Inclusive classrooms: What practicing teachers want to know. *Action in Teacher Education, 25,* 20–26.

Kerns, G. (1996). Preparation for role changes in general education and special education: Dual certification graduates' perspectives. *Education, 117,* 306–315.

Kincheloe, J. (2003). Critical ontology: Visions of self-hood and curriculum. *Journal of Curriculum Theorizing, 19,* 47–64.

—— (2004). The knowledges of teacher education: Developing a critical complex epistemology. *Teacher Education Quarterly, 31,* 49–66.

Kleinhammer-Trammill, J. (2003). An analysis of federal initiatives to prepare regular educators to serve students with disabilities: Deans' grants, REGI, and beyond. *Teacher Education and Special Education, 26,* 230–245.

Laarhoven, T., Munk, D., Lynch, K., Wyland, S., Dorsch, N., Zurita, L., Bosma, J., & Rouse, J. (2006). Project ACCEPT: Preparing pre-service special and general educators for inclusive education. *Teacher Education and Special Education, 29,* 209–212.

Lim, L., Thaver, T., & Poon, K. (2008). Adapting disability studies within teacher education in Singapore. In S. Gabel & S. Danforth (Eds.), *Disability and the politics of education: An international reader* (pp. 583–597). New York: Peter Lang.

Mastropieri, M. (2001). Is the glass half full or half empty? Challenges encountered by first-year special education teachers. *The Journal of Special Education, 35,* 66–74.

McCormick, L., Noonan, M., Ogata, V., & Heck, R. (2001). Co-teacher relationship and program quality: Implications for preparing teachers for inclusive preschool settings. *Education and Training in Mental Retardation and Developmental Disabilities, 36,* 119–132.

McCormick, L., Noonan, M., Ogata, V., & Heck, R. (2001). Co-teacher relationship and program quality: Implications for preparing teachers for inclusive preschool settings. *Education and Training in Mental Retardation and Developmental Disabilities, 36,* 119-132.

Mock, D., & Kauffman, J. (2002). Preparing teachers for full inclusion: Is it possible? *The Teacher Educator, 37,* 202–215.

National Collaborative on Diversity in the Teaching Force (2004). *Assessment of diversity in America's teaching force: A call to action.* Washington, DC: Author.

National Comprehensive Center for Teacher Quality (2008). *Lessons learned: New teachers talk about their jobs, challenges and long range plans* (Teaching in Changing Times, Issue #3). Washington, DC: Author.

National Council on Disability (1994). *Inclusionary education for students with disabilities: Keeping the promise.* Washington, DC: Author.

National Council on Disability (1995). *Improving the implementation of the Individuals with Disabilities Education Act: Making schools work for all of America's children.* Washington, DC: Author.

National Council on Teacher Quality (2004). *Attracting, developing and retaining effective teachers: Background report for the United States.* Washington, DC: Author.

——— (2007). *2007 State Teacher Policy Yearbook.* Washington, DC: Author.

Nevin, A. (2000). Emerging collaborative and creative roles and processes in inclusive schools: Collaborating to connect the inclusion puzzle. In R. Villa & J. Thousand (Eds.) *Restructuring for caring and effective education: Piecing the puzzle together* (pp. 249–253). Baltimore, MD: Paul H. Brookes.

Nevin, A., Cohen, J., Salazar, L., & Marshall, D. (2007). Student teacher perspectives on inclusive education. Annual Conference of the American Association of Colleges of Teacher Education, New York.

Pierson, M., & Howell, E. (2006). Pre-service teachers' perceptions of inclusion. *Academic Exchange, 10,* 169–173.

Praisner, C. (2003). Attitudes of elementary school principals toward the inclusion of students with disabilities. *Exceptional Children, 69,* 135–145.

Reusen, A., Shoho, A., & Barker, K. (2001). High school teacher attitudes toward inclusion. *The High School Journal, 84,* 7–20.

Rice, N. (2006). Teacher education as a site of resistance. In S. Danforth & S. Gabel (Eds.), *Vital questions facing disability studies in education* (pp. 17–31). New York: Peter Lang.

Salisbury, C. (2006). Principals' perspectives on inclusive elementary schools. *Research & Practice for Persons with Severe Disabilities, 31,* 70–82.

Scott, L., Jellison, J., Chappell, E., & Standridge, A. (2007). Talking with music teachers about inclusion: Perceptions, opinions and experiences. *Journal of Music Therapy, 44,* 38–56.

Shippen, M., Crites, S., Houchins, D., Ramsey, M., & Simon, M. (2005). Preservice teachers' perceptions of including students with disabilities. *Teacher Education and Special Education, 28,* 92–99.

Short, C. & Martin, B. (2005). Case study: Attitudes of rural high school students and teachers regarding inclusion. *The Rural Educator, 27,* 1–10.

Silverman, J. (2007). Epistemological beliefs and attitudes toward inclusion in pre-service teachers. *Teacher Education and Special Education, 30,* 42–51.

Singh, D. (2006). Preparing general education teachers for inclusion. 29th Teacher Education Division of the Council for Exceptional Children Conference, San Diego, CA.

Singh, D. (2007). General education teachers and students with physical disabilities. *The International Journal of Learning, 14,* 205–210.

Smith, P. (2004). Whiteness, normal theory, and disability studies. *Disability Studies Quarterly, 24*(2) (n.p.).

Smith, P., & Routel, C. (2008). Constructing meaning: Including students with disabilities in general education classrooms. 20th Annual Ethnographic and Qualitative Research Conference. Cedarville, IL.

220   SMITH

Snyder, L., Garriott, P., & Aylor, M. (2001). Inclusion confusion: Putting the pieces together. *Teacher Education and Special Education, 24*, 198–207.

Sprague, M., & Pennell, D. (2000). The power of partners preparing preservice teachers for inclusion. *The Clearing House, 73*, 168–70.

Thompson, S. (2007). A community just for practice: A case of an inclusive/special education course. *Canadian Journal of Education, 30*, 171–192.

Thousand, J., & Villa, R. (2000). Collaborative teaming: A powerful tool in school restructuring. In R. Villa & J. Thousand (Eds.) *Restructuring for caring and effective education: Piecing the puzzle together* (pp. 254–291). Baltimore, MD: Paul H. Brookes.

Titone, C. (2005). The philosophy of inclusion: Roadblocks and remedies for the teacher and the teacher educator. *Journal of Educational Thought, 39*, 7–32.

Torres, J., Santos, J., Peck, N., & Cortes, L. (2004). *Minority teacher recruitment, preparation, and retention*. Providence, RI: Educational Alliance, Brown University.

Voltz, D. (2001). Preparing general education teachers for inclusive settings: The role of special education teachers in the professional development school context. *Learning Disability Quarterly, 24*, 288–296.

Walsh, K. (2001). *Teacher certification reconsidered: Stumbling for quality*. Baltimore, MD: Abell Foundation.

Ware, L. (2005). Many possible futures, many different directions: Merging critical special education and disability studies. In S. Gabel (Ed.) *Disability Studies in Education: Readings in theory and method* (pp. 103–124). New York: Peter Lang.

Young, K., & Mintz, E. (2008). A comparison: Difference, dependency, and stigmatization in special education and disability studies. In S. Gabel & S. Danforth (Eds.), *Disability and the politics of education: An international reader* (pp. 499–511). New York: Peter Lang.

Yssel, N., Engelbrecht, P., Oswald, M., Eloff, I., & Swart, E. (2007). Views of inclusion: A comparative study of parents' perceptions in South Africa and the United States. *Remedial and Special Education, 28*, 356–365.

CHAPTER 11

Future Directions

Policy, Practice, and Research

PHIL SMITH

> In an authentic democracy we would expect to find schools defined by a spirit of cooperation, inclusion, and full participation, places that honor diversity while building unity. (Ayers, 2007, p. xiii)

The authors writing in this book assert that inclusion for people with intellectual and other disabilities is not just best practice but a human and civil right and a moral imperative. Yet people labeled as having intellectual disabilities remain marginalized and oppressed in our society and, for the most part, are educated outside of general education classrooms. How, then, do we change civil and educational communities to ensure that they are fully included in schools and other settings?

It will likely take a change, not just a systemic adjustment in services and supports, but a substantive cultural shift in perspectives, values, and thinking, one that is "part of a transformative political project" (Barton, 2007). This kind of transformation will require work in at least three areas of importance: policy (law, regulation, process, and procedure, in federal, state, and local arenas); practice (the how of it all—putting inclusive education into action, in schools, and in ensuring the adequacy of teacher education); and research (what works? what doesn't? why, and how?). Here, then, I will highlight the most important transformations in policy, in practice, and in research, to ensure and enable these essential rights.

Future Directions: Policy

> More than a decade ago, the National Council on Disability said that the field of special education needs to undergo a paradigm shift, from its current status as a system apart from regular education to one which is an integral part of regular education, providing a wide array of supports and services within the context of regular education programs and facilities. (National Council on Disability,1995)

These words are just as important and just as true today as they were then. Though, I must say, it might be easier and perhaps more productive to simply start over: blow up education, in particular special education, as we currently understand it in the United States and begin fresh with something that starts from a completely different place.

But how do we do that? How do we create the kind of real "systemic, transformative change" (Barton, 2007) in education (as well as in civil communities) necessary to ensure that people with intellectual disabilities are fully included? One mixed-methods project exploring policy implications of state-level reform legislation for students with disabilities and at-risk students found that reforms need to focus on positive outcomes for all students, not just for those with disabilities or who were at-risk. It also suggested that appropriate professional development resources need to be made available for all educators and administrators, not just for those in special education (Furney, Hasazi, & Clarke/Keefe, 2005). It is essential that we develop education policy that systematizes shared responsibility for the needs of all students and ensures that preservice and inservice teachers and administrators have the knowledge, resources, and experience to deliver differentiated instruction to all students (Furney, Hasazi, Clark/Keefe, & Hartnett, 2003).

Close to ten years ago, Bobby Silverstein (who has had a hand in crafting much of the important disability legislation over the last couple of decades) outlined a framework for understanding and analyzing public disability policy (2000). He based his framework on four critical values:

> Equality of opportunity: understanding that while each person has unique needs and abilities, people with disabilities should have the same access to supports, services, resources, and capacities in our society as those who do not have disabilities.

> Full participation: empowering individuals and families: people with disabilities and their families need to be full and real participants in decisions about what happens with their lives.

> Independent living: people with disabilities need appropriate services, supports, accommodations, and assistance in order to live meaningfully and independently in the community.

> Economic self-sufficiency: people with disabilities need the same kinds of economic stability and security that we all require in our lives. (Silverstein, 2000)

Any public policy work—whether related to special education or not—that explores issues related to disability would do well to keep those four key values in mind. Silverstein's guidelines are a key component for developing a new way of thinking about educating all students.

A foundational step would be creating a national policy conversation in which special education is "reconceptualized as a set of services that are available to children who need them, without the need for a disability label" (Harry & Klingner, 2006, p. 175). The notion of disability is, in its essence, metaphorical, based on language features that construct deficits inherent in individuals and that stigmatize, reify, and commodify those deficits (Danforth, 2007; Smith, 2006). These metaphors are principally ableist, creating systems of oppression, discrimination, devaluation, and exclusion for students with disabilities and their families (Hehir, 2002). Stepping outside these constructs requires looking at disability, not from a medical model of inherent deficit, but from a social model that understands disability as culturally constructed, something that society does to people rather than being something that resides in their bodies or minds. Such a portrayal allows us to explore ways in which cultural understandings (rather than individual differences) create difficulties for students. From this perspective, providing the supports necessary to meet the needs of all students, regardless of learning difference, creates opportunities for outcomes that are positive for all within particular cultures.

As Harry and Klingner (2007) point out, "Language in itself is not the problem. What is problematic is the belief system that this language represents" (p. 16). Changing the labels that we use to name students with disabilities from one set of words to another set of words will not eliminate stigma, oppression, discrimination, or segregation. Eliminating labels will. More importantly, changing cultural understandings of disability will begin a process of healing that can respond in important ways to the oppression and segregation of people with intellectual disabilities and their families.

I'd recommend doing away with special education altogether. That sounds really crazy coming from a guy who teaches in the largest university special education program in the United States. But with my disability studies hat on, and in thinking about what I and others have talked about in this book, I can see no real benefit to students with intellectual disabilities and their families of the kinds of special education policies in the United States that have formulated since federal special education law was enacted. Oh, sure there have been little pockets here and there of success—but those have been in spite of, not because of, special education. Until, or unless, *all* educators take responsibility for *all* students—until *all* communities take responsibility for *all* of their members—people with intellectual disabilities will be left by the wayside. What we need is the kind of policy discussions that will ensure that those kinds of goals can and will be met. And they won't be met from within special education, at either policy or practice positions.

Does that mean we need to give up special knowledge about disability, or teaching? No. That would be like saying that we should give up physicians, in order to eliminate the medical model of disability. If I have trouble with my heart, I'd want to go to my doctor and then probably to a cardiac specialist—somebody who knows what they're talking about. There is knowledge about how to teach people with intellectual disabilities that will be useful to have. But much of that knowledge will be useful for *all* teachers to have (not all of it, probably, but most of it). It would be useful to get that knowledge into the hands of all teachers, not just some.

Follow the Money: Policy Changes in School Finance to Create Inclusion

Given what has been discussed in this text, "careful scrutiny of governmental policies and mandates related to school financing" (Harry & Klingner, 2006, p. 176) may appear to be an almost unnecessary recommendation. Yet, though we know that

educational resources are not equitably distributed across schools and districts and that culturally and linguistically diverse children living in high-poverty areas are more likely than their peers to attend schools that are inadequately funded and staffed. (Harry & Klingner, 2006, p. 176),

we have done little to address substantive funding concerns.

While there have been large increases in special education funding over the last decade, funding levels continue to fall short of what is necessary to address the need. When Congress initially enacted special education legislation in the 1970s, it decided that it wanted to fund up to 40% of the "excess" cost of special education, the cost of educating a student with disabilities over and above the cost of educating a student without a disability, which was felt then to be approximately twice the cost of educating students without disabilities[1] (Apling, 2005).

While Congress has steadily increased its funding levels over time, it has never come close to reaching its goal at the 40% level. In FY2005, special education funding of Part B of IDEA (both as proposed by the president and as actually appropriated by Congress) at only 18.6% did not reach even half of the excess cost. Given a federal appropriation of $10.6 billion for IDEA Part B in FY2005, this left a balance of the estimated excess cost for students with disabilities of $46.2 billion (Apling, 2005). This balance is borne typically by local school districts already overwhelmed by budget shortfalls (Kusler, 2003).

We know that incentive and disincentive features are inherent in any funding program, local, state, or federal, including those related to special education (Parrish, 1993; 1995b). We also know that current federal funding structures encourage the labeling of students with disabilities, in order to capture federal and state dollars (Greene & Forster, 2002). It is essential, then, that federal, state, and local laws, policies, rules, and procedures be looked at closely to see ways in which they either support or get in the way of the efforts made to include students with intellectual disabilities in general education classrooms (National Council on Disability, 1994; Williamson, McLesky, Hoppey, & Rentz, 2006). As part of this project, eliminating funding disincentives to inclusion will be an essential goal in ensuring that students with intellectual and other disabilities are increasingly educated in general education settings (National Council on Disability, 1994). Perhaps even more importantly, creating actual funding INCENTIVES for inclusion, at federal, state, and local levels, will be necessary to ensure that inclusion happens.

One way of creating increased control of dollars at local levels is through so-called demand-oriented models. Although demand-oriented funding models do not make inclusion a certainty, such approaches make it more likely that families might have control over whether their students with intellectual (or other) disabilities are included in general education classrooms (Pijl & Dyson, 1998), taking control out of the hands of professionals who for so long have dominated the discourse and practice of education.[2]

At minimum, a clear set of principles should be applied to funding structures, whether at state or national levels. Funding should be understandable, equitable, adequate, predictable, flexible, identification neutral, fiscally accountable, cost-based, placement neutral, cost controlled, outcome accountable, connected to general education funding, and politically acceptable, as well as have a reasonable reporting burden (Parrish, 1994; 1995a; 2001; Parrish, Harr, Anthony, Merickel, & Esra, 2003).

How do we resolve the ongoing overrepresentation of students of color in segregated special education programs? A piece of the solution, of course, would be to adequately fund schools attended predominantly by students from racial and ethnic minorities or by those who live in poverty. But the reality is probably that such a solution would be like putting a small bandage on an injury requiring major surgery: it'd help, but its not much good in the long term.

Michael Apple has a vision of a better set of solutions:

> This is not to dismiss either the possibility or necessity of school reform. However, we need to take seriously the probability that only by focusing on the exogenous socioeconomic features, not simply the organizational features, of successful schools can all schools succeed. Eliminating poverty through greater income parity, establishing effective and much more equal health and housing programs, and positively refusing to continue the hidden and not so hidden politics of racial exclusion and degradation that so clearly still characterize daily life … only by tackling these issues together can substantive progress be made. (2004, p. 28)

To which I'd add ways of eliminating structural and institutional ableism in our culture.

An important initiative for students with intellectual disabilities, especially as they begin to move from school to postsecondary opportunities (whether toward further education or into the workforce), is to streamline and maximize the synergy of combining funding from various sources to enable students to move seamlessly from one set of supports to another. This will require collaboration across a variety of federal and state funding streams to support individual students to maximize their potential (President's Committee for People with Intellectual Disabilities, 2004).

Moving from Least Restrictive to Nonrestrictive Environments

As has been pointed out in several ways and in several places in this text and elsewhere, although the notion of the least restrictive environment may have begun as a potentially progressive notion, it has become a loophole for ensuring that students with disabilities remain in segregated educational settings (Connor, Chapter 8; LeRoy and Lacey, Chapter 5; Mintz, Chapter 6; Mutua and Siders, Chapter 7; Owen & Gabel, Chapter 4; Taylor, 2004; Taylor, Racino, Knoll, & Lutfiyya, 1987). What are the policy implications of this for federal and state law and regulation regarding inclusive education? The idea of least restrictive environment as outlined and required there should be eliminated. In its place, the notion of nonrestrictive environments should be implemented (Taylor, Racino, Knoll, & Lutfiyya, 1987).

Rewriting IDEIA

Much of what I've outlined so far will, at the very least, require a substantial rewriting of the Individuals with Disabilities Education Improvement Act (if not, in fact, just completely starting over—certainly a daunting but perhaps useful task). An important place to start is to insert a definition of inclusion, along with supporting legislation. Again, as I've said, we could do worse than start with Giangreco's (2006) definition (see Chapter 2).

Families and people with disabilities indicate that changes in the IDEA legislation and supporting regulations have over time moved laws farther away from protecting the rights of students with disabilities and their families, and closer to protecting the interests of school systems (Consortium for Citizens with Disabilities, 2005). Too often, families need to fight to enable their children with disabilities to be included in regular education classrooms (Kluth, Villa, & Thousand, 2002). Restoring and extending these rights to students with intellectual disabilities and their families would clearly be the right thing to do. Core concepts of disability policy that affect families must be examined closely whenever policy initiatives are undertaken (Turnbull, Beegle, & Stowe, 2001).

In a Special Education Expenditure Project analysis, school districts spent $146.5 million in the 1999–2000 school year on legal proceedings, due process actions, and mediation activities related to special education. These cases occurred in 38% of the country's school districts. Urban districts were more likely to have procedural safeguard cases, as were larger districts, indicating that they may not be as responsive to the needs of families because of bureaucratic structures. Results also indicate that districts with families with more income, and thus more resources and knowledge, had higher levels of procedural safeguard cases (Chambers, Harr, & Dhanani, 2003).[3] This raises a concern about the availability of redress for families who are impoverished.

The Governmental Accountability Office looked at how the U.S. Department of Education handled situations when states were found to be out of compliance with IDEA and its regulations. Typically, the Department of Education worked with states through technical assistance processes, rather than applying sanctions. The department worked with states to develop action plans to correct problems—a goal that was to be accomplished in one year. However, most often, corrective action plans remained open for two to seven years. This, coupled with long waits to issue monitoring reports, and with time lags involved with the development and approval of corrective action plans, meant that resolution times for problems were extremely long (Governmental Accountability Office, 2004).

Restoring rights to families and students with disabilities will save schools money, not make education more expensive (as school professionals often fear). Effective monitoring by the federal Department of Education must be implemented to ensure that states do what they are legally required to do.

In this discussion of families, I do not mean to imply that *all* families want school inclusion for their students with intellectual disabilities. I don't think they do—in fact, slightly more parents do not believe full inclusion is a good thing, either in general or for their child specifically (Palmer, Borthwick-Duffy, Widaman, & Best, 1998). What I *do* think is that families believe that their children with intellectual and developmental disabilities can function and achieve in real-world settings, and that they want their children to have as much contact with their peers without disabilities in order to get modeling of appropriate behaviors and skills (Gallagher, Floyd, Stafford, Taber, Brozovic, & Alberto, 2000). And parent opinions about inclusion are strongly influenced by child and parent characteristics, previous school placement history, and the kinds of inclusive opportunity explored (Palmer, Borthwick-Duffy, Widaman, & Best, 1998)—a complex set of values and perceptions that cannot be anything except heavily influenced by cultural constructions of disability that are inherently ableist. What is important to recognize is that almost half of all parents *do* want full inclusion for their children with intellectual disabilities (Palmer, Borthwick-Duffy, Widaman, & Best, 1998) and should have the right to make that happen.

Future Directions: Practice

Peters (2004) outlined Lipsky and Gartner's (1997) set of best practices for what is essential for making inclusion happen:

A Sense of Community: philosophy & vision that all children belong & can learn

Leadership: school administrators play a critical role in implementation

High Standards: high expectations for all children appropriate to their needs

Collaboration and Cooperation: support and co-operative learning

Changing Roles and Responsibilities: of all staff

Array of Services: e.g., health, mental health and social services

Partnership with Parents: equal partners in educating children

Flexible Learning Environments: pacing, timing, and location

Strategies Based on Research: best-practice strategies for teaching and learning

New Forms of Accountability: standardized tests & multiple sources

Access: physical environment and technology

Continuing Professional Development: on-going. (p. 10)

While these are principles that are essential to make inclusive education a real possibility, they are, to my mind, critical to making *all* education a real possibility.

Chief among these principles, I think, is the need for creating a sense of community in schools. We have known for a long time that learning happens in social contexts—it's all about relationships (Gibbs, 1987; F. Smith, 1998). Things happen—action is taken—when people support each other, through formal or informal circles (networks) of support (Falvey, Forest, Pearpoint, & Rosenberg, 1997; Ludlum, 2002; Perske, 1998). Community is about a sense of belonging—of being "members of each other":

> People recognized as members benefit from everyday exchanges of support that create opportunities to play socially valued roles and chances to form personally significant relationships. People excluded from membership risk loneliness, isolation, and powerlessness. (O'Brien & O'Brien, 1996, p. 5)

Community building—whether it occurs in schools or civic communities—is about discovering and supporting the assets that already exist in communities. It's about finding individual people with the skills, experiences, and knowledge needed to get the work of communities done (Green, 2006).

Leadership and administrative support are essential for making inclusion happen in schools (Kamens, Loprete, & Slostad, 2003). To create that kind of support, administrators will need training and experience in tools that encourage inclusion (Praisner, 2003; Reusuen,

Shoho, & Barker, 2001). And they'll need to understand the philosophical foundations of inclusion as well as gain experience with collaborative decision-making models (Doyle, 2003; Foley, 2001; Salisbury, 2006).

Expectations—of teachers, administrators, related support providers, families, community members—are critical to the success of educating students with intellectual disabilities in general education classrooms. Too often, educators have low expectations for students with disabilities and so don't provide them with access to the general curriculum (Downing, 2008). So it will be essential that pre- and inservice educators participate in experiences where high expectations are modeled.

Cooperation and collaboration are core habits of the mind for creating and maintaining the inclusion of students with disabilities. Robust and powerful models for developing collaborative groups have proven successful around the world; educators and others need experience and knowledge about them (Villa & Thousand, 2000; Thousand, Villa, & Nevin, 2002).

Educators, support providers, and administrators will need to rethink their roles in schools in fundamental ways. Collaborative strategies, such as co-teaching, in order to be successful, require special educators and general education teachers to explore new modes of working with students and to develop a fresh professional relationship with their colleagues (Villa, Thousand, & Nevin, 2008). A broad and diverse array of supports and services, from a variety of support providers, will need to be used to create successful inclusive opportunities. Wraparound approaches, for example, which use diverse providers from multiple service systems, both in and out of education, support families to participate in decision making and allow students to remain in nonrestrictive environments (Eber, Breen, Rose, Unizycki, & London, 2008). Related service providers, engaged and used carefully, can ensure that students with intellectual (as well as other) disabilities are included fully in general education classrooms (Giangreco, Prelock, Reid, Dennis, & Edelman, 2000).

Developing partnerships with families means seeing families as the real experts in the lives of their children with disabilities and understanding that they should have the tools and power to make decisions for students. In family support models, educators understand that families are the only real constant in the lives of students with disabilities and that their role is to support the priorities of families, thus ensuring that their needs are met in ways that they trust and value (Hanson & Lynch, 2004).

Flexible learning environments and strategies based on research too are important for ensuring the success of inclusion. One set of best practices for including students with disabilities in schools that meet the needs of all is a Universal Design for Learning (UDL) (CAST, 2008; Rose & Meyer, 2006; Villa, Thousand, Nevin, & Liston, 2005). The advantage of UDL is that its approach meets the needs of a truly diverse set of learners, not just those with disabilities (Jiménez, Graf, & Rose, 2007). In general education classrooms, UDL has positive practical implications for the education of students with intellectual disabilities, including those with the most significant disabilities (Downing, 2006; Spooner, Dymond, Smith, & Kennedy, 2006; Wehmeyer, 2006).

To create a real universal design for learning, one that meets the needs of all students, means that change directed at special education must include change in education overall, pay attention to adequate resources, and reflect movement toward a noncategorical approach.

As pointed out elsewhere (see Chapter 3), the so-called No Child Left Behind Act has had unintended negative consequences for the inclusion of students with disabilities in general education classrooms. Although the need for holding educators and schools accountable for the education of all students is critical, how we go about doing that is even more important. The use of high-stakes testing approaches has little value for students with disabilities, or for any student for that matter. Developing culturally competent accountability strategies that also encourage values of community and inclusion seems essential to meeting the real needs of students with intellectual disabilities and their families.

Although the federal government has proposed new regulations that will broadly change whether people with disabilities can physically access community environments, local communities continue to resist such essential changes, and immense hurdles remain related to basic means of access (Brock, 2008; Gentile, 2008). Although the Americans with Disabilities Act has done much to ensure the possibility of access for people with disabilities in the United States, it is clear that disability advocates and their allies still have much work to do in changing legislation and the thinking of people without disabilities.

As I've pointed out elsewhere in this book (see Chapter 10), all of this will require ongoing professional development activities for educators, administrators, and related support providers. The kinds of knowledge and experience necessary to make the changes needed to allow for inclusive opportunities cannot be delivered in one shot. It will take a long-term commitment by development providers and others to make it happen.

Teacher Preparation: Changing the Way We Do Business

In order to meet the educational needs of all children, we'll need to make real and substantial changes in the way that we do teacher preparation. All educators need to take responsibility for all students. In order to accomplish this goal, we need to dramatically transform our institutions for teacher education (Griffin, Jones, & Kilgore, 2007; Laarhoven et al., 2006; Nevin, Cohen, Salazar, & Marshall, 2007; Walsh, 2001).

At the foundation of this kind of transformed teacher preparation program must be—will be—a focus on a critical complex epistemology and critical ontology (Kincheloe, 2003; 2004). In order to eradicate notions of a medical model of disability from education, disability must also be at the center of teacher preparation programs that seek to create real inclusive educational opportunities, both in and out of university.

Teacher educators must model the kinds of educational practices that we know are successful in creating and maintaining inclusive education (Nevin, Cohen, Salazar, & Marshall, 2007; Ware, 2005). This will be difficult work: "the tensions in schools of education specific to disability and 'inclusive education' parallel those in K–123 settings where educators are constrained by institutional structures that insure exclusion and where cultural barriers obscure alternative understandings of disability" (Ware, 2005, p. 105).

Because of the importance of collaboration among educators in order for students with intellectual (as well as other) disabilities to be included in general education classrooms, both general and special educators will need theory, information, and experience in collaboration, consultation, and co-teaching in inclusive classrooms (Bradley & Monda-Amaya, 2005; DeSimone & Parmar, 2006; Downing & Peckham-Hardin, 2007; Kamens, 2007; Shippen, Crites, Houchins, Ramsey, & Simon, 2005; Short & Martin, 2005; Silverman, 2007; Thompson, 2007). And because of the centrality of families in the lives of students with intellectual disabilities, all educators must have a clear understanding of the important principles necessary to support them adequately (Turnbull, Beegle, & Stowe, 2001). What might the curriculum of teacher education look like if it were to be infused with disability studies approaches? Rice (2006) suggests that it would be radically different from the kinds of curricula that focuses on teaching educators the methods of instructing students with disabilities. Instead, she suggests, such a curriculum should point toward "disrupting the 'common sense' knowledge about disability and the professional discourses that produce teachers as 'subjects'" (Rice, 2006, p. 18). This kind of curriculum would explore cultural texts to unpack ableist elements and use as critical resources texts written by people with disabilities and their families. Rice calls for a new kind of teacher education that explores the meaning of normalcy and looks at disability from interdisciplinary perspectives.

Ware (2006) also asserts the need for teacher education that is critical of special education, that is, working "to expose the mythology of 'special' in education" (p. 271). She calls for the use of disability studies scholarship that is focused on the humanities across a wide range of form, media, content, and theory, and away from the professionalized discourse of special education. She insists that teacher education must model the kinds of basic and simple tenets that inclusive education recommends for K–12 educators (Ware, 2005). And she posits that the biggest hurdle to restructuring education, special or otherwise, is its continued reliance on behaviorist underpinnings, which must be summarily and totally rooted out and eliminated (Ware, 2005).

Also seeking a way out of the manner in which special education reifies both disability and education, Ferri (2006) uses a humanities-based approach, critiquing normative views of disability and in so doing problematizing ideas such as inclusion. She notes that "even in inclusive models the dominant group retains the power to include or exclude" (p. 292). She also notes the problems of "doing" disability studies in a current milieu that is without traditional textbook resources and confined within traditional teacher education programs.

It will be important for this new kind of disability-studies-infused teacher education to contextualize the social construction of disability. This sort of teacher education praxis will need to understand and explore disability as an interactive (and not just another) part of one's identity—one that is not separate from other aspects of identity, such as race or gender (Ferri & Connor, 2006).

Around the world, students with disabilities remain locked outside of institutions of higher education for a variety of institutional
and cultural reasons (Powell, Felkendorff, & Hollenweger, 2008; Marshall, 2008; Burgstahler & Corey, 2008). In any real teacher education
program that is truly adherent to a disability studies approach, it
seems to me, actively recruiting and supporting students with disabilities to become future educators would be an important, if not essential, element.

Future Directions: Research

Barton (2007) asks us to consider "to what extent is research a political
act?" If we accept, as many disability studies, critical theory, and
postmodern scholars suggest, that research is inherently a value-
laden human endeavor, then its political and ideological nature must
be foregrounded (Smith, 1999; 2006; 2008).

To better support students with intellectual disabilities, it will be
essential to explore the ideological nature of what we understand as
intelligence itself and to grasp the political nature of the psychology
that creates, reinforces, and enforces the notion. For "the concepts of
intelligence and cognitive development often used by mainstream
educational psychology are relics from another era" (Kincheloe, 1999,
p. 1). This will require researchers

> to document and validate types of reasoning and intelligence that differ from
> those now recognized by the field and the instruments used to measure them.
> Such a practice democratizes intelligence by admitting new members to the ex-
> clusive community of the talented. In this reconceived context, the central crite-
> rion for aptitude no longer involves simply how closely the individual comes up
> to "*our* norms." (Kincheloe, 1999, p. 1)

Kincheloe goes on to assert that intelligence is learnable and that it
needs to be taught in schools, universities, and other social institutions to increasingly diverse sets of learners. He calls for the creation
and exploration of a "critically grounded, postmodern, postformal
educational psychology" (p. 16).

An early exploration of the provision of special education incentives proposed a research agenda outlining factors necessary to understand the efficacy of special education funding and to provide
sound, research-based advice regarding special education policy and
practice. This research agenda included exploring

> adequacy of funding in relation to need in terms of both quantity and quality of
> services; equity of fund distribution; anticipated effects of service delivery in

terms of quality of life and in terms of future economic benefits; comprehensive-
ness of types of services and programming arrangements in relation to need;
control and coordination of services; compatibility with regular-education finance and service delivery; and efficiency. (Kakalik, 1979, p. 197)

Little had been done to that point to explore those issues. In the
more than thirty years since the passage of IDEA, little more has been
added to the base of research related to that agenda. Sound policy,
practice, and funding proposals cannot be made without answers to
those questions. In addition to quantitative explorations of these issues, their meaning for educators, people with disabilities and their
families, and policymakers must be explored, for which qualitative
research methods will be required.

At the core of all research into the meaning of inclusive education
for students with intellectual disabilities, or for students with any
other disability label, for that matter, must be a focus on disability
studies approaches. We've proven over decades that special education and the research agendas that it has promulgated have done little
if anything to ensure or enhance the rights of students with disabilities and their families. It's time for a new approach. Disability studies
is just that.

We don't have time to wait—it's long past time for waiting.

Baby Steps

I lived in New England for most of my life, spending greater or lesser
time in almost all of its states. I lived for almost half of my life in
Vermont, and it was there that I learned the values that have become
important to me as a community member, a disability studies scholar,
and a critical theorist and educator. I met and became friends and colleagues with a host of self-advocates (people with developmental disabilities who speak for themselves), learning from them and their
families. I learned about the work that it takes to be sure that they are
fully included in civic and educational communities—about the tire-
less and endless support and effort that is needed to make that happen. I learned about the baby steps that individual people and whole
communities have taken on the path to get there. I was fortunate to
live in Vermont—it was the second state to have closed its large institution for people with developmental disabilities, right next to the
first state to have done so (New Hampshire). These two states have
long been in the lead for including people with significant disabilities,
even those with intellectual disabilities, in general education class-

rooms. I learned from the people of those two northern New England states a tremendous amount about inclusion, how to make it happen, and its importance and value in the lives of us all.

I've lived now for five years in Michigan. I have a terrific job—in fact, I tell my colleagues and my students that it's the best job in the world (and its true). The sadness (and sometimes hopelessness) that I feel is not because I'm homesick for where I grew up. Rather, it's because Michigan still has large institutions (big group homes) for people with developmental disabilities. And the state ranks far down at the bottom of the list of states for including students with *any* disability, not just intellectual disabilities, in general education classrooms. So many adults live in group homes here (there's one just down the street from my house)—places that I consider to be mini-institutions. I feel sad for people that I value (though I don't know many of them) and deplore the lives they are forced to lead.

I argue with my colleagues and students constantly—they tell me that segregating students with disabilities is often necessary, perhaps essential. One of my students, who now teaches at a separate school for students with significant disabilities, tells me that inclusion is flat out wrong for her "kids" (who are really young adults). A colleague told me yesterday that I was "misguided" (and he is still a good friend, someone with whom I share an occasional beer). They laugh with (mostly not at) me when I bake an occasional "inclusion coffee cake" for breakfast at our monthly department faculty meeting.

It's frustrating, in so many ways, in spite of my self-deprecating laughter. Yet this is the work that I wanted and still want—this is *exactly* why I got into this field—to engage in the kind of social justice and human rights struggles that I find myself working on, trying to change the hearts and minds of people around me. A couple of days ago, in one of my graduate classes, we all brought in blank t-shirts. I made up a bunch of iron-on transfers that said "end the r-word." Someone brought in a tool that attaches rhinestones. Another student brought in fabric paints. We laughed, made crazy t-shirts, put them on, wore them proudly in the halls, and talked about why this was the right thing to do.

Will it change the world? Make inclusion happen overnight? Nope. It's a baby step, another teensy-weensy move in the direction of social and ethical goodness. The seventeen students in that graduate class got it. With luck, they'll go out and help some other people get it—a viral change of ways of thinking and new ideas that will, eventually, lead to giant steps (knock on wood).

Also with luck, this book will further that same kind of viral change. It's another kind of baby step in figuring out what the issues are, a movement in the direction of social justice for all people—in schools, in communities. I guess that's what it's all about—taking those first steps, on the way to learning to walk.

Come to think of it, as I write this, it's a beautiful spring day outside. The snow is finally gone (except for one lonely pile in the yard down the street), crocuses are blooming and daffodils are poking out of the warming earth. I just noticed buds on the maple tree in the front yard.

So, perhaps you'll think I'm being presumptuous, but still, let me extend to you an invitation, on this lovely spring day: let's go for a walk. Ah, but not just any walk. Let's take a walk in the spirit of my New England forebear Henry David Thoreau who wrote, in his essay "Walking," that "we should go forth on the shortest walk, perchance, in the spirit of undying adventure." Let's walk into a future where people with intellectual disabilities are fully included into all of our communities, school and civic—a future where we can struggle with and eliminate the core of ableism that is at the foundation of our culture. Baby steps or giant strides, wheelchair or scooter or walker—it's a walk we can *all* take.

To me, *that* walk sounds like an adventure.

Notes

1   The cost of providing services to students with disabilities is approximately twice the cost of education for a student without a disabilities, based on information from the Special Education Expenditure Project (OSERS, 2003).

2   The issue here is not (just) about whether or not all, most, many, or some families want inclusion. Rather, it is about who has control over that decision—where the power in decision-making lies. In this context, decision-making power lies in the hands of professionals. That being said, while I've not found any research about how many family members want inclusive educational and community opportunities for their sons, daughters, or siblings with disabilities, qualitative research indicates that family members believe that their siblings and children with intellectual and developmental disabilities have the ability to learn and grow in the real world, and that they must have as much contact as possible with their peers without disabilities in order to have models for appropriate skills and behavior (Gallagher, Floyd, Stafford, Taber, Brozovic, & Alberto, 2000).

3   Because of the way data was collected, it was unclear whether expenditures reported included reimbursements to families for legal costs, as required under IDEA (Chambers, Harr, & Dhanani, 2003).

References

Apling, R. (2005). *Individuals with Disabilities Education Act (IDEA): Current funding trends.* Washington, DC: Congressional Research Service, The Library of Congress.

Apple, M. (2004). Creating difference: Neo-liberalism, neo-conservatism and the politics of educational reform. *Educational Policy, 18,* 12–44.

Ayers, W. (2007). Foreword. In A. Winfield, *Eugenics and education in America: Institutionalized racism and the implications of history, ideology, and memory* (pp. xi–xiv). New York: Peter Lang.

Barton, L. (2007). Inclusive education and disability studies: Observations and issues for debate. 7th Annual Second City Disability Studies in Education Conference, Chicago, IL.

Bradley, J., & Monda-Amaya, L. (2005). Conflict resolution: Preparing preservice special educators to work in collaborative settings. *Teacher Education and Special Education, 28,* 171–184.

Brock, E. (2008). Feds to redefine ADA accessibility rules: Proposed changes could cost locals millions. *American City & County, 123*(10), 8, 10.

Burgstahler, S., & Corey, R. (2008). Moving in from the margins: From accommodation to universal design. In S. Gabel and S. Danforth (Eds.), *Disability and the politics of education: An international reader* (pp. 561–582). New York: Peter Lang.

CAST (2008). *Universal design for learning guidelines version 1.0.* Wakefield, MA: Author.

Chambers, J., Harr, J., & Dhanani, A. (2003). *What are we spending on procedural safeguards in special education, 1999–2000?* Palo Alto, CA: Center for Special Education Finance.

Consortium for Citizens with Disabilities (2005). *CCD Education Task Force* recommendations for IDEA regulations. Washington, DC: Author.

Danforth, S. (2007). Disability as metaphor: Examining the conceptual framing of emotional behavioral disorder in American public education. *Educational Studies, 42,* 8–27.

DeSimone, J., & Parmar, R. (2006). Issues and challenges for middle school mathematics teachers in inclusion classrooms. *School Science and Mathematics, 106,* 338–348.

Downing, J. (2006). On peer support, universal design, and access to the core curriculum for students with severe disabilities: A personnel preparation perspective. *Research and Practice for Persons with Severe Disabilities, 31,* 327–330.

——— (2008). Inclusive education: Why is it not more prevalent? *TASH Connections, 34*(2), 8–10, 13.

Downing, J., & Peckham-Hardin, K. (2007). Inclusive education: What makes it a good education for students with moderate to severe disabilities? *Research and Practice for Persons with Severe Disabilities, 32,* 16–30.

Doyle, L. (2003). Inclusion: The unifying thread for fragmented metaphors. Annual Meeting of the American Association of Educational Research, Chicago, IL.

Eber, L., Breen, K., Rose, J., Unizycki, R., & London, T. (2008). Wraparound as a tertiary level intervention for students with emotional/behavioral needs. *Teaching Exceptional Children, 40,* 16–22.

Falvey, M., Forest, M., Pearpoint, J., & Rosenberg, R. (1997). *All my life's a circle—Using the tools: Circles, MAPS, & PATHS* (2nd ed.). Toronto, ON: Inclusion Press.

Ferri, B. (2006). Teaching to trouble. In S. Danforth & S. Gabel (Eds). *Vital questions facing disability studies in education* (pp. 289–306). New York: Peter Lang.

Ferri, B., & Connor, D. (2006). *Reading resistance: Discourses of exclusion in desegregation and inclusion debates.* New York: Peter Lang.

Foley, R. (2001). Professional development needs of secondary school principals of collaborative-based service delivery models. *The High School Journal, 84,* 10–23.

Furney, K., Hasazi, S., & Clark/Keefe, K. (2005). Multiple dimensions of reform: The impact of state policies on special education and supports for all students. *Journal of Disability Policy Studies, 16,* 169–176.

Furney, K., Hasazi, S., Clark/Keefe, K., & Hartnett, J. (2003). A longitudinal analysis of shifting policy landscapes in special and general education reform. *Exceptional Children, 70,* 81–94.

Gallagher, P., Floyd, J., Stafford, A., Taber, T., Brozovic, S., & Alberto, P. (2000). Inclusion of students with moderate or severe disabilities in educational and community settings: Perspectives from parents and siblings. *Education and Training in Mental Retardation and Developmental Disabilities, 35,* 135–147.

Gentile, A. (2008). Disabled residents sue over sidewalks: California advocates want statewide improvements. *American City & County, 123*(7), 17–18 .

Giangreco, M. (2006). Foundational concepts and practices for educating students with severe disabilities. In M. Snell & F. Brown (Eds.) *Instruction of students with severe disabilities* (6th ed.) (pp. 1–27). Upper Saddle River, NJ: Pearson Prentice Hall.

Giangreco, M. F., Prelock, P., Reid, R., Dennis, R., & Edelman, S. (2000). Roles of related services personnel in inclusive schools. In R. Villa & J. Thousand, (Eds.), *Restructuring for caring and effective education: Piecing the puzzle together* (2nd ed.) (pp. 360–388). Baltimore, MD: Paul H. Brookes Publishing Co.

Gibbs, J. (1987). *Tribes: A process for social development and cooperative learning.* Santa Rosa, CA: Center Source Publications.

Government Accountability Office (2004). *Special education: Improved timeliness and better use of enforcement actions could strengthen Education's monitoring system* (GAO Report #GAO-04-879). Washington, DC: Author.

Green, M. (2006). *When people care enough to act: ABCD in action.* Toronto, ON: Inclusion Press.

Greene, J., & Forster, G. (2002). *Effects of funding incentives on special education enrollment.* New York: Manhattan Institute for Public Research.

Griffin, C., Jones, H., & Kilgore, K. (2007). The unintended side effects of including students with learning disabilities for teacher educators. *Learning Disabilities, 14,* 195–204.

Hanson, M., & Lynch, E. (2004). *Understanding families: Approaches to diversity, disability, and risk.* Baltimore, MD: Paul H. Brookes Publishing Co.

Harry, B., & Klingner, J. (2006). *Why are so many minority students in special education? Understanding race and disability in schools.* New York: Teachers College Press.

——— (2007). Discarding the deficit model. *Educational Leadership, 64*(5), 16–21.

Hehir, T. (2002). Eliminating ableism in education. *Harvard Educational Review, 72,* 1–32.

Jiménez, T., Graf, V., & Rose, E. (2007). Gaining access to general education: The promise of universal design for learning. *Issues in Teacher Education, 16,* 41–54.

Kakalik, J. (1979). Issues in the cost and finance of special education. *Review of Re-*

search in Education, 7, 195–222.

Kamens, M. (2007). Learning about co-teaching: A collaborative student teaching experience for preservice teachers. *Teacher Education and Special Education, 30,* 155–166.

Kamens, M., Loprete, S., & Slostad, F. (2003). Inclusive classrooms: What practicing teachers want to know. *Action in Teacher Education, 25,* 20–26.

Kincheloe, J. (1999). The foundations of a democratic educational psychology. In J. Kincheloe, S. Steinberg, & L. Villaverde (Eds.), *Rethinking intelligence: Confronting psychological assumptions about teaching and learning* (pp. 1–26). New York: Routledge.

——— (2003). Critical ontology: Visions of self-hood and curriculum. *Journal of Curriculum Theorizing, 19,* 47–64.

——— (2004). The knowledges of teacher education: Developing a critical complex epistemology. *Teacher Education Quarterly, 31,* 49–66.

Kluth, P., Villa, R., & Thousand, J. (2002). "Our school doesn't offer inclusion" and other legal blunders. *Educational Leadership, 59*(4), 24–27.

Kusler, M. (2003). The imperative of fully funding IDEA. *School Administrator, 60*(3), 47.

Laarhoven, T., Munk, D., Lynch, K., Wyland, S., Dorsch, N., Zurita, L., Bosma, J., & Rouse, J. (2006). Project ACCEPT: Preparing pre-service special and general educators for inclusive education. *Teacher Education and Special Education, 29,* 209–212.

Lipsky, D., & Gartner, A. (1997). *Inclusion and School Reform: Transforming America's Classrooms.* Baltimore, MD: Paul H. Brookes Publishing Co.

Ludlum, C. (2002). *One candle power: Seven principles that enhance the lives of people with disabilities and their community.* Toronto, ON: Inclusion Press.

Marshall, K. (2008). The reasonable adjustments duty for higher education in England and Wales. In S. Gabel and S. Danforth (Eds.), *Disability and the politics of education: An international reader* (pp. 541–560). New York: Peter Lang.

National Council on Disability (1994). *Inclusionary education for students with disabilities: Keeping the promise.* Washington, DC: Author.

National Council on Disability (1995). *Improving the implementation of the Individuals with Disabilities Education Act: Making schools work for all of America's children.* Washington, DC: Author.

Nevin, A., Cohen, J., Salazar, L., & Marshall, D. (2007). Student teacher perspectives on inclusive education. Annual Conference of the American Association of Colleges of Teacher Education, New York.

O'Brien, J., & O'Brien, C. (1996). *Members of each other: Building community in company with people with developmental disabilities.* Toronto, ON: Inclusion Press.

Office of Special Education and Rehabilitative Services (2003). *25ᵗʰ annual report to Congress on the implementation of the Individuals with Disabilities Education Act.* Washington, DC: Author.

Palmer, D., Borthwick-Duffy, S., Widaman, K., & Best, S. (1998). Influences on parent perceptions of inclusive practices for their children with mental retardation. *American Journal on Mental Retardation, 103,* 272–287.

Parrish, T. (1993). *State funding provisions and least restrictive environment: Implications for federal policy.* (CSEF Brief #2). Palo Alto, CA: Center for Special Education Finance.

— — — (1994). *Fiscal issues in special education: Removing incentives for restrictive placements* (CSEF Policy Paper #4). Palo Alto, CA: Center for Special Education Finance.

— — — (1995a). *Criteria for effective special education funding formulas.* Palo Alto, CA: Center for Special Education Finance.

— — — (1995b). *Fiscal issues related to the inclusion of students with disabilities* (CSEF Brief #7). Palo Alto, CA: Center for Special Education Finance.

— — — (2001). *Special education in an era of school reform: Special education finance.* Washington, DC: Federal Resource Center, Academy for Educational Development.

Parrish, T., Harr, J., Anthony, J., Merickel, A. & Esra, P. (2003). *State special education-finance systems, 1999–2000, Part I.* Palo Alto, CA: Center for Special Education Finance.

Perske, R. (1998). *Circles of friends.* Nashville, TN: Abingdon Press.

Peters, S. (2004). *Inclusive education: An EFA strategy for all children.* Washington, DC: World Bank.

Pijl, S., & Dyson, A. (1998). Funding special education: A three-country study of demand-oriented models. *Comparative education: 34,* 261–279.

Powell, J., Felkendorff, K., & Hollenweger, J. (2008). Disability in the German, Swiss, and Austrian higher education systems. In S. Gabel and S. Danforth (Eds.), *Disability and the politics of education: An international reader* (pp. 517–540). New York: Peter Lang.

Praisner, C. (2003). Attitudes of elementary school principals toward the inclusion of students with disabilities. *Exceptional Children, 69,* 135–145.

President's Committee for People with Intellectual Disabilities (2004). *A charge we have to keep: A road map to personal and economic freedom for people with intellectual disabilities in the 21st century.* Washington, DC: Author.

Reusen, A., Shoho, A., & Barker, K. (2001). High school teacher attitudes toward inclusion. *The High School Journal, 84,* 7–20.

Rice, N. (2006). Teacher education as a site of resistance. In S. Danforth & S. Gabel (Eds). *Vital questions facing disability studies in education* (pp. 17–32). New York: Peter Lang.

Rose, D., & Meyer, A. (2006). *A practical reader in universal design for learning.* Cambridge, MA: Harvard Education Press.

Salisbury, C. (2006). Principals' perspectives on inclusive elementary schools. *Research & Practice for Persons with Severe Disabilities, 31,* 70–82.

Shippen, M., Crites, S., Houchins, D., Ramsey, M., & Simon, M. (2005). Preservice teachers' perceptions of including students with disabilities. *Teacher Education and Special Education, 28,* 92–99.

Short, C., & Martin, B. (2005). Case study: Attitudes of rural high school students and teachers regarding inclusion. *The Rural Educator, 27,* 1–10.

Silverman, J. (2007). Epistemological beliefs and attitudes toward inclusion in preservice teachers. *Teacher Education and Special Education, 30,* 42–51.

Silverstein, R. (2000). Emerging disability policy framework: A guidepost for analyzing public policy. *Iowa Law Review, 85,* 1691–1796,

Smith, F. (1998). *The book of learning and forgetting.* New York: Teacher's College Press.

Smith, P. (1999). Ideology, politics, and science in understanding developmental disabilities. *Mental Retardation, 37,* 71–72.

— — — (2006). Split------ting the ROCK of {speci [ES]al} e.ducat.ion: FLOWers of lang[ue]age in >DIS<ability studies. In S. Danforth and S. Gabel (Eds.), *Vital Questions in Disability Studies in Education*, (pp. 31–58). New York: Peter Lang.

———— (2008). an ILL/ELLip(op)tical *po*—ETIC/EMIC/**Lemic**/litic *post*® uv ed DUCAT ion *recherché repres©entation. Qualitative Inquiry, 14*, 706–722.

Spooner, F., Dymond, S., Smith, S., & Kennedy, C. (2006). What we know and need to know about accessing the general curriculum for students with significant cognitive disabilities. *Research and Practice for Persons with Severe Disabilities, 31*, 277–283.

Taylor, S. (2004). Caught in the continuum: A critical analysis of the principle of the least restrictive environment. *Research and Practice for Persons with Severe Disabilities, 29*, 218–230.

Taylor, S., Racino, J., Knoll, J., & Lutfiyya, Z. (1987). *The nonrestrictive environment: On community integration for people with the most severe disabilities*. Syracuse,NY: Human Policy Press.

Thompson, S. (2007). A community just for practice: A case of an inclusive/special education course. *Canadian Journal of Education, 30*, 171–192.

Thousand, J., Villa, R., & Nevin, A. (2002). *Creativity and collaborative learning: The practical guide to empowering students, teachers, and families* (2nd ed.). Baltimore, MD: Paul H. Brookes Publishing Co.

Turnbull, H., Beegle, G., & Stowe, M. (2001). The core concepts of disability policy affecting families who have children with disability. *The Journal of Disability Policy Studies, 12*, 133–143.

Villa, R., & Thousand, J. (2000). *Restructuring for caring and effective education: Piecing the puzzle together* (2nd ed.). Baltimore, MD: Paul H. Brookes Publishing Co.

Villa, R., Thousand, J., & Nevin, A. (2008). *A guide to co-teaching: Practical tips for facilitating student learning*. Thousand Oaks, CA: Corwin Press.

Villa, R., Thousand, J., Nevin, A., & Liston, A. (2005). Successful inclusive practices in middle and secondary schools. *American Secondary Education, 33*, 33–50.

Walsh, K. (2001). *Teacher certification reconsidered: Stumbling for quality*. Baltimore, MD: Abell Foundation.

Ware, L. (2005). Many possible futures, many different directions: Merging critical special education and disability studies. In S. Gabel (Ed.), *Disability studies in education: Readings in theory and method* (pp. 103–124). New York: Peter Lang.

Ware, L. (2006). A look at the way we look at disability. In S. Danforth & S. Gabel (Eds). *Vital questions facing disability studies in education* (pp. 271–287). New York: Peter Lang.

Wehmeyer, M. (2006). Beyond access: Ensuring progress in the general education curriculum for students with severe disabilities. *Research and Practice for Persons with Severe Disabilities, 31*, 322–326.

Williamson, P., McLesky, J., Hoppey, D., & Rentz, T. (2006). Educating students with mental retardation in general education classrooms. *Exceptional Children, 72*, 347–361.

CONTRIBUTORS

David J. Connor: David J. Connor is an associate professor in the School of Education, Hunter College, City University of New York. A "critical (special) educator," his research interests include learning disabilities; inclusive education; urban education; and race, class, and (dis)abilities in general. He is the co-author of *Reading Resistance: Discourses of Exclusion in Desegregation & Inclusion Debates* (Peter Lang, 2006), and the author of *Urban Narratives: Life at the Intersections of Learning Disability, Race, and Social Class* (Peter Lang, 2008).

Susan L. Gabel: Susan L. Gabel, PhD, is a professor of special education at National-Louis University where she is the former director of the Disability and Equity in Education (DEE) doctoral program. She teaches in the Masters of Special Education and DEE doctoral programs and serves on the University Diversity and Inclusion Council. Prior to coming to NLU in 2001, Dr. Gabel was on the faculty of the University of Michigan and Cleveland State University. She has been a teacher educator for 13 years. Her doctorate is from Michigan State University in Curriculum, Teaching, and Educational Policy/Social Analysis in 1997. Her doctoral area of emphasis was educational policy and social analysis. Dr. Gabel taught special education for 15 years in Kentucky and Michigan, where she has worked with students with a variety of special educational needs, including high- and low-incidence disabilities from pre-kindergarten through middle school. Dr. Gabel's research interests focus on the social contexts of disability in education. She has received numerous private and internal research grants. She has published peer reviewed articles in the *Journal of Teacher Education, Mental Retardation, Curriculum Inquiry, Disability Studies Quarterly*, and *Disability and Society*. She is the co-editor of a book series with Peter Lang—Disability Studies in Education and is currently editing her third book. Dr. Gabel is on the editorial board of *Disability Studies Quarterly* and the editorial review board of *Mental Retardation*. She regularly reviews for numerous peer reviewed journals. Dr. Gabel is a disabled woman and mother of three adult disabled children.

Barbara LeRoy: Dr. Barbara LeRoy is the director of the Developmental Disabilities Institute and on the Graduate Faculty, College of Education, Wayne State University. In her 30+ years of experience in disability policy and program development, she has implemented systems change projects in supported employment, inclusive education, and self-determination. She sits on 15+ boards, including the Governor's Council on Developmental Disabilities, the United States International Council on Disabilities, the Education Commission of Rehabilitation International, and the WHO Research Group on Disability and Aging. Dr. LeRoy has consulted on disability programs in New Zealand, Australia, Malaysia, Japan, Hong Kong, Europe, and the Caribbean region. She is a policy and program consultant to OECD, Paris.

Kagendo Mutua: Kagendo Mutua is an associate professor of special education at the University of Alabama. Her research revolves around cross-cultural studies of Transition and secondary programming for adolescents with severe/multiple disabilities and their families in the United States and in Kenya. Her work is published in several journals including, *Journal of Special Education, International Journal of Disability, Development and Education,* and *Educational Studies.* She has also co-edited a volume, *Decolonizing Research in Cross-Cultural Contexts: Critical Personal Narratives* and is a co-editor of the book series, Research in Africa, Caribbean, and the Middle East. Kagendo is also co-director of CrossingPoints, a model transition demonstration program for adolescents with intellectual and other developmental disabilities located on the University of Alabama campus.

Emily A. Nusbaum: Emily A. Nusbaum is an assistant professor of special education at California State University, Fresno. Prior to beginning her position at CSU Fresno she lectured and supervised student teachers at California State University, East Bay, San Francisco State University, and San Jose State University. She previously worked as an inclusion support teacher, as well. Her research interests are focused on inclusive education and school reform, disability studies in education, and general educator's work with students with disabilities. Her dissertation research used ethnographic methods to uncover how general educators conceptualize "inclusive education" and demonstrated the utility of a disability studies perspective as a means to reveal and understand dominant discourse of disability and normality in schools and to identify the structural mechanisms and social processes through which these constructs are reified.

Valerie Owen: Valerie Owen, Ph.D., an associate professor at National-Louis University, is the director of the Disability and Equity in Education Doctoral Program and teaches in NLU's special education programs. She has been a faculty member at NLU since 1990 and has served in numerous leadership positions including Department Chair, Faculty Senate Chair, and compiler/author of the last two NLU Special Education accreditation reports to CEC. She began her career 30 years ago as a classroom teacher of children with autism and those considered the most significantly disabled. She currently serves on the Professional Advisory Board of the International Rett Syndrome Association and the Illinois Autism/PDD Training and Technical Assistance Leadership Team. She is the immediate past president of IL-TASH, a research and advocacy organization for individuals with severe disabilities. She is a founding member and former officer in the Disability Studies in Education Special Interest Group of the American Educational Research Association, and a founder of the Second City Disability Studies and Education Conference. She is a sought-after consultant and expert witness, advocating for disabled students' rights to access to education in due process hearings and other litigation. As a consultant to numerous schools and school districts, she continues to work closely with teachers in reimagining teaching and providing access to the curriculum for students who have often been denied access. Her scholarship, publications, and presentations focus on differentiated instruction and assessment of children identified as disabled in school and critical perspectives of professional teaching standards.

Jim Siders: Jim Siders is an associate professor and head of the Department of Special Education and Multiple Abilities at the University of Alabama. Dr. Siders is currently a member of the Board of Directors for the Council for Exceptional Children, Arlington, Virginia, and has served on the Board of Directors for Mississippi School Boards Association and the Lamar County Board of Education, Hattiesburg, Mississippi. During a stint with the Southern Regional Educational Service Agency as Associate Director of Technology Initiatives, Jim realized firsthand the current inclusive in/activities regarding inclusive practices in southern public schools. Jim is also co-director of CrossingPoints, a model transition demonstration program for adolescents with intellectual and other developmental disabilities located on the University of Alabama campus.

Phil Smith: Phil is an associate professor of special education at Eastern Michigan University, with an emphasis on inclusive education, families with members with disabilities, disability studies, and over-representation. He describes himself as being post-everything and after boundaries, but sometimes works as a critical ethnographer, poet, and visual artist. Both he and his daughter have disabilities. Phil's research interests include the representation of research; ways in which people with disabilities experience choice, control, and power in their lives; normal theory; disability and education policy; and cultural understandings of disability. He's been published widely in a variety of journals and books, presented locally and around the country, and does training and presentations on person-centered planning, circles of support, disability rights, family support, and a host of other areas. He has worked as an inclusion specialist in schools, a service coordinator, and an independent support broker. He was also director of Vermont's Self-Determination Project, and executive director of the Vermont Developmental Disabilities Council. Phil received the 2009 Disability Studies in Education Emerging Scholar Award. He's published a collection of poems, a book of plays, and a novel. A transplanted Yankee, Phil now lives, gardens, hikes, and bikes in Michigan, where he watches loons, wolves, moose, and bald eagles near Lake Superior, as well as endlessly (perseveratorily) renovating old houses.

INDEX

Disability Studies in Education

GENERAL EDITORS: SUSAN L. GABEL & SCOT DANFORTH

The book series Disability Studies in Education is dedicated to the publication of monographs and edited volumes that integrate the perspectives, methods, and theories of disability studies with the study of issues and problems of education. The series features books that further define, elaborate upon, and extend knowledge in the field of disability studies in education. Special emphasis is given to work that poses solutions to important problems facing contemporary educational theory, policy, and practice.

To order other books in this series, please contact our Customer Service Department:

(800) 770-LANG (within the U.S.)
(212) 647-7706 (outside the U.S.)
(212) 647-7707 FAX

Or browse by series:

WWW.PETERLANG.COM